Water, Electricity, and the Poor: Who Benefits from Utility Subsidies?

Water, Electricity, and the Poor: Who Benefits from Utility Subsidies?

Kristin Komives, Vivien Foster, Jonathan Halpern,
and Quentin Wodon
with support from Roohi Abdullah

THE WORLD BANK
Washington, DC

ISBN-10: 0-8213-6342-5
ISBN-13: 978-0-8213-6342-3
e-ISBN: 0-8213-6343-3
DOI: 10.1596/978-0-8213-6342-3

Cover photos by: Curt Carnemark (left) and Andrea Gingerich (right).
Cover design by: Serif Design Group, Inc.

Library of Congress Cataloging-in-Publication Data

Water, electricity, and the poor : who benefits from utility subsidies? / Kristin Komives ...
[et al.] ; with support from Roohi Abdullah.
     p. cm.-- (Directions in development (Washington, D.C.))
  Includes bibliographical references and index.
  ISBN 0-8213-6342-5
  1. Public utilities--Developing countries--Rates. 2. Subsidies--Developing countries. I.
Komives, Kristin. II. World Bank. III. Series.

HD2768.D444W38 2005
333.71'58'091724--dc22

2005050780

Contents

Boxes

Figures

Tables

Foreword

Subsidies for utility services are widespread in the water supply, sanitation, and electricity sectors. One motivation is to improve social welfare of the poor by facilitating their access to and use of such services, as well as by redistributing resources to augment their purchasing power. At the same time, such subsidies have often been seen as engendering resource use inefficiencies and financially weak utilities, which hobble efforts to expand and improve service. Those adverse consequences have often been used to argue against charging consumers less than the cost of service.

The impact of subsidies on both counts has been the subject of much controversy. The debate has gained renewed vigor as governments seek to ensure that all citizens have ready access to minimal levels of such services while striving to recover a larger share of the costs of utility operations to generate the resources required to sustain service and to improve its quality.

This book makes a substantive contribution to our thinking on a key facet of the debate: the distributional impact of consumer subsidies for urban water supply and electricity services. Drawing together empirical research across a wide range of countries, it documents the prevalence and variants of consumer subsidies found in the developing world and presents a number of indicators that are useful in assessing the degree to which such subsidies benefit the poor. The findings are placed in a broader social protection framework where comparisons are drawn with poverty-focused programs in other sectors using a common metric.

The book's findings are sobering. It concludes that the most common subsidy instruments (quantity-targeted subsidies such as those delivered through increasing block tariffs) perform poorly in comparison with most other transfer mechanisms. Alternative consumption and connection subsidy mechanisms show more promise, especially when combined with complementary nonprice approaches to making utility services accessible and affordable to poor households. Throughout, the authors dissect the many factors contributing to those outcomes, identifying those that policy makers can control and use to improve performance.

This book, a product of the Infrastructure Vice Presidency of the World Bank, is part of a larger effort to assess and promote cost-effective approaches to the financing and provision of infrastructure services to the poor in developing countries. It is a very useful resource for policy makers, utility regulators, and sector practitioners who are seeking ways to make utility services accessible and affordable to the poor. It will also be of considerable interest to those who view consumer utility subsidies as an instrument of social protection—for transferring resources to the poor where weak administrative structures make cash transfers infeasible or costly.

Jamal Saghir
Director, Energy and Water
World Bank

Acknowledgments

This book would not have been possible without the support and assistance of many people. It draws on existing work on the distributional incidence of utility subsidies. Many of the authors of those prior studies facilitated this comparative study by adapting their findings to the framework presented here. In this regard, special thanks are due to José Luis Aburto, Maria Caridad Araujo, José Gallardo, Andrés Gomez Lobo, Julian Lampietti, Marcela Melendez, Subhrendu Pattanayak, Linda Prokopy, V. Santhakumar, John Scott, Ian Walker, Jui-Chen Yang, and Tito Yepes. We are also grateful for the assistance of Doug Barnes, Diego Angel-Urdinola, Sudeshna Ghosh Banerjee, Walter Hall, Ellen Hamilton, Nicolas Okreshidze, Natalyia Pushak, and Maria Shkaratan, who helped bring new subsidy cases and additional supporting information into the analysis. The book also benefited from the thoughtful comments and suggestions received from Judy Baker, Fanny Missfeldt-Ringius, Mike Muller, John Nellis, Lee Travers, and Catherine Waddams-Price. Any errors that remain are the responsibility of the authors.

The preparation of this book was made possible through a grant from the Bank Netherlands Water Partnership (BNWP). The BNWP is a facility that enhances World Bank operations to increase delivery of water supply and sanitation services to the poor. The analytical framework on which the book is based was developed with funding from the Belgian Poverty Reduction Partnership. The dissemination of the book is supported by the Norwegian Trust Fund for Private Sector and Infrastructure.

Abbreviations and Acronyms

ACE	ASEAN Center for Energy
ADB	Asian Development Bank
ADERASA	Association of Water and Sanitary Regulatory Entities of the Americas
AFTES	Australasian Fluid and Thermal Engineering Society
BNWP	Bank Netherlands Water Partnership
CAESS	Companía de Alumbrado Eléctrico de San Salvador
Cargo SUMA	Cargo de Servicio Universal y Medio-Ambiente
CAS	Caracterisación Social
CDS	Centre for Development Studies
CFE	Comisión Federal de Electricidad
CIER	Comisión de Integración Energética Regional
DBT	decreasing block tariff
DEFRA	Department for Environment, Food, and Rural Affairs
DTI	Department of Trade and Industry
EEGSA	Empresa Eléctrica de Guatemala, S.A.
ERM	Environmental Resources Management
ERRA	Energy Regulators Regional Association
ESMAP	Energy Sector Management Assistance Programme
GDP	gross domestic product
GWHAP	Georgian Winter Heating Assistance Program
GWI	Global Water Intelligence
IBT	increasing block tariff
IEA	International Energy Association
IESA	Institute for Advanced Studies in Administration
IFPRI	International Food Policy Research Institute
INE	Instituto Nicaragüense de Energía
IRC	International Resource Center

KgOE	kilograms of oil equivalent
LAC	Latin America and the Caribbean
LPG	liquefied petroleum gas
MIDEPLAN	Ministry of Planning
NIUA	National Institute of Urban Affairs
OSINERG	Organismo Supervisor de la Inversión en Energía
O&M	operation and maintenance
OECD	Organisation for Economic Co-operation and Development
OLADE	Organización Latinoamericana de Energía
PFGMI	Policy Framework and Global Mapping Initiative
PPIAF	Public–Private Infrastructure Advisory Facility
QGC	quasi-Gini coefficient
SPSPs	small-scale private service providers
UN-ESCAP	United Nations Economic and Social Commission for Asia and the Pacific
VDT	volume-differentiated tariff
WEC	World Energy Council
WTP	willingness to pay

1
Introduction

Subsidies to utility customers are a salient feature of water and electricity services worldwide. In some cases, subsidized service is made possible by large transfers from general tax revenue, which can be in the form of either capital projects or regular transfers to cover revenue shortfalls. Utilities also benefit from a wide range of less visible subsidies, including underpricing of fuel inputs in electricity generation and of electricity and raw water inputs in water production. In addition, many utilities use cross-subsidization within their customer base to fund subsidies for specific groups of consumers. Other utilities simply absorb the financial loss from the general or targeted subsidies, gradually wearing down capital stock and pushing repair and maintenance costs off into the future.

The total value of subsidies provided to utility customers can represent a significant share of public expenditure and utility costs. The most striking examples of government-funded subsidy schemes come from the countries of the former Soviet Union. For example, power sector subsidies have been estimated to be more than 10 percent of gross domestic product (GDP) in Kazakhstan, Tajikistan, and Uzbekistan, and between 3 and 4 percent of GDP in Bulgaria and Georgia (Ebinger 2005). Power sector subsidies remain an important, although less-extreme, fiscal drain in many other regions of the world, exceeding 1 percent of GDP in India and Mexico. Fiscal transfers for drinking water and sanitation tend to be smaller as a percentage of GDP, although fewer estimates are available. In India, for example, drinking water subsidies have been estimated at 0.5 percent of GDP, or about half the value of power sector subsidies in the country. This figure does not imply superior financial performance for water utilities but rather the lower cost of water services, as well as a marked tendency for water utilities to defer otherwise essential expenditures—something not as easily accomplished in the electricity sector.

Subsidies to utility customers are widely popular among policy makers, utility managers, and residential customers alike, and yet subsidies remain the subject of much controversy. Are subsidies needed in the short or long term? Are they a good use of public and utility funds? Are they practical (if second-best) approaches to making utility services available to the poor or to transferring resources to poor households? Underlying this debate are differing perspectives on the policy objective behind subsidizing utility customers, as well as disagreement about the effects of subsidies on consumer and utility behavior. This book focuses on one major topic of discussion within this wider debate: the extent to which poor households benefit or could benefit from consumer utility subsidies.

Infrastructure Services Are Important to Economies and Households

One reason the debate over utility subsidies can become so heated is that the provision of adequate and reliable infrastructure truly matters—to economies, to households, and to poor households in particular. Improved water supply, sanitation, and electricity services are associated with raising productivity and living standards. More recently, the catalytic role of infrastructure in poverty reduction has received renewed recognition. The importance of infrastructure has been encapsulated in the Millennium Development Goals, which singled out increasing access to water supply and to sanitation service as explicit targets to be achieved by 2015. Although they were not explicit targets of the Millennium Declaration of the United Nations General Assembly, other infrastructure services such as electricity, transport, and telecommunications are widely acknowledged as key enabling factors for achieving the improved health, education, and income poverty goals spelled out in the Millennium Declaration (UN Millennium Project 2005).

Water supply, sanitation, and electricity contribute to poverty reduction and to improvements in the standard of living in several ways. First, the provision of those services has strong and direct links to improved health outcomes. Water-related illnesses account for a very substantial burden of disease in the developing world, exacting high costs in terms of death, malnutrition, stunting, and reduced productivity. Improving water and sanitation facilities has been shown to reduce those costs (Kelley 2003; Listorti 1996; Esrey and others 1991; Galiani and others 2005). Electricity enables improved health service delivery in several ways: electrification of health facilities enables safe storage of vaccines and medication, and electricity in the home enables safe preservation of medication and foods.

Access to these utility services is also often associated with improved educational outcomes. Electricity is strongly associated with improvement in adult literacy, as well as with primary school completion rates, because it enables reading and studying in the evening and early morning hours (Barnes 1988; Brodman 1982; Foley 1990; Venkataraman 1990). Lack of improved water facilities can work against educational outcomes, especially for girls. Many girls do not attend school because of a lack of adequate sanitary facilities at the schools or because of the demands on their time of chores such as collecting water. Water and sanitation improvements reduce those barriers to school attendance.

Water, sanitation, and electricity services contribute to improved productivity, both of individuals and of businesses. The time spent obtaining water and fuel or traveling to sanitation facilities outside the home can be significant. When household connections are available, household members, particularly women and children, can engage in more productive activities and leisure. Expansion in the quantity and improvement in quality of utility services can also lower costs and expand market opportunities for businesses and, thereby, increase productivity and investment that drive economic growth (de la Fuente 2004). Conversely, multicountry studies in Latin America and Africa find that underinvestment in infrastructure reduced annual growth by 1–3 percent per year and that the growth of output attributable to improvements in infrastructure, while relatively small (.15–.5 percent), is associated with significant reductions in poverty (Estache 2002).

Many Still Lack Access to Improved Water and Electricity Services

Despite the widespread acceptance of the importance of infrastructure services, billions of people in the developing world do not have access to improved water, sanitation, or electricity services. For every 10 people, 2 lack access to a safe water supply, 4 lack access to electricity, and 5 have inadequate sanitation. These statistics translate to an estimated 1.1 billion people without safe water, 2 billion without electricity, and 2.4 billion without sanitation (IEA 2002; WHO/UNICEF 2004).

Access to those services varies widely across regions and between urban and rural areas (table 1.1). Not surprisingly, those regions with a substantial share of middle-income countries tend to have broader access than do those in which low-income countries predominate. Electrification rates equal or exceed those for water supply in regions with a substantial share of middle-income countries. There are also regional differences in service levels. In Asia and Sub-Saharan Africa, many of the urban households estimated to have access to safe water do not have private water connections, but instead use other improved sources. Conversely, in Eastern Europe, Central Asia, Latin America, and countries of the Organisation for Economic Co-operation and Development (OECD), urban households with access to safe water typically obtain their water through household connections.

This snapshot of access to water, sanitation, and electricity services tends to underestimate the number of households without adequate services because such estimates are based on proximity to or use of a physical installation rather than on the quality and reliability of service that users actually obtain. In many countries where utility networks have been installed, the quality of service is poor. Many utility customers often have no water

Table 1.1. Percentage of the Population with Access to Improved Water Supply, Sanitation, and Electricity (and Percentage with a Household Water Connection)

	Water supply[a]		Sanitation[a]		Electricity[b]	
	Urban	Rural	Urban	Rural	Urban	Rural
East/Southeast Asia	92 (70)	69	71	35	99	81
South Asia	93 (53)	80	64	23	68	30
Sub-Saharan Africa	82 (39)	46	55	26	51	7
Middle East/North Africa	96 (92)	78	90	56	99	77
East Europe/Central Asia	98 (98)	78	93	64	N/A	N/A
Latin America	96 (95)	69	84	44	98	51
OECD	100 (100)	94	100	92	100	98

Sources: IEA 2002; WHO/UNICEF 2004.

Note:

IEA = International Energy Association; OECD = Organisation for Economic Co-operation and Development; WHO = World Health Organization.
a. Water supply and sanitation as of 2002.
b. Electricity as of 2000.

in the pipe, and when water is available, it is often unsafe to drink. Sanitation facilities are often inadequate, overloaded, in disrepair, or unused, and electricity service may be sporadic and of poor quality.

Are Subsidies the Answer?

Disparities in access to basic infrastructure services between countries and among income groups within a particular jurisdiction have often been invoked as a motivation for providing subsidies to utilities and to utility customers: households would be unable to afford those services if subsidies were not offered. In discussions about affordability, there is particular concern about the effect on the poor of raising tariffs to recover a greater share of costs in order to mobilize private finance or simply to reduce the use of scarce fiscal resources by utilities. This concern has prompted governments to maintain subsidies in the short term and only gradually to move toward cost-recovery pricing.

The counterargument is that subsidies have adverse consequences that can actually work against improving the quality of service to existing consumers and extending access to unconnected households. Subsidies engender distortions in the use of water and electricity, thereby leading to an inefficient use of resources and thus indirectly raising the costs of service provision. Subsidies can also induce inefficiency in utility operations, as utility managers face soft budget constraints. The costs of subsidies in terms of inefficiency may rival or exceed any benefit derived from the provision of the subsidy. Moreover, utility subsidies have tended to produce financially weak utilities with stagnant service areas and with declining service quality, because fiscal transfers are not always dependable and cross-subsidies are frequently insufficient to cover the subsidies provided to consumers. This endemic financial weakness means that the poorest unconnected households face the prospect of relying on alternative and often more expensive water and fuel sources for many years to come. Given the high cost of utility subsidies and their potential for creating this collateral damage to utilities and households, there is much interest in evaluating and improving utility subsidies.

Utility Subsidies Are Also Redistributive Mechanisms

The view that utility subsidies are an effective mechanism for expanding coverage and ensuring that the poor can use utility services is joined by another view that posits that utility subsidies are an important component of a broader social policy agenda: the redistribution of resources toward the poor. Particularly in countries where it is not administratively feasible to implement means-tested cash transfers, consumer utility subsidies appear to be a practical mechanism for delivering transfers to the poor. From this perspective, how utility subsidies affect utility behavior and household use of water, sanitation, or electricity services is less important than how subsidies compare with other social protection programs in terms of their ability to accurately target poor households and to reduce poverty levels.

Objective of This Book: Assessing the Targeting Performance of Subsidies

How well consumer utility subsidies target subsidies to poor households is an important consideration—both for those interested in those subsidies as a transfer mechanism and for those more interested in the sectoral objective of ensuring access to water and electricity for the poor. Better-targeted subsidies mean either lower subsidy budgets or larger discounts or transfers for the poorest people. This book examines the effectiveness of consumer utility subsidies in reaching and distributing resources to the poor.

The focus of the analysis is whether and why consumer utility subsidies are (or are not) able to target the poor. The relative targeting performance of different types of subsidies is assessed and conclusions are drawn as to how the design of such subsidies might be improved, if accurate targeting is the objective. The analysis is structured around a conceptual framework that decomposes the factors that influence the distributional incidence of consumer utility subsidies.

The distributional incidence of consumer utility subsidies admittedly allows only a partial look at the performance of utility subsidies. There are inevitably multiple objectives at work in the design of tariffs for water and electricity services, only one of which is concern for providing subsidies and affordable service to the poor. The objective is thus not to make recommendations about the best approach to charging for or subsidizing utility services. Rather it is to draw together empirical evidence to address a long-standing question in the ongoing debate about the design of utility tariffs and subsidies: to what extent do or could consumer utility subsidies benefit the poor?

The book is intended to make the findings of recent research accessible and to provide guidance to policy makers, utility regulators, and utility managers who are contemplating introducing, eliminating, or modifying subsidies for water, sanitation, and electricity service. The analysis is built on a recent body of empirical studies (many of them unpublished) that examine the targeting performance of consumer utility subsidies in developing countries. The context of those studies is generally urban in the case of water utilities and national in the case of electricity, mirroring the service areas of the utilities studied.

The analysis shows that consumption subsidies are ubiquitous in the water and electricity sectors and that the most common types of subsidies—quantity-based subsidies such as increasing block tariffs—are regressive in their distribution, favoring the nonpoor over the poor. Many factors contribute to this outcome, only some of which can be controlled or manipulated by those who design subsidy programs. Some modifications to the design of quantity-based subsidies would generate limited improvement in the targeting performance of the subsidies. Moving away from increasing block tariffs toward tariff structures that do not provide a lifeline for all households is one example. Using administrative selection, rather than the quantity of water or electricity consumed, to target benefits is another alternative (though one with well-known hurdles in implementation). In contrast, reducing the size of the first lifeline block of an increasing block tariff, a modification that is often advocated in policy circles, would have very limited effect on the targeting performance of consumption subsidies.

Connection subsidies are more promising than consumption subsidies when coverage is low, but their targeting performance depends on whether they actually induce households to connect to the system, an issue that has been little studied to date. Moreover, from a sectoral perspective, there are important differences in how connection and consumption subsidies affect coverage and usage patterns. In this sense, the two types of subsidies are not strictly substitutes. Another promising alternative to the standard consumption subsidies is to link subsidies to service level (for example, subsidies for low-voltage electricity service or service from communal water taps). The few such subsidies evaluated here do a better job of targeting the poor, but more such evaluations are clearly needed.

The book is structured as follows. Chapters 2 and 3 present a typology of the various kinds of consumer utility subsidies, examine the prevalence of different subsidy models, and take a closer look at the rationale for subsidizing services for the poor. The empirical analysis of the distributional incidence of consumer utility subsidies begins in chapter 4 with a conceptual framework and a discussion of the methodology used to measure and evaluate the targeting performance of the subsidies. Chapters 5 and 6 apply this framework to the analysis of subsidies distributed through quantity targeting (for example, increasing block tariffs), administrative targeting (for example, geographic and means testing), and service-level targeting (for example, subsidies for public water taps). Chapter 7 extends the analysis to connection subsidies. Chapters 8 through 10 reassess the extent to which consumer utility subsidies are effective in achieving social policy and sectoral objectives in light of the findings of the earlier chapters and then discuss some policy implications of the research findings.

2
A Typology of Consumer Utility Subsidies

Consumer utility subsidies, as defined in this book, are subsidies that result in some or all residential consumers paying less than the cost of the electricity, water, or sanitation services that they receive. Consumer utility subsidies can be distinguished from subsidies to utilities (fiscal transfers, guarantees, concessional credit), which are treated here as a potential mechanism for funding consumer subsidies. Although it is convenient to refer to consumer utility subsidies as a general label, in practice there is an enormous variety in the forms that such subsidies can take. Such differences matter, because the details of the subsidy design ultimately determine the targeting performance of the subsidy. With a view to establishing an adequate terminology for distinguishing between different variants of subsidies, this chapter lays out a general taxonomy of consumer utility subsidies and discusses their prevalence.

What Types of Consumer Utility Subsidies Exist?

Table 2.1 presents a general typology of consumer utility subsidies. Few subsidy programs fit perfectly into any one category in this typology. Most existing subsidy mechanisms combine a number of the elements in the table. Nonetheless, the typology helps illustrate two important ways in which subsidy models differ from one another, each of which is the result of a policy decision made in the process of designing the subsidy. The two dimensions of subsidy design are consumption versus connection subsidies, and targeted versus untargeted subsidies.

Subsidies May Facilitate Connection or Consumption

A distinguishing feature of subsidies is whether they seek to reduce the cost of consumption or the cost of connecting to the network. Consumption subsidies help make service less expensive to existing utility customers on a continuing basis. Consumption subsidies may be provided to all those with private household connections. Some consumption subsidy models,

| | Untargeted subsidies | Implicit targeting | Targeted subsidies | | |
| | | | Explicit targeting | | |
			Self-selection: quantity targeting (See chapter 5)	Self-selection: service-level targeting (See chapter 6)	Administrative selection (See chapter 6)
Consumption subsidies	*Across-the-board price subsidies* ⇒ all consumers *Charging for variable but not fixed costs* ⇒ all consumers	*Low collection rate with no disconnection policy* ⇒ all consumers who do not pay their bills *Illegal connections* ⇒ those with illegal connections *Flat fees for unmetered connections* ⇒ high-volume consumers with unmetered connections *Combined water and sewer tariffs* ⇒ households with water and sewer connections *Single volumetric charge* (when costs vary by customer or time of use) ⇒ high-cost customers	*Increasing block tariffs* ⇒ low-volume consumers with meters *Volume-differentiated tariffs* ⇒ households with metered private connections who consume less than x units per month	*Free water at public water taps* ⇒ households using public taps *Low rates for low-voltage electricity service* ⇒ households with connections to low-voltage electricity services	*Geographically differentiated tariff* ⇒ customers who live in certain areas *"Social tariffs"* ⇒ customers classified as poor *Merit discounts and discounts for pensioners* ⇒ qualifying customers *Burden limit cash transfers* ⇒ households whose utility bills and housing expenditure exceed a defined burden limit
Connection subsidies (See chapter 7)	*No connection fee* ⇒ all new customers *Subsidized interest rate for financing connections* ⇒ all new customers	*Flat connection fee* ⇒ new customers who are more costly than average to connect		*Reduced connection fee for households providing labor or materials* ⇒ households that choose to provide labor *Reduced connection fee for lower service level* ⇒ households that chose this service level	*"Social connections"* ⇒ households classified as poor

Source: Authors' elaboration.

however, deliver subsidies only to metered customers or only to users of a communal form or lower level of service (for example, public water taps or low-voltage electricity). Consumption subsidies may operate through the tariff structure (as a reduction in the price faced by all or some households), may appear as a percentage discount applied to customer bills, or may take the form of a cash transfer to reimburse households for utility expenditures. The defining feature of consumption subsidies is that they are available only to current utility customers.

Connection subsidies, by contrast, are available only to unconnected households, which are households that are not currently utility customers. Connection subsidies are one-time subsidies that reduce or eliminate the price that customers pay to connect to the system.

Subsidies May Be Targeted or Untargeted

Connection and consumption subsidies may be targeted or untargeted. Untargeted subsidies occur when there is general underpricing of utility services, such as when certain costs are not passed on to customers. By contrast, targeted subsidies benefit only a subgroup of utility customers. In practice, targeted and untargeted subsidies are often combined: there may be an across-the-board price subsidy for all customers, but some customers may be targeted to receive greater discounts than others.

Within the category of targeted subsidies, a distinction can be made between those that rely on implicit targeting and those that rely on explicit targeting. Explicit targeting represents a conscious attempt to reduce the cost of service or the cost of connection for customers with a particular characteristic (for example, poor households, households in informal settlements, or households that use little electricity). By contrast, implicit targeting is the unintentional result of common pricing practices of utilities.

The most basic form of implicit targeting arises from charging one flat connection fee or one flat monthly service fee to all households for water supply or electricity service. Some households are inevitably more expensive to connect because they are farther from the network, or they are more expensive to serve because they consume more electricity or water than other households. Flat fees subsidize those expensive-to-serve customers, relative to those who are inexpensive to serve. When water and electricity connections are not metered, this form of implicit targeting is unavoidable. It is difficult to know the exact cost that a particular unmetered customer imposes on the system, so it is not possible to charge full cost to each customer. In the case of connection fees, it is possible to avoid implicit targeting of subsidies—each customer could be charged the exact cost of his or her connection—but making this calculation for each new customer imposes a significant administrative burden on the utility. In practice, many utilities prefer to use a flat connection fee, which will overcharge some new customers and undercharge others.

Implicit targeting does not arise only from flat fees. Even when connections are metered and all customers pay the same unit prices, some customers may be paying more than the cost they impose on the system, and others may have their service subsidized. In the case of electricity service, for example, failure to differentiate between peak and off-peak demand in the tariff subsidizes those consumers with heavy peak-period demand. A common example of implicit targeting in the water supply and sanitation sector is the practice of charging one combined tariff for water supply and sewer service. Where not all households have both water and sewer connections (which is usually the case in developing countries), those combined tariffs lead to subsidies for households with sewer connections. Low collection rates (with no disconnection for nonpayment) and tolerance of illegal connections are two other practices that lead to implicit targeting of subsidies, because, in practice, customers who pay for the service they receive subsidize those who do not pay.

The value of the subsidies that arise through implicit targeting can be quite substantial, making them worthy of inclusion in a study of the distributional incidence of utility subsidies. One might expect, for example, that the subsidy provided to those with illegal connections would be a well-targeted subsidy because illegal connections are very common in informal settlements. Likewise, the subsidies to sewer users, which arise from the practice of charging one combined price for water and sewer service, would probably be regressive in most cases: wealthy households are more likely than poor households to have sewer connections. Unfortunately, it is very difficult, in practice, to measure the distributional incidence of implicit subsidies precisely because the costs that different consumers impose on the system are not known. For example, the most common forms of implicit targeting arise in situations where the quantity of water or electricity used by subsidy beneficiaries is not known (for example, unmetered or illegal connections). Because of this practical limitation in available data, it was generally not possible to study implicit subsidies in detail in this book.

The focus of the book is instead on explicit targeted subsidies. Explicit targeting involves an intentional policy to charge some consumers more and other consumers less for the same service. When policy makers debate the benefits and costs of consumer utility subsidies, they are usually talking about explicit targeted subsidies.

There Are Several Approaches to Explicit Targeting

Various forms of explicit targeting exist, as table 2.1 shows. One approach is administrative selection: the government or the utility decides which consumers will receive the subsidy. The administrative decision could be to subsidize all customers in a particularly deserving group, such as pensioners or veterans (categorical targeting), all residential customers living in a certain region or neighborhood (geographic targeting), or all households that are determined to be or thought to be poor (targeting through means testing or proxy means testing).

Self-targeting can be an alternative or a complement to administrative selection. On one level, all consumer utility subsidies are self-targeted: to the extent that households choose whether or not to be utility customers, they play an important role in determining whether they are eligible for consumer utility subsidies. In the subsidy models identified as self-targeted in table 2.1, however, households play an even larger role in determining whether they receive a subsidy and how large that subsidy is. In such cases, subsidies are allocated to some households on the basis of how much water or electricity they consume (quantity targeting—see box 2.1) or of what level or type of utility service they use (service-level targeting). Quantity-targeted subsidies, such as increasing block tariffs, are the most widely used type of consumer utility subsidy.

Why Target Subsidies?

Targeting subsidies to the poor has three potential benefits. First, targeting has the potential to lower the subsidy budget or the cost of providing the subsidy. If only some households receive the subsidy, the amount of revenue the utility needs to obtain through cross-subsidies or from some external source to fund the subsidies it provides is reduced. Second, targeting means a greater potential impact on poor households for a given subsidy budget, because such targeting should allow a larger proportion of the total subsidy budget to benefit the poor. Third, subsidies that are targeted to fewer households have the potential to cause fewer distortions in consumption decisions than untargeted or poorly targeted subsidies (but are still more distorting than no subsidies at all).

Targeting does have its costs, however. Four generic costs are often cited (Sen 1995; Subbarao and others 1997). First, targeting programs may receive little political support and thus may run the risk of being eliminated. In the case of utility subsidies, there would likely be more support for a broad-based subsidy that protected all customers from potential tariff increases than for a narrowly targeted subsidy that provided such protection only to low-income households. Second, when benefits are targeted only to the poor, poor households may choose not to take advantage of the benefits because of the stigma associated with being categorized as needy. Third, administrative costs are associated with targeting, both for the agencies in charge of the targeted program and for the households receiving the targeted benefit. It is administratively more difficult to limit who receives a benefit than to provide the benefit to all. If households have to apply for or be

Box 2.1 Quantity-Targeted Subsidies in Tariff Structures

There are two basic types of tariffs that incorporate quantity targeting. One is a block tariff and may be either an increasing block tariff (IBT) or a decreasing block tariff (DBT). The second is a volume-differentiated tariff (VDT).

A block tariff is a stepped tariff in which a different price per unit is charged for different blocks of consumption. In the case of an IBT, the price charged rises with each successive consumption block, while in the case of a DBT, the price charged falls with each successive consumption block. A specific example of an IBT would be a tariff under which households were charged US$0.10 per cubic meter for the first 10 cubic meters of water consumed, then US$0.20 per cubic meter for any additional units of water used during the billing period. If US$0.20 represents the average cost of water service, then this IBT provides a subsidy to all customers for the first 10 cubic meters of water they use each month.

A VDT uses quantity targeting in a different way. It could take the form of two different tariffs, for example, a flat rate of US$0.10 per cubic meter and a flat rate of US$0.20 per cubic meter. Customers consuming less than 10 cubic meters would have their bills calculated on the basis of the first price. For customers consuming more than 10 cubic meters, the second tariff would be applied. The higher-volume customers would be charged US$0.20 for all units of water consumed, including the first 10. Unlike the IBT, the VDT does not provide any subsidy to the households that consume more than 10 cubic meters a month. This tariff is sometimes referred to as a tariff with a "disappearing first block."

A common misconception about quantity-targeted tariff structures is that they somehow seek to represent the underlying cost structure for the relevant services, which is generally not, in fact, the case. For the water sector, the marginal cost is determined by the total consumption in the system, not the amount consumed by each customer. A water user does not impose an increasingly high cost on the system with each unit of water consumed. For the electricity sector, it is a customer's load profile rather than the total volume of consumption that primarily affects his or her contribution to system costs. In this sense, quantity-based tariff structures merely represent alternative ways of allocating system costs across customers to meet cost recovery or social objectives. They cannot be justified in terms of reflecting underlying economic costs. The exception would be a case in which quantity consumed was correlated with another factor that drives the cost a user imposes on the system, such as a correlation between quantity consumed and the load profile of a customer (that is, time of day or seasonal usage patterns).

screened for subsidies, they incur real private costs (time, transport, etc.) in doing so. Finally, incentive costs arise if households change their behavior—or even falsify their status—in order to qualify for the subsidy.

How Are Subsidies Funded?

How to fund subsidies is another decision that must be made in the process of designing a subsidy program. Subsidies may come directly from the government, may be funded by other customers, or may not be funded at all.

Government-funded subsidies can be delivered in a variety of ways. Governments may transfer the subsidies directly as a cash payment to the beneficiary household, as is the case with the burden limit subsidies common in the countries of the former Soviet Union. Alternatively, the government may make a cash payment to the utility against proof that a subsidy was provided to a specific consumer, as is the case in the Chilean water supply sector. Such payments are the cleanest approaches to funding subsidies with government transfers, because the money flows directly to the intended beneficiary.

A more common approach to channeling government funding for utility subsidies is for the utility to receive general financial support (grants, tax exemptions, guaranteed low prices for inputs, loan guarantees, support for research and development, etc.) and then to make subsidy allocation decisions. The government provides the financial support to the utility, and the utility is expected to pass this benefit on in the form of lower prices to customers in general or to some particular privileged customer group. An alternative approach is for utilities to incur losses by providing subsidies to consumers and then to be reimbursed by the government. This arrangement is often unplanned, as when governments assume the debt obligations of utilities that are in bad financial shape.

Each approach carries the risk that the government will fail to deliver the promised resources. This risk is borne directly by the customer in the case of burden limit subsidies and directly by the utility in the other options considered, and the risk is particularly high in the case of unplanned subsidies to the utility. Where governments fail to deliver subsidies, utilities may end up in an unfunded subsidy situation. Unusually, the Chilean water subsidy program addresses this problem by allowing utilities to stop providing subsidies to consumers if the utilities are not adequately reimbursed by the government. Because such a move would be politically unpopular, this requirement provides strong incentives for government officials to ensure that it does not happen.

In the case of government financial support for utilities, consumers face an additional risk that resources transferred by the government to the utility will be absorbed in the form of inefficiency and will fail to filter through in the form of lower prices. Where utilities rely on state transfers, utility managers experience a soft budget constraint that undermines incentives to manage resources efficiently, because higher costs may be accommodated by larger state transfers. Utility managers may have significant power in budget negotiations because of the potential threat of service interruptions if adequate financing is not forthcoming. In such situations, subsidies may effectively be captured by utility employees and contractors in the form of excess costs, rather than being transferred to customers in the form of lower prices.

For example, in the case of the Hyderabad Municipal Water Supply and Sewerage Board, it was estimated that about 40 percent of the annual subsidy transfer from the state government in 2001 was absorbed by utility employees in the form of excess labor costs (Foster and Homman 2001). The remaining 60 percent of the subsidy benefited consumers in the form of utility tariffs that were below the true costs of efficient service provision. Nevertheless, the unreliability of government funds led to underfinancing of maintenance and capital programs, so that the utility was able to provide water for only a couple of hours every other day. Consumers spent a sum equivalent to about half of the subsidy they received on storage systems and tanker water so they could cope with intermittent service (figure 2.1).

Figure 2.1 Who Ultimately Captures Government-Funded Subsidies to Utilities?

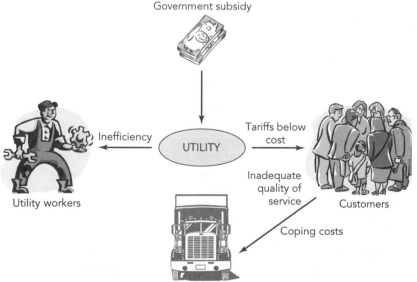

Source: Foster and Homman 2001.

Subsidies for capital projects are another common form of government support for utility operations. Like the fiscal transfers and other financial support for utilities, capital subsidies have the potential to lower the utility's costs (and thus lower prices) or to avoid burdening customers with the cost increases associated with improved service levels. Capital subsidies are unique among government-funded subsidies, however, in that the choice of the capital project (not just the utility's decision about how to allocate the cost savings across customers) has an effect on the distributional incidence of the subsidy. For example, capital projects that lead to service expansions will benefit unconnected customers, whereas capital projects aimed at improving the reliability of service will benefit only existing customers.

It is sometimes argued that financing subsidies from government funds is desirable because it avoids distortions in utility price structures. While this is true, it overlooks the fact that raising taxation revenue can also introduce important distortions into the economy as a whole—for example, by diluting incentives to work or to save, or by reducing consumer spending. Empirical studies suggest that this cost of public funds can actually be quite high. It has been estimated that in the United States each dollar of public funds that is raised has an opportunity cost of US$1.30 of private consumption (Ballard and others 1985), while more recent estimates for 38 African countries find an average opportunity cost of US$1.17 for each dollar of tax revenue raised (Warlters and Auriol 2005).

A politically attractive alternative to funding subsidies with government funds is to rely on *cross-subsidies* generated within the utility. Revenue earned in excess of costs from some customers or in one part of the utility's business is used to offset losses created by the subsidy programs. Cross-subsidization may take many forms. The two most common forms of this practice are for industrial customers to pay prices in excess of costs to subsidize residential consumption, and for high-volume consumers within the residential customer class to subsidize low-volume users. There are other types of cross-subsidies. Existing customers may subsidize the expansion of the water supply network into unserved areas. Depending on how the fixed costs of electricity service are allocated, high-density areas might subsidize low-density areas. In multiservice utilities, surcharges on one service can be used to keep prices low for another service. In Ecuador, for example, a surcharge on telecommunications is used to fund investments for water utilities. In Gabon, the national water and electric utility uses profits from urban electricity supply to subsidize water and electricity service in small towns and rural areas. Thus, even though the water business generates only 15 percent of the utility's total revenues, it accounts for 60 percent of the overall investment plan (ERM 2002; Tremolet 2002).

Cross-subsidies are popular because they appear to permit utilities to achieve cost recovery without relying on central government transfers. Cross-subsidies are not without their own risks, however. Achieving cost recovery by using cross-subsidies requires having the right balance between subsidy recipients and cross-subsidizers; otherwise, the utility will not be able to recoup the revenue lost through subsidy provision. Because consumers react to the price distortions entailed by establishing a cross-subsidy mechanism, this balance is hard to predict and sustain over time.

In some situations, reaching a balance is simply not possible because of the socioeconomic composition of the customer base. For example, this is the case where there are simply not enough industrial consumers or enough high-income, high-consumption residential consumers to compensate for the mass of low-income consumers who are thought to be deserving of subsidization. In general, industrial customers account for 10 to 15 percent of water utility revenues and 40 to 60 percent of electric utility revenues. For example, in Colombia, only 15 percent of water customers are net contributors to the national cross-subsidy scheme, compared with 55 percent of electricity customers, because of greater industrial demand for power than for water supply (World Bank 2004a).

This more favorable balance between industrial and residential customers makes electricity appear to be a more promising sector for applying this type of cross-subsidy. However, growing liberalization of electricity markets for larger industrial customers has at the same time made such cross-subsidization increasingly difficult to sustain. By contrast, in the water supply sector, which remains a monopoly, industrial customers are more exposed to this type of policy. Nevertheless, even in the water supply sector, industrial customers still have the option of reacting to cross-subsidization by disconnecting themselves from the public network and by arranging their own private supply of water, or perhaps by relocating to a different service area.

This option can lead to a vicious circle in which the shrinking base of subsidizing customers leads to even more punitive prices on the remaining cross-subsidizers, which further accelerates the contraction of the customer base. This situation arose in Côte d'Ivoire during the 1980s, when a policy of free water connections for urban and rural customers was funded by imposing hefty surcharges on a few hundred industrial customers. Although the scheme was initially successful in expanding access, it ultimately collapsed as industrial customers exited from the public network (Lauria and Hopkins 2004). For this reason, having a sense of the price elasticity of demand of both the subsidized customers and the cross-subsidizers is a critical step in designing any tariff that relies on cross-subsidies.

Much of the empirical evidence regarding price elasticity of demand in different cases indicates that industrial customers may be more price sensitive on average than residential customers (table 2.2). Where this is so, high markups on industrial customers may ultimately be counterproductive, so that cross-subsidy schemes predicated on cross-subsidies from industrial customers

Table 2.2 Summary of Evidence on Price and Income Elasticity

Sector and customer class	Price elasticity			Income elasticity		
	Median (number of observations)	Mean	Standard deviation	Median (number of observations)	Mean	Standard deviation
Electricity						
Residential	−0.32 (57)	−0.39	0.25	0.28 (38)	0.47	0.45
Industrial	−0.42 (10)	−0.42	0.20	n.a.	n.a.	n.a.
Water						
Residential	−0.38 (155)	−0.38	0.22	0.35 (69)	0.36	0.22
Industrial	−0.54 (17)	−0.54	0.32	n.a.	n.a.	n.a.

Source: Authors' elaboration based on a survey of published studies.

Note: Residential values for electricity are based on data from 31 countries and 57 separate estimates of elasticities. Residential values for water are based on data from 18 countries and 155 separate estimates of elasticities.

n.a. = not applicable.

may be on shaky financial ground. The burden placed on cross-subsidizers can be minimized (and the financial stability of cross-subsidy mechanisms thus improved) by funding cross-subsidies across a relatively broad customer base and by keeping the associated surcharge as low as possible.

When transfers or cross-subsidies fail to fully cover the financial losses associated with subsidizing consumers, consumer utility subsidies are termed *unfunded subsidies*. Loss-making utilities are forced to reduce expenditures on system expansion, maintenance, or asset renewal when their budgets run short. Such cutbacks have serious long-run effects on the quality of service and on the ability of the utility to meet demand growth. The lower the quality and reliability of service, the less valuable the service is to households and the higher are the coping costs they face. Households are forced to turn to alternative fuels or to alternative water sources in times of outages, to filter or boil water, to buy water storage containers, and to find ways to protect appliances against power surges.

The Funding Mechanism Affects the Net Distributional Incidence of Subsidies

It is important to note that only a subgroup of the general public ultimately pays for utility subsidies, whether in the form of higher taxes, higher utility prices, or deteriorating utility service. The distribution of costs across society may differ substantially according to how taxes are raised, how cross-subsidies are structured, and how service restrictions are allocated across the population. Thus, funding mechanisms can play important roles in determining the distribution of the net benefits of the subsidy.

For example, if all nonpoor households were cross-subsidizers and if all poor households received the subsidy, then a cross-subsidy structure would increase the progressivity of the subsidy. If, however, some poor households become cross-subsidizers, the cross-subsidy structure could work against the objective of targeting benefits to the poor. The same is true for subsidies funded from general tax revenue or from property taxes. If the tax system is progressive, then the funding mechanism will improve targeting of the poor. A regressive tax system, however, can have the opposite impact—any benefits that poor households receive from their utility subsidy may be lost through general taxation. Unfunded subsidies transfer the subsidy burden to future generations of utility consumers or taxpayers who will be responsible for repairing run-down systems.

Measuring the net benefit of a subsidy to a particular household (the subsidy received minus the contribution to the subsidy pool) is very difficult, in practice, because information on contributions to the subsidy pool is rarely available. In most of this book, the focus is on the distribution of the utility subsidies themselves, but where possible the impact of the funding mechanism on the distribution of subsidy benefits is also examined.

How Prevalent Are Different Types of Subsidies?

Little systematic information is available about the prevalence of untargeted subsidies, implicit targeted subsidies, and explicit targeted subsidies in water supply and electricity sectors around the world. This is due in part to the lack of comparable data across cases and in part to the lack of careful analysis of subsidies in the literature. To analyze prevalence, data were collated from a variety of regional databases and country case studies to obtain a global overview of subsidy practice based on evidence for some 80 large cities in the case of water and some 50 countries in the case of electricity. The analysis of increasing block tariffs presented below is based on evidence on tariff structures for 50 water utilities and 66 electric utilities from around the world (presented in appendix H).

Underpricing and Increasing Block Tariffs
Are Common for Water Sector

A recent survey by Global Water Intelligence (GWI) covering water utilities in 132 major cities worldwide revealed that underpricing of water supply services is widespread, even in high-income and upper middle-income

Box 2.2 Indicative Cost-Recovery Ranges for Water Services

GWI (2004) developed the following ranges for identifying the probable
degree of cost recovery in developing and industrialized countries. The
box table differentiates between tariffs that are in most cases insufficient to
reach even basic operation and maintenance (O&M) costs, tariffs that are
probably high enough to be covering operation and some maintenance
costs, and tariffs that may be high enough to be covering O&M plus some
capital costs. Cost estimates for developing countries are somewhat lower,
reflecting lower labor costs.

	Developing countries	Industrialized countries
<US$0.20/m^3	Tariff *insufficient* to cover basic operation and maintenance (O&M) costs	Tariff *insufficient* to cover basic O&M costs
US$0.20–0.40/m^3	Tariff *sufficient* to cover operation and some maintenance costs	Tariff *insufficient* to cover basic O&M costs
US$0.40–1.00/m^3	Tariff *sufficient* to cover operation, maintenance, and most investment needs	Tariff *sufficient* to cover O&M costs
>US$1.00/m^3	Tariff *sufficient* to cover operation, maintenance, and most investment needs in the face of extreme supply shortages	Tariff *sufficient* to cover full cost of modern water systems in most high-income cities

Source: GWI 2004.

countries (GWI 2004). According to survey data and estimates of tariff levels
that would be needed to achieve varying degrees of cost recovery (box 2.2),
it appears that 39 percent of water utilities have average tariffs that are set
too low to cover basic operation and maintenance (O&M) costs. A further
30 percent have tariffs that are set below the level required to make any
contribution toward the recovery of capital costs (table 2.3). The average
tariff rises substantially across country income levels, from US$0.11 per
cubic meter in low-income countries to about US$0.30 in middle-income
countries, reaching US$1.00 in high-income countries. Nevertheless, even
in high-income countries, only 50 percent of water utilities charge tariffs

Table 2.3 Overview of Average Water Tariffs and Probable Degree of Cost Recovery

Grouping of water utilities	Average water tariffs (US$/m³)						Percentage of utilities whose average tariffs appear to be . . .[a]		
	Mean	Median	Min.	Max.	25th percentile	75th percentile	Too low to cover basic O&M	Enough to cover most O&M	Enough for O&M and partial capital
Global	0.53	0.35	0.00	1.97	0.13	0.85	39	30	30
By country income level									
HIC	1.00	0.96	0.00	1.97	0.60	1.37	8	42	50
UMIC	0.34	0.35	0.03	0.81	0.15	0.57	39	22	39
LMIC	0.31	0.22	0.04	0.85	0.19	0.39	37	41	22
LIC	0.11	0.09	0.01	0.45	0.05	0.16	89	9	3
By region									
OECD	1.04	1.00	0.00	1.97	0.70	1.37	6	43	51
LAC	0.41	0.39	0.12	0.81	0.22	0.54	13	39	48
MENA	0.37	0.15	0.03	1.17	0.03	0.60	58	25	17
EAP	0.25	0.20	0.04	0.53	0.18	0.30	53	32	16
ECA	0.13	0.16	0.01	0.20	0.08	0.17	100	0	0
SAS	0.09	0.06	0.02	0.22	0.05	0.12	100	0	0

Sources: ADB 2004; ADERASA 2005; GWI 2004; NIUA 1999.

Note: Average tariffs are based on residential consumption of 15 cubic meters. Data are drawn from utilities serving 132 major cities worldwide, broken down geographically as follows: OECD, 47; South Asia (SAS), 24; Latin America and Caribbean (LAC), 23; East Asia and Pacific (EAP); 19; Middle East and North Africa (MENA), 12; Europe and Central Asia (ECA), 6. The same group of countries is broken down by income group as follows: high-income (HIC), 52; upper-middle-income (UMIC), 18; lower-middle-income (LMIC), 27; lower-income (LIC), 35.

O&M = operation and maintenance.

a. Based on GWI 2004 (box 2.4).

high enough to cover more than O&M costs. In low-income countries, barely
3 percent of water utilities were able to achieve this level. Some degree of
general subsidy is thus the norm.

These findings are confirmed by additional data collected for this study.
Those data show that many countries, including Organisation for Economic
Co-operation and Development (OECD) countries, still provide grant subsidies for constructing water infrastructure. The subsidies involved are quite
substantial and even reach 100 percent in some cases. There is also further
evidence that many water utilities are not recovering even O&M costs from
customers. Evidence compiled on Asian water utilities in the late 1990s
showed that the operating ratio (annual O&M costs relative to annual billing)
was less than 1 for 35 of 49 utilities (McIntosh and Yñiquez 1997). Canada
has an estimated $1.2 billion per annum shortfall in tariff revenues in water
utilities (OECD 1999).

Implicit subsidies are also omnipresent in the water supply and sanitation sectors. Implicit subsidies associated with unmetered service are very
common, producing widespread subsidies for high-volume unmetered customers. Of 50 water utilities reviewed for this study for which information
on metering was available, about a quarter had meter coverage below 50 percent. Metering coverage varies widely, from 0 percent in Calcutta and Ireland,
to 100 percent in Chile. A recent survey of 22 major urban water utilities in
Latin America found an average meter coverage of 78 percent, with an
interquartile range from 65 percent to 95 percent (ADERASA 2005). A similar survey of metropolitan water utilities in India found that only a handful of cities had come close to achieving universal metering, and elsewhere
average meter coverage was about 62 percent in larger cities and 50 percent in smaller cities (Ragupathi and Foster 2002). The practice of combining water and sewer tariffs—another source of implicit subsidies—is quite
common in both Latin America and Asia, but in Latin America, at least,
many utilities have taken steps to avoid charging households without sewer
connections for sewer service. Finally, many water utilities have low collection rates and many illegal connections, which means that nonpaying
households are subsidized by those that do pay.

As regards explicit subsidies, it is quite common to find higher average
prices for industrial than residential customers across all geographic regions,
possibly indicating the presence of cross-subsidies between customer classes.
This price differential exists in 90 percent of the utilities in our sample for
which information is available. A recent survey in Latin America found that
in 17 major urban water utilities, industrial customers were charged
2.24 times as much as residential customers for an equivalent volume of
water (ADERASA 2005). A similar study of 23 metropolitan cities in India
found that the ratio was 5.42 times as much (Ragupathi and Foster 2002).

Most water tariff structures are block tariffs, which means that quantity
targeting is used to allocate subsidies within the residential customer base.

The majority of utilities surveyed in Latin America and Asia use increasing block tariff structures with two to four consumption blocks (table 2.4). In Latin America, and to a lesser extent in South Asia, increasing block tariff structures also often include fixed charges that are relatively high compared with the average consumer bill. In most Latin American cases, the tariff for the last consumption block begins to be high enough to cover a significant proportion of capital costs, while in Asia the tariff for the last block is commensurate only with O&M costs. However, in both cases, the last tariff block begins to apply only at consumption levels of about 70 cubic meters per month, which is about three times as high as typical residential consumption. In OECD countries, linear tariff structures are more common, although increasing block tariff structures are still found in a significant percentage of utilities. North America is the only region of the world where decreasing block tariff structures are found, albeit in a minority of cases.

In Latin America, the majority of utilities surveyed offer a separate social tariff structure for disadvantaged customers. Eligibility for this tariff is often determined on the basis of proxy means tests of various kinds. Social tariffs are also known to be widely practiced in Europe and Central Asia.

There is only limited information available about service-level targeting for water supply services. Such targeting seems to be most common in Africa and Asia, where it is common for water supplied through public standpipes to be provided free of charge.

Electricity Sector Achieves Better Cost Recovery and Targeting

Generalized underpricing is less prevalent in the electricity sector than in the water supply sector. A global survey of cost recovery using a methodology similar to the GWI study for water (see box 2.3) found that 15 percent of electricity utilities had average tariffs below the level likely required to cover O&M costs, and a further 44 percent had tariffs below the level required to make any contribution toward the recovery of capital costs (table 2.5). The average tariff rises substantially across country income levels, from US$0.05 per kilowatt-hour in low-income countries to about US$0.07 in middle-income countries, reaching US$0.12 in high-income countries. In high-income countries, more than 80 percent of electric utilities charge tariffs high enough to more than cover O&M costs, while in low-income countries, only 25 percent of electric utilities achieve this level.

However, it should be noted that many industrialized countries that charge cost recovery prices for electricity have—in parallel—developed substantial social safety nets to help cover electricity and heating fuel charges. Those programs are funded directly by fiscal transfers. Examples include the U.S. Low-Income Home Energy Assistance Program (amounting to US$1.7 billion per year), the French energy funds for low-income households (amounting to US$175 million per year), and the British fuel poverty

Table 2.4 Overview of IBT Tariff Structures for Residential Water Customers

	Fixed charges, with or without minimum consumption		Block structure				
	Minimum consumption (m³/month)	Fixed charge (% of 15m³/month)	Number of blocks	Size of first block (m³/month)	Size of last block (m³/month)	Price of first block (US$/m³)	Price of last block (US$/m³)
Latin America	5	36	4	24	72	0.32	0.82
Bolivia	4	43	7	23	195	0.22	0.75
Brazil	10	26	5	20	70	0.40	1.59
Colombia	0	34	2	20	40	0.38	0.44
Costa Rica	15	100	4	25	60	0.31	0.70
Nicaragua	0	6	2	20	20	0.24	0.54
Peru	4	31	4	18	80	0.22	0.73
South Asia	3	73	2	13	79	0.08	0.32
Bangladesh	0	0	1	n.a.	n.a.	0.08	n.a.
India	3	100	2	17	134	0.06	0.15
Nepal	10	45	1	n.a.	n.a.	0.16	n.a.
Sri Lanka	0	0	5	10	25	0.01	0.48
East Asia	1	44	4	17	74	0.13	0.35
Cambodia	0	0	4	7	50	0.14	0.33
China	0	0	2	12	62	0.08	0.47
Indonesia	0	0	3	10	20	0.13	0.20
Korea, Rep. of	0	28	4	30	100	0.24	0.60
Malaysia	0	44	3	20	35	0.15	0.45
Mongolia	0	0	1	n.a.	n.a.	0.12	n.a.
Philippines	10	59	8	20	200	0.04	0.12
Vietnam	0	0	4	20	50	0.11	0.27

Source: Adapted from appendix H.

Note: n.a. = not applicable.

Box 2.3 Indicative Cost-Recovery Ranges for Electricity

Following the Global Water Intelligence methodology for the water sector described in the text, Foster and Yepes (2005) developed indicative ranges for cost recovery in the electricity sector. Their analysis, presented in the box table below, was based on discussions with international experts on electricity tariffs. Different thresholds are provided for residential and industrial customers to reflect the lower cost of service provision to the latter group.

Tariff	Residential customers	Industrial customers
< US$0.04/kWh	Tariff insufficient to cover basic O&M costs	Tariff insufficient to cover basic O&M costs
> US$0.05/kWh		Tariffs likely to be making a significant contribution toward capital costs, in most types of systems
> US$0.08/kWh	Tariffs likely to be making a significant contribution toward capital costs, in most types of systems	

Source: Foster and Yepes 2005.

---

payments. The special welfare assistance programs for energy reflect the fact that this service has a relatively high weight in the household budget, particularly in cold countries where heating requirements are substantial.

The magnitude of implicit subsidies is also lower in the electricity sector than in the water supply sector. Metering levels are typically much higher—and close to universal—thereby avoiding implicit cross-subsidies between metered and unmetered customers. Moreover, the issues presented by joint charging of water and sewerage services do not arise. Nevertheless, collection rates and theft through illegal connections remain a problem for many electrical utilities, generating significant implicit subsidies for non-paying households and for those with illegal connections.

As regards explicit subsidies, differential pricing between industrial and residential customers is less common in the electricity sector than it is in the water supply sector. Of the electricity utilities in Europe and

Table 2.5 Overview of Average Electricity Tariffs and Probable Degree of Cost Recovery

Grouping of electricity utilities	Average electricity tariffs in US$/m³						Percentage of utilities whose average tariffs appear to be...[a]		
	Mean	Median	Min.	Max.	25th percentile	75th percentile	Too low to cover basic O&M	Enough to cover most O&M	Enough for O&M and partial capital
Global	0.08	0.07	0.01	0.21	0.05	0.10	15	44	41
By income									
HIC	0.12	0.11	0.06	0.21	0.09	0.13	0	17	83
UMIC	0.07	0.06	0.04	0.14	0.05	0.09	0	71	29
LMIC	0.06	0.05	0.03	0.14	0.04	0.08	27	50	23
LIC	0.05	0.05	0.01	0.13	0.04	0.06	31	44	25
By region									
OECD	0.12	0.11	0.06	0.21	0.09	0.13	0	17	83
LAC	0.09	0.09	0.05	0.14	0.06	0.10	0	47	53
ECA	0.06	0.04	0.02	0.14	0.04	0.08	31	38	31
EAP	0.05	0.05	0.01	0.08	0.04	0.06	29	65	6
SSA	0.05	0.06	0.03	0.08	0.04	0.06	29	71	0
SAS	0.04	0.04	0.04	0.05	0.04	0.05	33	67	0

Sources: ERRA 2004; Estache and Gassner 2004; OECD 2004; OLADE 2004; UN-ESCAP 2004.

Note: Data drawn from 84 countries worldwide, broken down as follows by region: OECD, 23; Latin America and Caribbean (LAC), 19; Europe and Central Asia (ECA), 18; Sub-Saharan Africa (SSA), 13; East Asia and Pacific (EAP), 8; South Asia (SAS), 3. The same group of countries is broken down by income group as follows: high-income (HIC), 23; upper-middle-income (UMIC), 18; lower-middle-income (LMIC), 26; lower-income (LIC), 17.

O&M = operation and maintenance.

a. Based on Foster and Yepes 2005 (box 2.3).

Central Asia, the Middle East, Sub-Saharan Africa, and South and East Asia for which information is available, 30 percent charge different tariffs to residential and industrial customers, possibly resulting in cross-subsidies to residential consumers. In Latin America, only 1 of 14 utilities charges higher average prices to industrial customers than to residential ones. In all the others, residential customers pay higher rates than industrial clients.

The use of special social tariffs in electricity for low-income households is relatively common in Latin America and in Europe and Central Asia. In Latin America, the most common criterion used to determine eligibility for social tariffs is the volume of consumption. However, in Eastern Europe, there is greater use of proxy means tests, categorical targeting, and administrative selection in general. Information on the prevalence of social tariffs in Africa and in South and East Asia is not available.

The use of quantity targeting to distribute the benefits of explicit subsidies is quite common in electricity services—though not omnipresent, as in water services. About 70 percent of countries surveyed applied increasing block tariff structures for electricity. Analysis of the tariff structures in place show that such structures typically comprise three to four blocks (table 2.6). The first block tends to vary between 50 and 100 kilowatt-hours per month, with a tariff of about US$0.05 to US$0.06 per kilowatt-hour. The size of the last block varies enormously, from about 200 to 2,000 kilowatt-hours per month. A handful of countries, including the United Kingdom and several countries in Asia, apply decreasing block tariff structures. Most regions present isolated cases of volume-differentiated tariff structures (multiple tariffs applied to customers in different consumption ranges).

There is little information on service level targeting, but available information suggests that it is comparatively rare. Only one or two of the countries surveyed reported that they differentiated domestic tariffs according to load, or according to whether single-phase or triple-phase service was provided.

The Majority of Subsidies for Water and Electricity Apply Quantity Targeting

To summarize, available evidence suggests that quantity-targeted subsidies are by far the most common form of explicit subsidy in both the water supply and the electricity sectors. Because general underpricing is still present in many utilities, quantity targeting and other alternative measures are often combined with a general subsidy so that all households are subsidized and the targeting mechanism is used to distribute the subsidy between households.

Table 2.6 Overview of IBT Tariff Structures for Residential Electricity Customers

	Fixed charges, with or without minimum consumption		Block structure				
	Minimum consumption (kWh/m)	Fixed charge (% of 100kWh)	Number of blocks	Size of first block (kWh/m)	Size of last block (kWh/m)	Price of first block (US$/kWh)	Price of last block (US$/kWh)
Latin America							
Brazil	13	22	4	93	308	0.06	0.11
Colombia	0	0	3	30	125	0.03	0.07
Ecuador	0	0	2	200	200	0.05	0.07
Honduras	0	20	6	50	300	0.08	0.11
Mexico	20	50	3	100	300	0.05	0.08
Nicaragua	0	18	3	50	100	0.11	0.15
Paraguay	0	0	6	25	1,000	0.04	0.26
Peru	0	0	3	50	150	0.05	0.06
Venezuela, R. B. de	100	100	3	300	500	0.07	0.10
Asia							
Cambodia	1	n.a.	4	54	255	0.06	0.07
Indonesia	0	0	3	40	105	0.06	0.11
Lao PDR	0	n.a.	3	23	60	0.16	0.17
Malaysia	0	14	3	50	151	0.03	0.04
Philippines	10	9	3	103	533	0.07	0.11
Sri Lanka	0	n.a.	5	10	300	0.07	0.08
Thailand	0	5	6	30	180	0.03	0.13
Vietnam	0	0	5	78	400	0.04	0.16
Africa							
Cape Verde	0	n.a.	3	95	2,250	0.15	0.19
Kenya	0	0	2	40	n.a.	0.02	0.19
Uganda	0	7	4	50	7,000	0.03	0.10
São Tomé and Príncipe	0	n.a.	2	30	300	0.07	0.17
Zambia	0	n.a.	3	300	700	0.01	0.03
Zimbabwe	0	n.a.	4	50	1,000	0.02	0.05

Source: Adapted from appendix H.

Note: n.a. = not applicable; m = month; IBT = increasing block tariff.

Table 2.7 Summary of Prevalence of Different Types of Subsidies in Water and Electricity

	Water	Electricity
Untargeted subsidies	39% of utilities fail to cover O&M; 69% fail to cover full capital costs	15% of utilities fail to cover O&M; 59% fail to cover full capital costs
Implicit subsidies	Widespread as a result of low meter coverage, lack of separate accounts for sewerage, low revenue collection, and illegal connections	Less widespread as a result of higher metering, but low revenue collection and illegal connections remain problematic
Explicit subsidies with quantity targeting	Widespread IBTs, used by 80% of utilities, suffer from high fixed charges and shallow price gradients	Widespread IBTs, used by 70% of utilities; lesser prevalence of high fixed charges and steeper price gradients
Explicit subsidies with service-level targeting	Significant use of public standpipes	Occasional use that is based on load profile
Funding	Combination of government transfers, cross-subsidies, and unfunded subsidies	Combination of government transfers, cross-subsidies and unfunded subsidies

Source: Authors' elaboration.

Note: IBTs = increasing block tariffs; O&M = operation and maintenance.

When one compares the water supply and the electricity sectors, it is evident that consumer utility subsidies are much more prevalent in the former than in the latter (table 2.7). The water supply sector has a much lower degree of cost recovery and metering coverage than the electricity sector, leading to more untargeted and implicit subsidies in the water sector. It is also more common in the water sector to charge different prices to industrial and residential customers and to apply increasing block tariff structures that subsidize all but the very highest levels of residential consumption. The lower prevalence of industrial to residential cross-subsidies for electricity reflects the increasing liberalization of power markets, as well as the greater sensitivity of industries to electricity pricing.

Why Are Subsidies So Prevalent?

Why are consumer utility subsidies so prevalent, and why are they more prevalent for water than for electricity? The idea of subsidizing water and electricity services (the latter particularly in cold climates) has widespread support among politicians, policy makers, utility managers, and the public at large. Subsidies for basic services—particularly subsidy mechanisms such as increasing block tariffs—are considered fair and even necessary for ensuring that poor households enjoy the use of those services. They are also seen as an alternative instrument of social policy, as a way to increase the purchasing power of the poor. The next chapter considers policy rationales for subsidizing the poor in more detail. However, irrespective of the policy motivation, it is important to understand how the cost structure of water and electricity services makes them tempting candidates for subsidization, especially when there is political interest in subsidization.

Three characteristics of the cost structure are considered here. The first is the relatively high proportion of fixed costs to total costs, which means that the economically efficient pricing solution (marginal cost pricing) will, in many situations, not lead to full cost recovery. The second is the relatively high percentage of nonattributable or common costs, which are difficult to allocate precisely to different customers. The third is the high capital intensity of water and electric industries, combined with long asset lives, which collectively make it feasible to get away with underpricing services in the short or medium term. Each of those characteristics of the water and electricity sectors is considered in more detail below.

High Fixed Costs Complicate the Determination of Prices

The theoretical ideal for utility pricing is marginal cost pricing. The most efficient consumption level and allocation of consumption across customers are obtained when all customers face the marginal cost of using an additional unit of water or electricity as they decide how much to consume. Under marginal cost pricing, each customer will consume up to the point that the marginal cost of using another unit of water or electricity is greater than the value he or she places on that additional unit of consumption.

In practice, marginal cost pricing is rarely implemented, however, because it is not always compatible with other objectives of tariff design. For example, marginal cost pricing will not necessarily lead to full cost recovery. The high proportion of fixed costs in the total cost structure of utilities means that marginal costs decline with the scale of production, thus making the marginal cost lower than the average cost. As a consequence, marginal cost pricing would not allow firms to break even financially. Strict implementation of marginal cost pricing in this situation would result in an untargeted, across-the-board price subsidy. In the longer run, of course, marginal costs tend to rise as the capacity limits of current infrastructure are reached and as the need to develop new (often more costly) facilities becomes apparent. When the marginal cost exceeds the average cost, marginal cost pricing is consistent with recovering all costs.

The potential incompatibility between marginal cost pricing and cost recovery gives rise to much discussion and controversy about how to recover the costs of service without deviating too far from the ideal rule for marginal cost pricing. Two possible solutions to this problem have been identified in the economics literature. The first is to cover the deficit arising from marginal cost pricing by using a budget transfer from the state. This school of thought gives rise to the tendency toward government-funded subsidies that was documented above. The second possible solution is to allow some markup of prices over marginal costs to allow the firm to break even. This school of thought opens the door for cross-subsidization between different customer categories, as was also documented earlier.

In principle, there are many different ways in which prices could be marked up over marginal costs to ensure full cost recovery. The economics literature has focused on developing pricing rules that minimize the distortions caused by raising prices above marginal costs. Building on the work of Boiteux (1971), Ramsey (1927) showed that the best way to close the gap was to apply markups over marginal cost pricing that were inversely proportional to the price elasticity of demand of each customer, thereby minimizing the deviations from what each customer would have consumed under marginal cost pricing. This markup effectively entails charging higher prices to those customers with the most inflexible demands on the system, which in practice are often domestic customers. Coase (1946) later showed that it was possible to improve on Ramsey-Boiteux pricing by using two-part tariffs when the elasticity of connection is zero. In this way, all consumers continue to face marginal cost prices on each unit consumed, and fixed costs are recovered through a flat entry fee, which is akin to a lump-sum tax. However, a potential disadvantage of two-part tariffs is that small consumers may be discouraged from using the network because it may not be worth their while to pay the flat entry fee.

In practice, the wide range of potential solutions for recovering fixed costs means that more often than not those degrees of freedom are used to advance social and political objectives, rather than to promote economic efficiency. This means that fixed costs are recovered primarily from those customer groups with the perceived highest ability to pay for the service, generally industrial customers. From the policy maker's perspective, one of the attractions of determining utility prices in this way is that it often gives the impression that social policy objectives can be achieved at zero fiscal cost. However, there is clearly an economic cost associated with this approach, which leads to distortions in economic behavior. The reason is that determining prices in this way typically involves charging the highest prices to the largest consumers (commerce, industry, and high-volume domestic consumers). If those are the customers whose consumption decisions are most sensitive to price (that is, those who have the highest price elasticity, as table 2.2 suggests might be the case), they should—according to Ramsey-Boiteux principles—face the lowest marginal prices, not the highest ones.

Nonattributable Costs Lead to Discretion in Cost Allocation

The costs of providing utility services are difficult to attribute uniquely to different customers or even customer groups. The reason is that water and electricity can flow freely across networks that are shared by large numbers of customers; thus, it is not feasible or meaningful to say which water molecules or electrons go to specific customers or exactly which parts of the network were used to reach those customers. Moreover, strictly speaking, the cost of serving each individual customer is different, because the cost will be affected both by the precise geographic location and by the time profile of consumption.

This situation creates a considerable degree of discretion in allocating costs across customer groups, and it is always tempting to use this discretion to further social and political objectives. There are, however, economic limits on the extent to which costs can be arbitrarily assigned to politically convenient customer categories.

Faulhaber and Levinson (1981) use a game-theoretic bargaining framework to shed light on this issue. This framework is based on the concepts of stand-alone cost and incremental cost. *Stand-alone cost* is defined as what it would cost a particular customer or group of customers to abandon the network and to provide its own utility services on an independent basis. *Incremental cost* refers to the additional costs placed on the system to attend to the needs of a new customer or group of customers who decide to connect to the system. As a result of the cost structure of utility services, stand-alone costs are often quite high, while incremental costs are often quite low.

Faulhaber and Levinson (1981) show that any set of prices that will ensure that no group of consumers will pay more than its stand-alone cost and that each group of consumers will pay at least its incremental costs would be acceptable to all parties involved as the outcome of a bargaining process. The reason is that it is no longer in the interest of any group of consumers to break away from the utility's client base because, by definition, those customers are being offered a price that is lower than their stand-alone cost. At the same time, it is not in the interest of any group of consumers to try to exclude any other group from the utility's customer base because, by definition, all are paying more than their incremental cost. Hence, all groups are making some contribution toward common costs, thereby reducing the burden to be shared among other customers.

Given the high fixed costs of utilities as noted above, the range defined by incremental and stand-alone costs can be a very wide one, meaning that a wide range of potential prices could emerge and be justifiable in principle. This range varies considerably according to the local context. Cities with good-quality, shallow groundwater—such as many in Asia—have a very low stand-alone cost for urban water supply. As a result, network connections may be very sensitive to the design of tariff structures. More generally, commercial and industrial customers may face a lower stand-alone cost than the cost to residential customers, owing to the larger volume of consumption within commercial and industrial areas. They are thus more likely to abandon network services as utility prices increase.

Long Asset Lives Make It Tempting to Underfinance

Utility services are characterized by a high degree of capital intensity and by long asset lives (table 2.8). The table shows that—in the network components of the electricity and water services—70 percent to 90 percent of costs can be capital costs. Such assets typically last for much longer than 20 years.

High capital intensity and long asset lives make it possible to get away without covering the full capital costs of service provision—at least for some period of time. This opens the door to unfunded subsidies of the type described above. The problem is more severe in the case of water utilities than electric utilities because water networks and their associated services deteriorate quite gradually, without necessarily threatening the continuity of provision. Power systems, however, are more sensitive. Inadequate maintenance can lead relatively quickly to outright failure and prolonged blackouts—which are, moreover, politically unpopular. For this reason, it is easier for politicians to underfinance water and sewerage services than electricity services.

Table 2.8 Capital Intensity and Asset Lives for Utility Services

	Capital intensity (% of total costs)	Typical asset lives (years)
Electricity		25–30
Generation	35–75	
Transmission	90	
Distribution	70	
Water	65	20–40
Sewerage	80	40–60
Telecommunications	25–45	10–15

Source: Authors' elaboration that is based on consultations with World Bank specialists.

As a point of contrast, it is interesting to examine the equivalent parameters for the telecommunications sector, which has a much lower level of capital intensity and substantially shorter asset life (table 2.8). This explanation is one of several potential reasons those services have been less vulnerable to underpricing than water or electricity services. Because capital represents a lower proportion of total costs, there is less scope for reducing prices by squeezing capital maintenance. Moreover, because asset lives are shorter, equipment needs to be replaced more frequently in order to ensure service continuity.

In summary, the cost structure of utility services means that there is no unique, widely accepted formula for utility pricing that will achieve cost recovery. Therefore, there is considerable scope for modifying the way that costs are recovered. Furthermore, the long-lived nature of network assets makes it possible to defer the recovery of capital costs for some time before service quality begins to decline. As a result, it can be politically tempting to sustain general price subsidies for water and electricity services or to use utility prices as a vehicle for income redistribution.

Summary

This chapter presented a general typology of utility subsidies. Utility subsidies can be used to reduce the cost of either consuming or connecting to utility services. Subsidies may be untargeted, involving generalized underpricing of the service, or may be targeted to benefit specific groups. Although many common utility practices lead to implicit subsidization, the focus of this book is on explicit targeted subsidies, which represent a deliberate attempt to benefit certain groups of customers. Explicit subsidies can be targeted on the basis of categorical variables, geographic zones, or individual means testing, or may be designed to allow beneficiaries to self-select the subsidy through their choice of the quantity or type of service that they consume.

Three different vehicles of subsidy finance were defined and distinguished, involving direct transfer of government funds, cross-subsidy among customer groups, and unfunded subsidies that entail running down the capital stock. Each has its drawbacks. Government transfers are often unreliable and may undermine managerial incentives, so that subsidies are ultimately absorbed by inefficiencies within the utility rather than passed on to customers. Cross-subsidies create distortions in pricing that affect consumer behavior and that may ultimately undermine financial sustainability of the utility by creating incentives for customers to turn to self-provision. Unfunded subsidies ultimately impose a heavy nonfinancial burden on consumers in the form of deteriorating service quality and reduced service expansion.

Utility subsidies were found to be quite prevalent across most regions of the world—particularly in developing and transitional countries. Quantity targeting, built around the increasing block tariff structure, is by far the most common approach to subsidization. However, it is typically combined with general underpricing, so that all customers benefit from subsidies to varying degrees. Subsidies tend to be more prevalent in the water supply sector than in the electricity sector. Electric utilities tend to recover a higher proportion of costs, to make much greater use of metering, to be less reliant on quantity targeting, and to be much less likely to charge different prices to industrial and residential customers.

One of the reasons utility services are so prone to subsidization lies in the very cost structure of such network industries, in particular the preponderance of fixed and nonattributable costs, as well as the high capital intensity and long asset lives. A high share of fixed costs means that marginal cost pricing does not necessarily allow full cost recovery in the short run, thus providing a justification for government transfers or price markups to close the financial gap. At the same time, a high share of common or nonattributable costs introduces substantial discretion in the allocation of such costs across different customer groups, making it politically tempting to use utility tariffs as an off-budget vehicle for financing social objectives. Finally, high capital intensity and long asset lives mean that expenditures can often be quite easily deferred by underfunding ongoing operations and postponing capital maintenance activities, the negative effect of which becomes apparent only gradually as service levels decline.

For all those reasons, the central policy question with regard to utility subsidies is typically not whether to introduce them but how to deal with those that are already in place. In particular, can and should utility subsidies be scaled back or radically overhauled in their design? The answer depends on how well the subsidies perform in meeting the sectoral and social objectives that are typically used to justify their existence. The nature of those motivations is the topic of the next chapter.

3

The Rationale for Subsidizing
Services for the Poor

There are essentially two distinct rationales for subsidizing water and electricity services for the poor. The first rationale is based on a sectoral perspective: utility subsidies help to make (or keep) services affordable for poor households and thus facilitate the achievement of universal access and broader cost recovery for the sector. The second rationale is based on a social policy perspective: utility subsidies are an effective way to address income poverty and inequality, particularly in countries that may lack the administrative capacity to implement more sophisticated means-tested cash transfer schemes. The purpose of this chapter is to explore both of those perspectives in greater depth.

Both perspectives can be understood within a social welfare framework. If income is seen to be the primary determinant of social welfare, then utility subsidies present simply one more vehicle for boosting the income of poor households. However, if social welfare is conceived as multidimensional—encompassing income and monetary components such as health, dignity, and social participation—then utility subsidies may provide a means of facilitating household access to the other aspects of social welfare.

Subsidies Are Instruments of Sectoral Policy

It is widely assumed among policy makers in developing countries that utility services represent basic needs that would not be affordable to a substantial segment of the population if charged at cost recovery prices. If tariffs remain or become unaffordable, it is argued, a significant segment of the population will be unable to connect to utility services or to keep up with their utility bills once connected. As a result, subsidization of those services, at least for the poor, is necessary. Three questions can be raised about this argument:

1. What is an affordable tariff?; 2. Are tariffs unaffordable?; 3. Would affordable tariffs and connection charges make services accessible to the poor?

Affordability Is a Subjective Notion

From an economic perspective, households choose the bundle of goods and services that maximizes their utility, subject to preferences and budget constraints. Preferences differ substantially across households, reflecting varying income levels, demographics, and health, as well as social and cultural factors, and can, therefore, lead to widely diverging choices about how much to spend on a given service. There is thus no economic basis for judging whether a particular household is spending too much on, or consuming too little of, any particular utility service. Thus, the concept of an affordable tariff has no real basis in economic theory.

Rather than focusing on normative concepts of affordability, economists attempt to measure willingness to pay for services. Willingness to pay indicates the maximum price at which a household would still be willing to use the service, and, as such, it provides a measure of affordability that avoids making value judgments about how much households should be spending. What each household is willing to pay for water supply, electricity, or sanitation varies and depends on household preferences and the quality of existing service alternatives (for example, wells, rivers, and kerosene). It is, therefore, not possible to make blanket statements about what households in one city, much less households in general, would be willing to pay.

Willingness-to-pay studies have been used to try to measure how much connected and unconnected households would pay in practice for a connection to a water supply or electricity system or for a basic block of water supply or electricity services. The results are then compared with cost recovery prices to determine to what extent those prices are affordable to different segments of the population. If a large percentage of the population is unwilling to pay the cost of service provision, and yet there is a political imperative to provide it, then fiscal transfers or cross-subsidies will be necessary to bridge the financial gap. In this sense, willingness-to-pay information can be very useful to policy makers who are trying to decide what level of service could be sustainably provided with a given subsidy budget. If a small proportion of users are unwilling to pay cost recovery prices, identifying those types of households can help in designing targeted subsidies. Numerous methodologies are available for measuring willingness to pay, and a huge literature exists on the advantages and disadvantages of each (box 3.1).

In the case of the water supply sector, there has been a recent review of willingness-to-pay studies using the contingent valuation methodology in Central America (Walker and others 2000). In about half the cities studied, water consumers were, on average, willing to pay substantially more than the current tariff but still significantly less than cost recovery levels. In the

---

Box 3.1 Methodologies for Measuring Willingness to Pay

Economists have developed numerous methodologies for measuring willingness to pay (Freeman 1994). Those methodologies fall into two broad categories: revealed preference approaches and stated preference approaches.

The revealed preference approaches rely on existing economic behavior in other markets to determine the preferences of the household with regard to the particular service in question. This approach is often used to place a lower bound on willingness to pay for utility services by currently unconnected households. For example, if households without access to water or electricity currently spend US$10 per month on tanker water or candles and batteries, then they must be willing to pay at least as much for a higher-quality network-based service. The drawback of this approach is that there may not always be evidence of this kind on which to draw, and, moreover, the evidence is seldom a perfect source of information about willingness to pay, given important qualitative differences in the services involved.

Stated preference approaches, such as contingent valuation, rely on asking households questions about carefully constructed hypothetical scenarios. In contingent valuation surveys, households are asked how much they would be willing to pay (or whether they would be willing to pay a certain sum) for a connection or for a block of water or electricity under a series of well-specified service conditions. The drawback of this approach is that, however carefully constructed the hypothetical scenario, it remains hypothetical and people's responses to such questions may not reflect how they would actually behave in a real situation.

Given the limitations of each approach and the significant differences between them, the results obtained for a given situation may differ substantially. As a result, economists sometimes prefer to use multiple methods to define a more credible range for willingness to pay.

---

other half of the study cities, consumers were willing to pay significantly more than cost recovery levels, on average (figure 3.1). However, in three of the six cases, an alternative methodology for estimating willingness to pay produced results that would lead one to the opposite conclusion. (In two of the cases, the contingent valuation method produced a higher result for willingness to pay than that obtained with revealed preference methods, while in the third case the opposite was true.) A similar study (Choe, Varley, and Biljlani 1996) in Dehra Dun, India, found that 80 percent of consumers

Figure 3.1 Willingness to Pay for Water against Full Cost Tariff in Central America

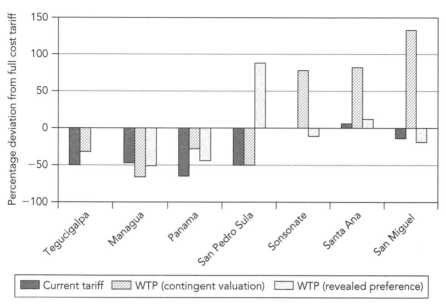

Source: Walker and others 2000.
Note: WTP = willingness to pay.

were willing to pay more than the current tariff (figure 3.2). Even so, the maximum willingness to pay—US$0.20 per cubic meter—still falls short of the likely full cost of service provision. New research on willingness to pay for water services in Sub-Saharan Africa finds that households are generally willing to pay between US$0.30 and US$0.40 per cubic meter for private connections, which is generally below the prevailing price (Keener and Banerjee forthcoming).

In the case of electricity, use of the contingent valuation approach has been much more limited. One of the reasons for that limitation is the relative ease of calculating existing household expenditures on electricity substitutes, such as candles and kerosene lamps. Those data appear to provide a solid lower bound on what households might be willing to pay for a superior electricity service, and thus the data reduce the need to depend on hypothetical survey questions. Recent research has served to develop a refined methodology for inferring the demand for lumens on the basis of current expenditure patterns of different types of households (Barnes, Fitzgerald, and Peskin 2002; ESMAP 2002). For the case of India, Barnes, Fitzgerald, and Peskin (2002) find that rural households connecting to electricity receive an average benefit (consumer surplus) of US$0.30 to

Figure 3.2 Willingness to Pay for Water Supply against Current Tariff in Dehra Dun, India

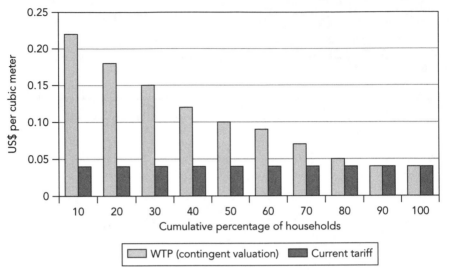

Source: Choe, Varley, and Biljlani 1996.

Note: WTP = willingness to pay.

US$0.40 per kilowatt-hour as a result of improved illumination as compared with a tariff of US$0.04 per kilowatt-hour. In the case of Indonesia, a benefit (consumer surplus) of US$36.75 per household per month is estimated for households that switch from kerosene lamps to electricity for lighting purposes.

Normative Burden Limits Are Often Invoked to Gauge Affordability

In practice, the willingness-to-pay approach is not so often applied to determine tariff and subsidy levels or subsidy design. Instead, a normative or basic needs perspective is often invoked on the pricing issue, arguing that certain services are not discretionary and that households should be able to pay for a subsistence level of consumption without jeopardizing the ability to pay for other goods and services, no matter how much the households would be willing to pay. Following this line of reasoning, a number of countries and organizations set burden limits, or upper thresholds, on the proportion of income that they consider a household can afford to spend to meet any specific basic need.

In the case of water supply and sanitation, a burden limit of 5 percent of income has been widely adopted as a rule of thumb for assessing affordability. Indeed, the Chilean government adopted this same rule of thumb as a basis for defining the magnitude of transfers needed under its direct water subsidy program (Gomez-Lobo and Contreras 2003). The U.K. government has determined a burden threshold of 3 percent of disposable income for water charges, judging any expenditure above this level to represent hardship (DEFRA 2004).

In the case of electricity, there is no such widely accepted rule of thumb. Nevertheless, in many former Soviet states, housing subsidies were often designed with reference to burden limits of 15–30 percent of income for combined housing and utility expenditures, including all fuels. Furthermore, in 2001, the U.K. government introduced the concept of fuel poverty, referring to households that need to spend more than 10 percent of their income to maintain a satisfactory heating regime of 21 degrees Celsius (DTI 2001).

In this context, it is interesting to examine current expenditure patterns for water supply and electricity in developing countries (figures 3.3 and 3.4). Comparing across regions, households in Africa, Latin America, and Eastern Europe spend two to three times more on average on water supply and electricity, in absolute terms, than do their counterparts in South Asia. Moreover,

Figure 3.3 Monthly Residential Electricity Expenditure Patterns by Region

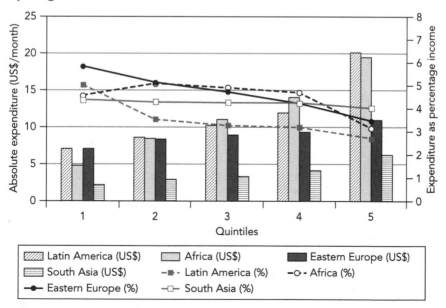

Source: Authors' calculations are based on data from appendixes B and C.

Figure 3.4 Monthly Residential Water Expenditure Patterns by Region

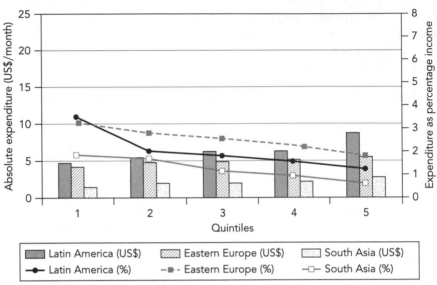

Source: Authors' calculations are based on data from appendixes B and C.

households in all regions spend two to three times as much on electricity as on water supply. When those expenditures are expressed as percentages of household income, the differences between regions are much smaller. Households in Latin America, Eastern Europe, and South Asia all spend on average about 4 percent of income on electricity and 1–2 percent of income on water supply. In almost all cases, the percentage of income spent on water supply and electricity decreases across quintiles as average household income rises. For the poorest households, electricity represents 4–6 percent of income, while water supply represents 1–3 percent of income. This finding would appear to indicate that service is affordable for many poor households, according to the rule of thumb and burden limits discussed above.

Current expenditure patterns reflect current tariffs, which often lie well below cost recovery levels. The patterns observed in figures 3.3 and 3.4 result from the combined effect of regional differences in the customer base, in average willingness to pay, and in the prevalence and magnitude of existing consumer subsidies. It is, therefore, relevant to consider what percentage of income households would have to dedicate to buy a subsistence block of water supply and electricity services, if tariffs were set at full cost recovery levels. Because both the full cost recovery price and the subsistence consumption level vary according to local conditions, a

Table 3.1 Estimated Cost Ranges for Subsistence Service Levels (US$)

Electricity	O&M cost = US$0.04/kWh	O&M plus some capital = US$0.08/kWh
Low subsistence (40 kWh/month)	1.60	3.20
High subsistence (120 kWh/month)	4.80	9.60
Water	O&M cost = US$0.40/m^3	O&M plus some capital = US$0.80/m^3
Low subsistence (8m^3/month)	3.20	6.40
High subsistence (16m^3/month)	6.40	12.80

Source: Authors' elaboration.

Note: O&M = operation and maintenance.

range of parameters is used to establish the potential costs of subsistence service (table 3.1).

In the case of electricity, estimates of monthly subsistence consumption range from 40 kilowatt-hours (equivalent to a few light bulbs and a radio) to 120 kilowatt-hours (equivalent to a few light bulbs, a small refrigerator, and a modest television). The tariffs considered are US$0.04 and US$0.08 per kilowatt-hour, thought to be the minimum price levels consistent with recovering operating costs and some capital costs respectively (see box 2.3).

In the case of water supply, reasonable estimates of monthly subsistence consumption from a private connection range from 8 cubic meters per month (equivalent to 50 liters per capita per day for a family of five, thought to be the minimum necessary to meet basic hygienic requirements) to 16 cubic meters per month (equivalent to 100 liters per capita per day for a family of five, which is equivalent to modest domestic use in urban settings) (Howard and Bartram 2003). In addition, US$0.40 per cubic meter is assumed to be a minimum cost of covering operation and maintenance (O&M) costs, and US$0.80 per cubic meter is the estimated cost of recovering a significant portion of capital costs as well (see box 2.2). These figures lead to estimates in the range of US$1.60 to US$9.60 a month as the cost of subsistence electricity service, and between US$3.20 and US$12.80 per month for basic water supply service (table 3.1).

The distribution of household income within each region was estimated by using household survey data for 32 countries from different developing regions of the world (Foster and Yepes 2005). On this basis, it is possible to calculate what percentage of households in each region have income below any particular level and, thus, to infer what percentage of households might experience affordability problems with full cost recovery charges for utilities.

When the arbitrary affordability threshold of 5 percent of income is adopted, results indicate that a monthly utility bill of US$6 would barely generate any affordability problems in Latin America. However, it would represent a problem for 20 percent of households in East Asia and about 35 percent of households in India and Sub-Saharan Africa (figure 3.5). Raising the monthly utility bill to US$13 would create affordability problems for about 15 percent of Latin American households, 45 percent of East Asian households, and 65 percent of households in India and Sub-Saharan Africa. A lower affordability threshold would increase the percentage of households in all regions expected to have trouble paying utility bills.

In summary, affordability threshold analysis suggests that a sizable percentage of the population in developing countries could face difficulties

Figure 3.5 Affordability of Full Cost Charges for Utility Services in Urban Areas (US$)

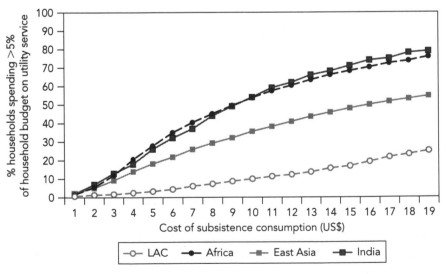

Source: Foster and Yepes 2005.

Note: LAC = Latin America and the Caribbean.

in paying the full operating, maintenance, and capital costs for water supply and electricity services. If tariffs are increased to cost recovery levels, the affordability problem is likely to be far worse in lower-income regions—such as South Asia and Sub-Saharan Africa—than in middle-income regions—such as Latin America.

Evidence from willingness-to-pay studies, however, points to the limitations of this analysis. Households are often willing to pay far more than current tariffs for a decent level of water supply or electricity service. Some households are willing to pay more than 3 to 5 percent of their monthly income for a utility service, but others would refuse to pay that much. In this sense, the affordability threshold analysis does not help determine how many households in a particular utility service area would see cost recovery prices as a barrier to continuing to use improved water and electricity services, nor whether affordable prices would be enough to induce unconnected households to use the services.

Affordability Is but One Barrier to Utility Services

As one assesses whether subsidies help expand coverage or prevent households from exiting the system in the face of price increases, it is important to realize that solving the affordability problem (however affordability is defined and measured) is just one piece of the puzzle. Households consider more than price in determining whether to use utility services. The quality and reliability of network service relative to existing alternatives are another important factor in their decisions. In areas with good cheap alternatives to conventional utility service, demand for connections may be low, even with subsidies. Likewise, if unfunded subsidies lead to a deterioration of service quality, fewer households (even poor households) may be interested in obtaining a connection.

Moreover, many of the households that currently do not use utility services would not be able to connect to services even if they wanted to and could afford to. Access to water networks and electricity grids is particularly limited in rural areas, but even many urban households live in neighborhoods that do not have the basic infrastructure backbone needed to enable connections. Service may be infeasible in some areas because of low density of settlements or technical constraints. In urban areas, it is also common to find legal or administrative barriers that prevent utilities from serving households that do not have secure tenure to their land or houses (see chapter 9 for more discussion of this issue). Financially weak utilities may not have had the resources to expand their distribution networks. Whatever the reason, many households—and many poor households in particular—do not have the option of connecting to utility services, even if subsidies might otherwise make connecting attractive and affordable.

Utility Subsidies Are Also Instruments of Broader Social Policy

The discussion above examined why subsidies for the poor are often advocated as an element of utility policy. Support for utility subsidies also comes from the social policy camp. There are essentially two alternative ways of providing assistance to low-income households: cash transfers (also known as income subsidies) and transfers in kind (such as utility subsidies) that involve providing specific goods or services at less than full market cost. One of the central findings of the social welfare literature is that cash transfers are the best instrument for addressing concerns about poverty and inequality. Cash transfers are preferred to transfers in kind because they respect the principle of consumer sovereignty, thereby allowing beneficiary households to allocate the additional income they receive to the good or service representing the highest priority for the household. Moreover, cash transfers avoid distorting economic decisions in the relevant markets by artificially changing relative prices of goods.

Notwithstanding the theoretical supremacy of cash transfers, the fact remains that transfers in kind are the prevalent instruments of social policy in the welfare systems of most countries. For example, Singh and Thomas (2000), find that more than 70 percent of resources spent on means-tested social assistance programs by the U.S. government was allocated to in-kind programs. The reason is that a number of practical considerations favor transfers in kind.

Transfers in Kind May Be Simpler to Implement Than Cash Transfers

The first consideration relates to the greater administrative ease of implementing transfers in kind. The implementation of cash transfer programs requires a relatively sophisticated apparatus for means testing, which is both costly to implement and prone to abuse. Such systems are often lacking in developing countries and may be slow and difficult to construct. In those situations, transfers in kind present a practical alternative to cash transfers, particularly if they can be delivered in the form of goods that have strong self-targeting properties.

Self-targeting goods are those that are widely and disproportionately consumed by the poor and are, therefore, most likely to ensure that the associated subsidies reach the desired target population (Subbarao and others 1997). The best candidates are goods that meet the following criteria. First, they have universal reach among poor households. Second, they constitute a significant percentage of the expenditure of the poor. Third, they are inferior goods with low (ideally negative) income elasticities, so that the amount consumed as a percentage of income declines as income rises. Fourth, they can be differentiated by quality, so that transfers can be targeted to lower-quality variants more likely to be used by the poor. Fifth, they are not readily tradable, so that the transfers remain with the intended beneficiaries.

The Presence of Externalities and Merit Good Characteristics Is a Further Justification

Over and above any administrative advantages associated with transfers in kind, there may also be theoretical arguments for providing subsidies to specific goods, in particular those that generate positive externalities (or spillover effects) in consumption—for example, by reducing the spread of contagious diseases or environmental pollution. Society as a whole benefits from having more people consume a good that generates positive externalities. Because individuals tend to overlook the spillover effects, they will not, in general, consume (or provide) enough of the good from a social perspective, thereby providing a rationale for its subsidization.

Another justification for transfers in kind arises in the case of so-called merit goods (Musgrave 1959). They have been defined as goods for which an individual's consumption matters to society as a whole, not necessarily because of any spillover effect to society but because they are central to the well-being of the individual. As a result, society takes a paternalistic interest in how much of the good each individual consumes and may, therefore, choose to intervene by subsidizing consumption.

There are a number of reasons why specific goods may be considered merit goods (Thurow 1974). All of them can be readily understood with reference to health and education, which are the two most classic examples of merit goods. The first reason is that individuals may (for diverse reasons and to varying degrees) lack the competence to correctly perceive their own welfare. Therefore, they may not consume as much of a good as they ideally need to, even if they can afford to do so. (Examples are children who do not want to go to school, or adults who avoid going to the dentist.) The second reason is that society may wish for certain goods and services to be equitably distributed even though income is not equitably distributed. (For example, everyone should be able to read and to enjoy a basic level of health.) A third reason is that consumption of certain goods and services (notably education) contribute to the formation of those values upon which society itself is based.

What Kind of Transfers in Kind Would Be Most Effective?

A number of arguments favor transfers in kind over cash transfers under real-world conditions. However, transfers in kind can be delivered through a

Table 3.2 Applicability of Arguments for Transfers in Kind across Different Goods

	Utilities			Other goods and services			
	Water	Sanitation	Electricity	Food	Education	Health	Transport
Administrative							
Universal reach	*		**	***	**	**	**
Inferior goods	*	*	*	***	*	*	*
Differentiable	**	**	*	***	***	***	**
Nontradable	*	**	*		***	***	*
Externalities	**	***		*	*	***	**
Merit goods	**	***	**	**	***	***	**

Source: Authors' elaboration.

Note: *** = often applies; ** = sometimes applies; * = occasionally applies.

wide variety of goods. Common examples include food, education, health, and utility services (such as water supply, sanitation, and electricity). Where fiscal resources are scarce, policy makers need to assess the relative efficacy of different goods and services as alternative vehicles for delivering transfers in kind.

One way of doing that is to compare alternative candidates for transfers in kind in terms of the arguments mentioned above (table 3.2). For example, goods that meet most of the administrative criteria for self-targeting are likely to make better candidates for transfers in kind. Similarly, goods that have strong externalities and the characteristics of merit goods make better candidates than those that do not. Consider first the extent to which different goods meet the administrative criteria for self-targeting transfers in kind.

As regards universal reach, basic foodstuffs (such as carbohydrates) are typically the most widely consumed foodstuffs among the poor. Electricity services also have relatively high coverage in urban areas in some parts of the world. However, that is less often the case for water supply nor for sanitation. Moreover, lack of access for all three services is disproportionately concentrated among the poor. Access to education, health, and transport services is typically high in urban areas, although poorer households are less likely to make use of those services when they are available.

As regards materiality, combined expenditure on electricity, water supply, and sanitation can readily absorb up to 7–12 percent of household income in poor households (see figures 3.3 and 3.4). For households with both network water and network electricity services, electricity generally makes up a larger component of the expenditure. That finding suggests that electricity is a

Table 3.3 Budget Shares for Different Categories of Goods in Africa (Percentage of Household Budget)

	Electricity	Health	Water	Education	Transport	Food
Cape Verde	2.50	1.48	3.24	0.84	4.37	38.27
Ghana	1.54	3.63	2.68	4.38	3.89	55.29
Kenya	0.78	0.22	2.17	3.72	5.19	56.92
Malawi	1.52	1.50	2.95	2.02	1.03	39.88
Uganda	0.73	3.35	3.26	5.05	4.09	43.54
Zambia	2.75	1.78	2.30	3.87	7.96	53.87
Average	1.64	1.99	2.77	3.31	4.42	47.96

Sources: Authors' calculations based on appendix tables B.4. and C.4, plus data from the following household surveys: Cape Verde (2002)—Inquerito as Despensas e Receitas Familiars, Years 2001/02, (Income and Expenditure Household Survey, Year 2001/02); Ghana (1998)—Living Standard Measurement Survey; Kenya (1997)—Welfare Monitoring Surveys III; Malawi (1997)—Integrated Household Survey; São Tomé and Principe (2000)—Inquerito Condicoes de Vida das Familias, Ano 2000 (Survey about Household Living Conditions, Year 2000); Uganda (1999)—National Household Survey; and Zambia (1998)—Living Conditions Monitoring Survey II.

better candidate for subsidization than water supply, if the goal is to increase the disposable income of the poor. However, other goods and services represent an even higher share of income among the poor than either of those utility services. This finding can be seen in some illustrative data on household budget shares from half a dozen African countries (table 3.3). The data show that food absorbs, on average, almost half of the household budget, while spending on transport is almost twice as high as spending on water supply or electricity. Education and health expenditures vary substantially across countries but are generally lower than transport expenditures.

As regards income elasticities, they tend to take values of about 0.3 to 0.5 in the case of water and electricity (see table 2.2 in chapter 2), indicating that water and electricity clearly are not inferior goods that are self-targeted to low-income households. While the amount consumed as a percentage of income declines as incomes rise, the absolute amount consumed generally rises with income. Comparable data on elasticities for other goods were not readily available. Instead, household survey data from the same set of African countries are used to calculate pseudo income elasticities that compare the difference in household spending on each good between the richest quintile and the poorest with the difference in incomes between the two groups (table 3.4). The results show that food has the lowest pseudo-elasticity, closely followed by water. However, electricity has by far the highest pseudo-elasticity of any of the goods considered, showing that it behaves as a luxury good, at least in the African context.

Table 3.4 Pseudo Income Elasticities for Different Categories of Goods in Africa

	Food	Water	Health	Education	Transport	Electricity
Cape Verde	0.55	0.53	1.81	2.80	1.81	3.80
Ghana	0.92	0.28	1.32	0.49	2.50	2.79
Kenya	0.64	1.03	3.18	3.20	4.24	—
Malawi	0.50	2.47	1.21	3.94	5.15	18.55
Uganda	0.65	0.34	1.25	5.37	8.22	19.90
Zambia	0.60	0.83	1.43	1.23	9.48	11.24
Average	0.64	0.91	1.70	2.84	5.23	11.26

Sources: Data for these calculations were drawn from the following household surveys: Cape Verde (2002)—Inquerito as Despensas e Receitas Familiars, Years 2001/02, (Income and Expenditure Household Survey, Year 2001/02); Ghana (1998)—Living Standard Measurement Survey; Kenya (1997)—Welfare Monitoring Surveys III; Malawi (1997)—Integrated Household Survey; São Tomé and Principe (2000)—Inquerito Condicoes de Vida das Familias, Ano 2000 (Survey about Household Living Conditions, Year 2000); Uganda (1999)—National Household Survey; and Zambia (1998)—Living Conditions Monitoring Survey II.

Note: Coefficients reported are the percentage differences in expenditure over the percentage differences in income between the first and fifth quintiles of the per capita expenditure distribution. Although they are not—strictly speaking—income elasticities, they provide similar information about the relationship between expenditure and income. Thus, a value greater than 1 suggests a luxury good.
— = not available.

Quality differentiation is likely to be much harder in the case of utilities than in the case of food, urban transport, and health and education services. For water supply and sanitation, at least some differentiation is possible between household connections and alternative services, such as standposts and latrines. However, quality differentiation between household connections is much harder, even though load limiters (electricity) and restricted-diameter connections (water) can be used to limit quality of service.

As regards tradability, food is most easily traded, while health and education services are least easily traded. Utility services are also relatively difficult to exchange, in that they are supplied to specific households through dedicated infrastructure. Nevertheless, resale of water and electricity to neighboring households through improvised network extensions of infrastructure is not unheard of and can take place on a significant scale, particularly in larger cities.

Merit good arguments may apply across the full range of goods and services considered. Electricity is perhaps the least obvious case. Nevertheless, because it facilitates access to modern information (radio, television, computers) and provides longer hours of light, electricity has been found to promote literacy and education (see chapter 1).

The main externality in the case of water supply and sanitation is reducing the spread of disease. Adequate health care and nutrition undoubtedly play an important role in doing so. However, the provision of safe water and sanitation is also known to have a major effect on public health (see chapter 1).

Summary

The rationale for providing consumer utility subsidies to the poor can be understood either in terms of utilities policy or as part of a broader social policy framework.

From the sectoral perspective, utility subsidies provide a way of making essential services affordable for a broad base of households, with the ultimate goal of expanding coverage and use of improved services. Economists do not work with a set criterion for assessing affordability. Policy makers, by contrast, frequently invoke more or less arbitrary burden limits to define normative criteria for affordability. The burden limit analysis presented in this chapter suggests that—although even poor households may not face significant affordability problems of paying tariffs at today's levels (often well below the cost recovery threshold)—a substantial proportion of the population of lower-income countries may find it difficult to pay the full cost of services. Nonetheless, subsidizing prices will not, on its own, be enough to eliminate all the barriers to service for poor households.

From the social policy perspective, utility subsidies represent a particular form of transfers in kind. Although cash transfers are theoretically preferable, there are a number of reasons that transfers in kind are so prevalent. First, they have much lower administrative costs, particularly when delivered through goods with self-targeting characteristics. Second, it may be desirable for society to encourage the consumption of goods that have positive externalities or the characteristics of merit goods, by reducing the costs that individuals face in doing so. Although utility services meet some of the criteria for transfers in kind, they are not the only goods and services to do so. Food, urban transport, health, and education are other strong candidates. Hence, where fiscal resources are scarce, governments need to prioritize among alternative vehicles for delivering transfers in kind on the basis of their relative efficacy as social policy instruments.

4

The Determinants of Targeting Performance: A Conceptual Framework

The rest of this book turns to the empirical assessment of the targeting performance of consumer utility subsidies. This chapter describes the data, the methodology, and the conceptual framework behind the analysis.

Data and Methodology

Subsidy cases from a variety of sources formed the empirical basis for the analysis. In changing the sample of cases, the objective was to examine as many cases of explicit targeted subsidies as possible. The majority of the existing explicit targeted subsidies studied in the literature are quantity-targeted consumption subsidies, which is not surprising because quantity targeting is widespread in both the water and the electricity sectors. Subsidy simulations were included in the sample of cases to broaden the analysis to other subsidy options.

In some instances, published or unpublished articles were used to explore a case. Information from the articles was used to create as complete a picture of the case as possible. For other cases, it was possible either to return to the original data and to estimate a wider range of parameters, or to build a new case from existing, unanalyzed household survey data. Wherever possible, the case was delimited by utility service area. Water utilities tend to serve one urban area; thus, the water cases are primarily city cases. For electricity cases, a mix of national cases, state cases, and municipal cases were analyzed.

Appendix A lists the cases of existing subsidies, as well as the simulations, and it categorizes them according to the subsidy typology presented in chapter 2. The sample includes 45 electricity subsidies from 13 utilities, plus 32 water subsidy programs from 13 utilities. The appendix also includes information about the original source of the subsidy analysis for each case. For simplicity of presentation, the sources are not cited throughout the rest of the book.

The Financial Value of a Subsidy Is the Measurement
Adopted for the Analysis

For this analysis, the value of a subsidy is defined as the *financial* value of the subsidy. The financial value of a subsidy is equal to the money that the utility loses by providing the subsidy. To operate in a sustainable manner, the utility needs to recoup this loss through government transfers or surcharges on nonsubsidized customers.

The financial value of a consumption subsidy received by household j is equal to $CQ_j - E_j$, where C is the average unit operating and capital cost of producing and distributing water or electricity, Q_j is the quantity consumed by household j, and E_j is that household's expenditure on utility service (that is, the utility bill).[1] This approach to estimating the financial value of a consumption subsidy incorporates two important assumptions. The first assumption is that the unit cost of serving a customer is constant across customers. In reality, costs may differ. For example, pumping water to households on steep slopes is more expensive than servicing households at an elevation lower than the water source. Although logic tells us that these cost differentials exist, the cost differences are rarely known. In practice, therefore, average cost is used to estimate the cost of serving any particular household.

The second assumption is that the cost of serving a customer is solely a function of the quantity of water or electricity consumed, and the cost increases linearly with consumption. This assumption is reasonable for large volumes of consumption but may not be accurate for low consumption levels. Part of the cost of serving a customer is billing, metering, and providing customer service to that client. This cost is likely to be high relative to consumption-based costs for small-volume customers. Unfortunately, information on the average fixed cost of serving a client is not available for any of the utility subsidy case studies. Client service costs are, therefore, combined with other costs in estimating the financial value of the subsidy, which may lead to an underestimation of the cost of serving low-volume customers and, therefore, may underestimate the value of the subsidy those customers receive.

The estimation of the financial value of a connection subsidy begins with an estimate of the average cost of a connection. There is, however, no universally accepted definition of exactly which costs are associated with the installation of a connection and should, therefore, be recovered through the connection charge. Moreover, the cost of connecting a household in an area that already has a network or grid is much lower than the cost of extending the network to connect customers in previously unserved areas. Most of the connection subsidy cases presented in this book assume that the value of the simulated connection subsidy would be constant across new residential customers and would simple equal the utility's current connection charge.

The financial value of a utility subsidy is central to understanding how subsidies affect the use of public funds and the financial health of water and electricity utilities. It is an appropriate measure of the cost to the government or the utility of providing the subsidy. From the subsidy recipient's perspective, however, the financial value of the subsidy may seem less relevant to his or her budgetary position. The recipient might instead focus on the cash value of the subsidy. Few households actually know how much the service they receive costs to provide. Households may perceive (if they understand the utility tariff structure) how much money they save on utility service each month or on a connection thanks to the subsidy. In many cases, this discount will be less than the financial value of the subsidy because generalized underpricing means that even the supposedly unsubsidized bills reflect charges below the average cost of service provision. As prices rise to cost recovery levels, the financial value of a consumption subsidy and this cash value of the subsidy move closer together.

Neither the financial value nor the cash value of the subsidy is equivalent to the welfare value of a utility subsidy—the net impact of the subsidy on household welfare. The estimation of the welfare value of a subsidy requires assumptions about the form of the household utility function, a level of analysis beyond the scope of this book.

Three Dimensions of Subsidy Performance Are Analyzed: Benefit Incidence, Beneficiary Incidence, and Materiality

To analyze how well consumer utility subsidies function as instruments of social policy and the extent to which they help make utility services affordable for households, one must examine three dimensions of subsidy targeting performance: benefit incidence, beneficiary incidence, and material value of the subsidy.

Benefit incidence is meant to address the question: "How well does the subsidy instrument target benefits to the poor versus other households?" A targeting performance indicator, called Ω, is defined to help readers measure the benefit incidence of the subsidy. This measure compares the actual targeting outcome with a neutral subsidy distribution.[2]

The benefit targeting performance indicator Ω is the share of the subsidy benefits received by the poor divided by the proportion of the population in poverty.[3] A value of 1.0 for Ω implies that the subsidy distribution is neutral, with the share of benefits going to poor households equal to their share of the population. For example, if 40 percent of the population is poor, then a neutral targeting mechanism would deliver 40 percent of the subsidy to the poor. It should be noted that neutral targeting is no better than random assignment of subsidies across the entire population or than a universal subsidy that delivers equal benefits to all.

A value greater than 1.0 implies that the subsidy distribution is progressive, because the poor benefit from a larger share of the total benefits than their share of the population. The higher the value, the better the targeting performance. For example, if 40 percent of the population is poor and if the bottom 40 percent of the income distribution receives 80 percent of the subsidy benefits, Ω would equal 2 (80/40). A value of 2 means that the poor are receiving twice as much as they would have received under a universal intervention that distributed the benefits equally to all households. A value below 1.0 implies that the subsidy distribution is regressive: the poor receive a smaller share of the benefits than their population share. If Ω equals 0, then none of the subsidy is accruing to poor households.

Beneficiary incidence is meant to address this question: "Do poor households receive the subsidy?" Two indicators measure how well utility subsidies target beneficiaries. The first is the error of exclusion, defined as the percentage of poor households that do not receive the subsidy. The second is the distribution of beneficiaries across income quintiles. The latter provides a more detailed picture of beneficiary incidence and is reported in appendixes D.1, E.1, F.1, and G.1.

The final dimension of subsidy performance is the material impact of the subsidy: How significant is the value of the subsidy received by poor households? The average value of the subsidy received by poor households as a percentage of household income is used as the primary indicator of materiality.

These three sets of measures provide a well-rounded view of the distributional incidence of subsidies. It would be possible, for example, to have a very well-targeted subsidy (in which nearly all of the benefits go to poor households) that reaches very few households and thus has a high error of exclusion. The most extreme example of accurate targeting but with high rates of exclusion would be a subsidy to only one poor household. Similarly, a subsidy might reach all poor households but provide a benefit that is very small relative to household income and thus will do little to reduce poverty levels.

The Definition of Poverty Can Affect the Results

The calculation of the performance indicators requires a definition of poverty that classifies households as either poor or nonpoor. The choice of poverty line can affect the results.

A distinct advantage of the targeting performance indicator Ω is that it permits a comparison of distributional outcomes across cases in which the percentage of households in poverty differs. For example, the targeting performance of a subsidy that allocates 60 percent of the benefits to the poor when 40 percent of the population is poor ($\Omega = 60/40 = 1.5$) would be the same as that of a subsidy allocating 30 percent of the benefits to the poor, where only 20 percent of the households live in poverty ($\Omega = 30/20 = 1.5$). In both cases, the subsidy delivers 50 percent more to the poor households than they would receive with a neutral (or random) distribution.

However, even with this indicator, the choice of poverty line affects the results. Imagine a case in which the poorest quintile received 40 percent of the subsidy; the second quintile, 30 percent; the third quintile, 20 percent; and the two remaining quintiles, 5 percent each. If the relative poverty line was drawn at 20 percent of the population, then Ω would equal 1.5 (40/20). If 40 percent of the households were considered poor, then Ω would equal 1.75 (70/40). The distributional incidence of the subsidy appears more progressive when the poverty line is set higher. (Of course, another hypothetical example could have led to a different outcome.)

This problem is addressed in three ways. First, to facilitate comparison across cases, the performance indicators are calculated with the poorest 40 percent of households defined as poor for as many cases as possible. Second, in some cases, it is possible to examine the effect of a change in the poverty line on the results. Finally, statistics are presented by quintile (either in the text or in the substantial data appendixes). This presentation gives a more fine-grained picture of distributional incidence than is provided by any single indicator.

Conceptual Framework: The Determinants of Subsidy Performance

The rest of this chapter presents a conceptual framework for analyzing the determinants of the three dimensions of subsidy performance described above. The framework is based on Angel-Urdinola and Wodon 2005a. A formal decomposition of the determinants is first presented. The framework differentiates between access factors, which determine which households are potential candidates for a subsidy, and subsidy design factors, which affect who actually receives a subsidy and the value of the subsidy received.

Consumption Subsidies

As described above, the targeting performance indicator Ω is defined as the share of subsidy benefits received by the poor (S_P/S_H) divided by the proportion of households in the total population (P/H) in poverty. This ratio can also be expressed as the average benefit per poor household, divided by the average benefit per household in the population as a whole:

$$\Omega = \frac{\dfrac{S_P}{P}}{\dfrac{S_H}{H}}, \tag{4.1}$$

where P is the number of poor households, H is the total number of households in the population, S_P is the value of subsidies accruing to the poor, and S_H is the total value of the subsidy received by the population as a whole.

To understand who is excluded from subsidy benefits, first consider A_H, which is the share of households that have potential access to the service. Households with potential access have the option of connecting to water or electricity service because the water network or electricity grid is present in the neighborhood. For households without access, using utility services is not an option.

Next consider $U_{H|A}$, the share of households that actually use the service because they decided (or received the opportunity) to connect to the network or grid. The value of $U_{H|A}$ is the uptake rate of connections among those with potential access, which is a subset of H, the total number of households. Thus, $A_H \times U_{H|A}$ is equal to the actual connection rate, or the percentage of households that are connected and use water or electricity service.

A and U are access factors: factors that determine which households are potential beneficiaries of consumption subsidies. Policy makers or utility managers who are designing a utility subsidy cannot immediately make changes to the number of households with access (A) and the number who use the services (U). Access and usage rates change over time as the result of network expansion and households' connection decisions. Access factors will always (in the short run, at least) affect the distributional incidence of the subsidy, regardless of what type of consumption subsidy is chosen or how it is structured.

Subsidy design factors, by contrast, influence the distributional incidence of the subsidy by interacting with the subsidy model chosen. One subsidy design factor is the targeting mechanism used. $T_{H|U}$ is the share of eligible utility service users (that is, households with access and a connection) who are targeted and, therefore, receive a subsidy. In the case of a general subsidy for all residential customers, $T_{H|U}$ would equal 1, indicating that all households with the potential to receive the subsidy do receive the subsidy.

A, U, and T together determine the beneficiary incidence of the consumption subsidy—that is, who actually receives the subsidy.[5] The share of all households receiving the subsidy is equal to $A_H \times U_{H|A} \times T_{H|U}$. A graphic illustration is provided in figure 4.1.

Figure 4.1 Decomposing Subsidy Performance

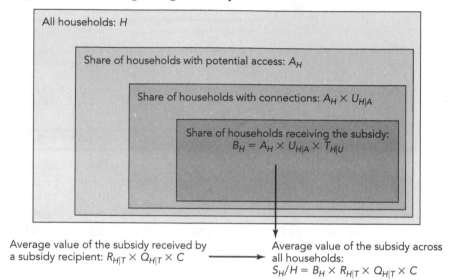

Source: Authors' elaboration.

For poor households, denoted by the subscript P, the share of poor households receiving a subsidy is $A_P \times U_{P|A} \times T_{P|U}$. The variable B is thus a measure of beneficiary incidence, so that

$$B_H = A_H \times U_{H|A} \times T_{H|U} \tag{4.2}$$

$$B_P = A_P \times U_{P|A} \times T_{P|U}. \tag{4.3}$$

Two additional subsidy design factors affect the value of the benefit that a subsidy recipient receives and thus influence the distribution of subsidy benefits between poor and nonpoor households. The first is the rate of subsidization. The average unit cost of producing and distributing the service is denoted by C. The total cost of serving a customer is a function of C and of the quantity consumed by that customer: Q. If the average quantity consumed by subsidy recipients is $Q_{H|T}$, and the average expenditure on water or electricity (that is, the bill paid by subsidy recipients) is $E_{H|T}$, then the average rate of subsidization is $R_{H|T} = 1 - E_{H|T}/(Q_{H|T} \times C)$.

The second factor is the average quantity of water or electricity consumed by subsidy recipients ($Q_{H|T}$). Though under the control of households rather than subsidy designers, the quantity consumed by subsidy recipients is a key determinant of the total value of the subsidy that each recipient will receive. If a household is eligible for a subsidy, the more water or electricity it consumes, the larger will be the total value of the subsidy that household receives. The value of the subsidy is determined by the rate of subsidization,

Table 4.1 Determinants of Consumption Subsidy Performance

	Benefit incidence	Beneficiary incidence	Materiality
Indicator	Ω	Error of exclusion (% of poor not benefiting from subsidy)	Subsidy as a percentage of total household income or consumption (among subsidy recipients who are poor)
Formula	equation 4.7	1 − equation 4.3	$(R_{P|T} \times Q_{P|T} \times C)/Y_{P|T}$, where Y_p is the average income of subsidy recipients who are poor
Access factors			
Access ratio: Access to network or grid in household's neighborhood	√	√	
Uptake ratio: Uptake rate among households with access	√	√	
Subsidy design factors			
Targeting ratio: Share of eligible households targeted for subsidy	√	√	
Subsidy rate ratio: Average rate of subsidization among beneficiary households	√		√
Quantity ratio: Average quantity consumed among beneficiary households	√		√
Cost: Average cost of production, transmission, and distribution			√

Source: Authors' elaboration.

the average quantity consumed by subsidy recipients, and the average unit cost. The average subsidy received by poor subsidy recipients would be $R_{P|T} \times Q_{P|T} \times C$.

Note that unless all households (a) have access to the network, (b) have connections to that network, and (c) qualify to be subsidy recipients on the basis of the targeting procedure used, the average value of the subsidy received by subsidy recipients is less than the average value of the subsidy across all households. The average subsidy benefit per household in the population is equal to

$$\frac{S_H}{H} = B_H R_{H|T} \times Q_{H|T} \times C \tag{4.4}$$

with $B_H = A_H \times U_{H|A} \times T_{H|U}$.

In other words, the average subsidy benefit per household in the population is the product of six terms: access, uptake, targeting, rate of subsidization, quantity consumed, and average cost. The same factors determine the average subsidy benefit per poor household:

$$\frac{S_P}{P} = B_P \times R_{P|T} \times Q_{P|T} \times C \tag{4.5}$$

with $B_P = A_P \times U_{P|A} \times T_{P|U}$.

Recalling equation 4.1, the benefit targeting performance indicator Ω, which represents the share of the benefits of the subsidy that accrues to the poor, is defined as

$$\Omega = \frac{B_P}{B_H} \times \frac{R_{P|T}}{R_{H|T}} \times \frac{Q_{P|T}}{Q_{H|T}} \tag{4.6}$$

or, if the components of beneficiary incidence are presented individually, as

$$\Omega = \frac{A_P}{A_H} \times \frac{U_{P|A}}{U_{H|A}} \times \frac{T_{P|U}}{T_{H|U}} \times \frac{R_{P|T}}{R_{H|T}} \times \frac{Q_{P|T}}{Q_{H|T}}. \tag{4.7}$$

Thus, Ω is simply the product of five ratios, each of which compares the situation of poor households with that of all households in the case area: the access ratio (A), uptake ratio (U), targeting ratio (T), subsidy rate ratio (R), and quantity ratio (Q).

Typically, one would expect the access ratio to be lower than 1 (the poor tend to live in areas with lower coverage of networks or grids than the population as a whole) and the uptake ratio to also be lower than one (when access is available in a neighborhood or village, the poor are less likely to be connected to the network than the population as a whole). Where coverage is not universal, the combined effect of the access ratio and uptake ratio produces an "access handicap," which can be expected to work against the targeting of subsidy benefits to the poor. Subsidy design factors need to overcome the access handicap if the subsidy distribution is to be progressive. To be progressive, the product of the subsidy design factor ratios must be larger than 1.

Complete data on all five factors are not available for most of the cases presented in the book. For most cases, therefore, subsidy performance is decomposed into three groups of factors. First, the combined effect of access (A) and uptake (U) is examined. This combination is equivalent to the connection rate in each service area. Second, targeting (T) is analyzed to reveal the percentage of connected households that are receiving the subsidy. Third, the product of the subsidy rate ratio (R) and the quantity ratio (Q) is examined to determine whether the average subsidy that the poor receive exceeds the average value accruing to all subsidy recipients.

Apart from analyzing the value and determinants of the distributional parameter Ω, beneficiary incidence and the material value of the water and electricity subsidies are also assessed. Table 4.1 indicates which access factors and subsidy design factors come into play in determining these aspects of subsidy performance.

An Illustration: Cape Verde's IBT for Water and Electricity

One of the cases for which near complete data are available is Cape Verde. This case is used to illustrate the application of the conceptual framework. The tariff structures for water and electricity in Cape Verde are both increasing block tariffs (IBTs) and are, thus, supposed to be beneficial to households with low levels of consumption. For electricity, as presented in table 4.2, the tariff structure for residential users consists of two blocks, with the first lifeline block defined as consumption below 40 kilowatt-hours. The water tariff has three blocks, with the changes in pricing occurring at consumption levels of 7 and 10 cubic meters per month. The tariffs in the top block of the IBT are assumed to represent the average cost in the case of both electricity and water. Different estimates of average costs are available, some of which are very close to the tariffs in the top blocks of the IBT. However, those estimates do not take into account an appropriate provision for the cost of capital; hence, it is likely that the full average cost is higher than the top block tariff.

Following the methodology used by the National Institute of Statistics in Cape Verde, a household is considered poor if its per capita consumption falls below a relative poverty line equal to 60 percent of the median household consumption in the 2001–2 survey. With that definition, roughly 37 percent of the population is considered poor. The analysis here assumes that 40 percent of the population is poor.

Results from the decomposition of the determinants of subsidy performance are provided in table 4.3. The benefit targeting performance indicator (Ω) takes a value of 0.24 for water and 0.48 for electricity. These results

Table 4.2 Residential Electricity and Water Tariff Structures in Cape Verde, 2001

Water		Tariff per cubic meter (US$)	Electricity		Tariff per kilowatt-hour (US$)
Consumption block (cubic meters per month)			Consumption block (kilowatt-hours per month)		
0	7	1.83	0	40	0.15
>7	10	2.57	>41		0.19
>10		3.21			

Source: Angel-Urdinola and Wodon 2005a.

Note: US$1 = CVEsc 108.96.

indicate that neither water nor electricity subsidies are pro-poor, because the share of the water subsidies that goes to the poor is five times lower than the share of the poor in the population, and the share of electricity subsidies is three times lower. The error of exclusion in both cases is also very high: 90 percent of poor households do not receive the water subsidy, and 76 percent receive no electricity subsidy.

These findings are due in large part to access factors. For electricity, the availability of access to the electricity network in neighborhoods or villages where households live is somewhat lower for the poor ($A_P = 0.72$) than for the population as a whole ($A_H = 0.82$). Moreover, within the neighborhoods with access, the uptake rate is much lower for the poor ($U_{P|A} = 0.34$) than for the population as a whole ($U_{H|A} = 0.54$). The product of the access ratio and the uptake ratio is 0.55, which means that those access factors put poor households at a significant disadvantage for receiving the electricity subsidy.

To overcome this handicap and to produce a progressive subsidy, the subsidy design factors would need to greatly favor the poor. That does not happen in this case. All residential customers receive some subsidy; none are net cross-subsidizers. As a result, targeting has no role in the final benefit or beneficiary incidence of the subsidy (the value of the targeting ratio is 1).

The remaining subsidy design factors are the rate of subsidization and the quantities consumed. Although the rate of subsidization is greater for the poor than for all households ($R_{P|T} = 0.11$ versus $R_{H|T} = 0.06$), the average quantity (in kilowatt-hours per month) consumed by poor households connected to the network is about half the quantity consumed in the population as a whole ($Q_{P|T} = 56.83$, versus $Q_{H|T} = 111.72$). Because the tariff structure provides greater subsidies to households that consume less, this difference in consumption levels leads to greater percentage discounts for poor households (which tend to be lower-volume consumers). However, the nonpoor still receive a larger absolute subsidy than the poor each month because the nonpoor consume more electricity and almost all of their

Table 4.3 Decomposition of Determinants of Subsidy Performance in Cape Verde

	Share of households with access (A)	Share of households with access who have connections (U)	Share of connected households who receive the subsidy (T)	Rate of subsidization (R)	Average quantity consumed (cubic meters or kWhs per month) (Q)	Average household expenditure (US$) (E)	Average cost (US$) (C)
Water							
Poor households	0.52	0.20	1.00	0.40	3.36	6.60	3.21
All households	0.65	0.41	1.00	0.33	6.37	13.93	3.21
Ratio	0.79	0.49	1.00	1.19	0.53	n/r	3.21
Electricity							
Poor households	0.72	0.34	1.00	0.11	56.83	9.56	0.19
All households	0.82	0.54	1.00	0.06	111.72	19.71	0.19
Ratio	0.88	0.63	1.00	1.70	0.51	n/r	0.19

Source: Angel-Urdinola and Wodon 2005a.

Note: US$1 = CVEsc 108.96.

n/r = not required for calcuation of Ω.

The reported information about poor households and all households has been reduced to two decimal places.

The ratios and Ω were calculated from the full numbers, which are not reported here or in the appendixes.

consumption is subsidized to some degree. The product of the subsidy rate ratio and quantity ratio is 0.87. Ironically, the large difference in average consumption between poor and nonpoor households contributes significantly to the regressivity of the electricity IBT in Cape Verde.

Similar results are obtained for the water IBT in Cape Verde. Although the geographic availability of the network is lower for the poor ($A_p = 0.52$) than for the population as a whole ($A_H = 0.65$), the larger difference is in uptake rates ($U_{P|A} = 0.20$ versus $U_{H|A} = 0.41$). As with the electricity IBT, all households receive the subsidy, so $T_{P|U} = T_{H|U} = 1$. The subsidy rate ratio is slightly above 1, again indicating that the IBT does lead to lower prices per unit on average for the poor than for the population at large. But the average quantity consumed by poor subsidy recipients is only half the quantity consumed in the whole population of subsidy recipients ($Q_{P|T} = 3.36$ cubic meters per month versus $Q_{H|T} = 6.37$). The product of the subsidy rate ratio and the quantity ratio is 0.63. As with electricity, the average subsidy going to poor subsidy recipients is much lower than that provided to all other connected households. The access factors and subsidy design factors combine to produce a highly regressive distribution of subsidy benefits: Ω equals 0.24.

Connection Subsidies

A framework similar to that presented for consumption subsidies can be applied to connection subsidies. As with consumption subsidies, the targeting performance of connection subsidies is determined by access factors and subsidy design factors, but the specific elements differ slightly.

The share of the population with access is denoted by $A_H \times U_{H|A}$ and the share of the population without access and that could potentially benefit from a new connection is $1 - (A_H \times U_{H|A})$. The share of the poor who could potentially benefit from a connection subsidy is $1 - (A_P \times U_{P|A})$. This is the access factor in the design of connection subsidies: the more households that are currently unconnected, the more potential beneficiaries of connection subsidies there are.

Three subsidy design factors come into play to determine the benefit incidence of the subsidies. The first is targeting ($T^C_{H|A}$ and $T^C_{P|A}$). Connection subsidies may be offered to all unconnected households (as would be the case if no connection charge were levied), or they may be targeted only to a subset of households that meet some criteria (such as households in a particular neighborhood).

The second factor is the future uptake of connections: among those households targeted to receive the subsidy, how many will actually decide to connect? Those that decide to connect ($U^C_{H|T}$ and $U^C_{P|T}$) become subsidy recipients; those that do not will not receive the subsidy. This household decision is not under the control of subsidy designers, but it is a powerful determinant of the benefit and beneficiary incidence of the subsidy.

The share of households that benefit from a connection subsidy is, therefore, a function of those households that currently lack connections, those households targeted for the subsidy, and those households that choose to connect when offered the subsidy:

$$B_H^C = (1 - A_H \times U_{H|A}) \times T_{H|A}^C \times U_{H|T}^C \qquad (4.8)$$

$$B_P^C = (1 - A_P \times U_{P|A}) \times T_{P|A}^C \times U_{P|T}^C \qquad (4.9)$$

The third subsidy design factor is the subsidization rate $(R_{H|T}^C)$.[6] This rate is a function of the difference between the average cost of installing a connection (C^C), which is assumed to be constant for all households, and the average connection fee paid by the subsidized households $(F_{H|U}^C)$, so that $R_{H|T}^C = 1 - (F_{H|U}^C/C^C)$.

Note that the rates of subsidization for the poor and for the population as a whole benefiting from the connection subsidies need not be the same. The rate of subsidization of connections for poor households is given by $R_{P|T}^C = 1 - (F_{P|T}^C/C^C)$.

The benefit incidence of connection subsidies, or Ω^C, is

$$\Omega^C = \frac{B_P^C}{B_H^C} \times \frac{R_{P|T}^C}{R_{H|T}^C}, \qquad (4.10)$$

or by decomposing the components of beneficiary incidence, it can be written as:

$$\Omega^C = \frac{1 - A_P \times U_{P|A}}{1 - A_H \times U_{H|A}} \times \frac{T_{P|U}^C}{T_{H|U}^C} \times \frac{R_{P|T}^C}{R_{H|T}^C} \times \frac{U_{P|T}^C}{U_{H|T}^C} \qquad (4.11)$$

The benefit targeting performance indicator for connection subsidies is the product of four ratios: the ratio of unconnected households $(1 - A \times U)$, the targeting ratio (T^C), the future uptake ratio (U^C), and the subsidy rate ratio (R^C).

With consumption subsidies, the a priori expectation is that access factors will tend to work against the progressivity of the subsidy. With connection subsidies, the opposite is true. Typically, one would expect that the ratio of potential poor beneficiaries to all potential beneficiaries to be greater than 1, because a smaller proportion of poor households have water and electricity connections. Unlike consumption subsidies, one could expect access factors to provide a solid basis for making connection subsidies for water or electricity progressive. The product of the remaining ratios must be close to 1 or greater than 1 to ensure that this advantage is sustained.

Table 4.4 presents the determinants of the various subsidy performance indicators for connection subsidies in summary form. This basic framework can be adapted in various ways to reflect differing circumstances.

Table 4.4 Determinants of Connection Subsidy Performance Indicators

	Benefit incidence	Beneficiary incidence	Materiality
Indicator	Ω^C	Error of exclusion (% of poor not benefiting from subsidy)	Subsidy as a percentage of household income or consumption (among subsidy recipients who are poor)
Formula	equation 4.12	1 − equation 4.9	$\dfrac{R^C_{P\|T} * C^C}{Y^C_{P\|T}}$, where Y is the average income of poor subsidy recipients
Access factors			
Ratio of unconnected households: Share of unconnected households (households with potential to connect)	√	√	
Subsidy design factors			
Targeting ratio: Share of households targeted for subsidy among households connecting	√	√	
Future uptake ratio: Share of households that decide to connect once offered the subsidy	√	√	
Subsidy rate ratio: Average rate of subsidization among households that benefit from a subsidized connection	√		√
Average cost: Average cost of a new connection			√

Source: Authors' elaboration.

In chapter 7, which examines the performance of connection subsidies, the framework is expanded to consider the case when not all unconnected households could benefit from a connection subsidy because they lack access to the water network or electricity grid or because they do not meet the utility's criteria for receiving a connection.

An Illustration: Connection Subsidies for Water and Electricity in Cape Verde

The Cape Verde case study can be used to illustrate the application of this framework for assessing the targeting performance of connection subsidies. Because the majority of poor households are unconnected, connection subsidies appear to be an effective way to reach the poor in this case.

No explicit connection subsidy program exists in Cape Verde, so an untargeted connection subsidy is simulated. Table 4.5 presents the key ratios that contribute to the benefit targeting performance of the simulated subsidies. The simulation assumes that the targeting(T^C), future uptake (U^C), and subsidy rate (R^C) ratios are all equal to 1, which means that only the access factor determines the performance of the subsidy. In this case, both the water and the electricity connection subsidies would be progressive (Ω would equal 1.22 for water and 1.35 for electricity).

Table 4.5 Decomposition of Determinants of Connection Subsidy Performance in Cape Verde

	Access factors		Subsidy design factors	
	Ratio of unconnected households	Targeting ratio	Future uptake ratio	Subsidy rate ratio
	$\dfrac{1 - A_P * U_{P\mid A}}{1 - A_H * U_{H\mid A}}$	$\dfrac{T^C_{P\mid A}}{T^C_{H\mid A}}$	$\dfrac{U^C_{P\mid T}}{U^C_{H\mid T}}$	$\dfrac{R^C_{P\mid T}}{R^C_{H\mid T}}$
Water	1.22	1.00	1.00	1.00
Electricity	1.35	1.00	1.00	1.00

Source: Angel-Urdionola and Wodon 2005a.

Summary

This chapter presented a methodology and conceptual framework used to assess the distributional impact of consumer utility subsidies. A few clear messages emerge from the conceptual framework, which foreshadow the empirical findings in subsequent chapters.

Access factors determine whom the potential beneficiaries of consumption and connection subsidies will be. One would expect to find fewer poor households than other households with connections in most developing countries. Thus, one hypothesis is that access factors will create a major hurdle to designing progressive consumption subsidies with low errors of exclusion. By contrast, where the access rate for poor households is less than for the population as a whole, connection subsidies would appear likely to have a progressive distribution.

In the short run, subsidy designers cannot adjust existing connection rates, which significantly limits the scope for improving subsidy performance in the short run. They can, however, decide how to target subsidies among potential beneficiaries and how much of a subsidy to provide. Because access factors work against the poor in the case of consumption subsidies, the effectiveness of the targeting mechanism is typically more critical in the design of consumption subsidies than of connection subsidies. Targeting must overcome the handicap imposed by access factors on consumption subsidies. Of course, targeting may also improve the distributional incidence of connection subsidies.

The framework also illustrates that who ultimately receives a subsidy and how large that subsidy will be is not entirely under the control of subsidy designers. Consumer utility subsidies may influence household decisions about how much water to use or whether to connect to the network or grid, but households make the final decision. In this sense, all consumer utility subsidies have an element of self-selection: household decisions have the power to improve or undermine the performance of subsidies. The art of subsidy design, therefore, requires careful analysis of how a subsidy might affect household behavior.

Notes

1. In the case studies reviewed in subsequent chapters, when information on average cost was not available, the value of the subsidy was estimated as the difference between the bill the household would have received on the basis of its consumption if it were not a subsidy recipient and the household's actual utility bill. Various methods were used to estimate the unsubsidized bill. In the case of IBTs (increasing block tariffs), for example, the price of consumption in the highest block was taken as the reference price for unit cost in many studies. The disadvantage of this approach is that it may overestimate or underestimate the actual financial value of the subsidy, depending on the relationship between this price and the actual average unit cost.

2. A similar targeting indicator was used by Coady, Grosh, and Hoddinott (2003) in their study of the targeting performance of social policy instruments.

3. Note that in some of the cases presented in this book, the analysis is population-weighted, so that the size of households is taken into account when analyzing the

distributional properties of utility subsidies. In other cases, information on household size was unavailable or not considered in the original subsidy analysis.

4. For some consumption subsidies, another subsidy design factor also determines who the beneficiaries of the subsidy will be: the metering rate. Price subsidies, such as those subsidies delivered through increasing block tariffs, are available only to households that have meters. Unmetered households would be ineligible for the subsidy. The importance of metering in explaining benefit and beneficiary incidence is discussed in more detail in chapter 5. It is not included in the general framework presented here, however, because it is feasible to provide subsidies to households who are not metered (for example, through a subsidized fixed monthly charge).

5. There is no quantity variable in this case because a household can have only one connection.

5

The Targeting Performance of Quantity-Based Subsidies

Quantity targeting is the most common mechanism used to explicitly subsidize certain consumers of utility services: most water and electricity tariff schedules are designed so that the price households pay for each cubic meter of water or kilowatt-hour of electricity that they consume varies with the total quantity consumed. Increasing block tariffs (IBTs) and volume-differentiated tariffs (VDTs) are attractive to those interested in subsidizing utility services for the poor for two primary reasons. First, it is often assumed that most poor households are small-volume consumers; targeting subsidies to small-volume consumers is thus tantamount to subsidizing the poor. Second, quantity-targeted subsidies are consistent with the idea of providing all households with access to a limited (or lifeline) quantity of water or electricity at a subsidized price.

In practice, quantity-based consumption subsidies for both water and electricity do a poor job of targeting benefits to the poor and exclude many households from the water or electricity lifeline they purport to provide. This chapter examines why actual practice falls short of expectations, following the model set out in chapter 4. The focus here is on subsidies that rely solely on quantity targeting to allocate benefits. The next chapter investigates to what extent the performance of quantity-targeted subsidies could be improved by combining them with other targeting methods or by redesigning the tariff structures.

A Snapshot of Performance: Quantity-Targeted Subsidies Are Regressive

The sample of quantity-targeted consumption subsidies examined in this chapter includes four cases of IBTs in the water sector: Bangalore, Cape Verde, Kathmandu, and Sri Lanka. The electricity sample is larger, with 18 examples of straight IBTs, 2 simulated IBTs, and 2 VDTs. Of the 18 straight IBTs, 15 are electricity subsidies in Indian states. The other three are in Cape Verde, Peru, and São Tomé and Principe. The simulated IBTs are from Hungary and Rwanda. The cases of VDTs come from Guatemala and Honduras.

Table 5.1 presents a snapshot of subsidy performance for these cases. It is striking that not a single case achieves a progressive, or even neutral, subsidy distribution. In all cases, the share of benefits accruing to the poor is smaller than their share of the population ($\Omega < 1$). The simulated electricity IBT in Hungary comes closest to a neutral distribution (with a benefit targeting performance indicator, Ω, of 0.98). The poorest performers are the water IBT in Cape Verde, where the poorest 40 percent of the population receives only 11 percent of the benefits, and the VDT for electricity in Guatemala (with a discount for all households consuming less than 300 kilowatt-hours per month), which manages to allocate only 8 percent of the benefits to the poorest 40 percent.

Moreover, most of these quantity-targeted subsidies also exclude large numbers of poor households from receiving any benefit. The four water IBTs all exclude more than half of the poor households. The African electricity IBTs exclude more than 70 percent of the poor. Errors of exclusion are somewhat lower in India, but one-third of poor households are still excluded in most cases because they remain unconnected. According to this evidence, the notion that quantity targeting through tariff structures is inherently pro-poor is clearly a misconception.

Figure 5.1 plots Ω against the share of poor households receiving the subsidy. There is a mild positive relationship between the two indicators of

Figure 5.1 Measures of Beneficiary and Benefit Incidence of Quantity-Targeted Subsidies

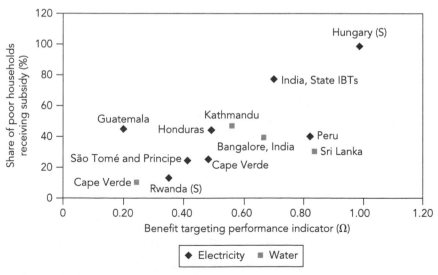

Sources: Appendixes D.1, D.6, E.1, and E.6.
Note: S = simulated.

Table 5.1 Performance Indicators for Quantity-Based Subsidies

Country, city	Type of subsidy	Benefit targeting performance indicator (Ω)	Error of exclusion (%)	Access factors	Subsidy design factors	
				Product of access and uptake ratios (A × U)	Targeting ratio (T)	Product of subsidy rate and quantity ratios (R × Q)
Electricity cases						
Guatemala	VDT	0.20	55.4	0.71	1.00	0.28
Honduras	VDT	0.49	56.0	0.65	1.12	0.68
Peru	IBT	0.82	59.9	0.79	1.24	0.84
Cape Verde	IBT	0.48	75.6	0.55	1.00	0.87
São Tomé and Principe	IBT	0.41	76.8	0.56	1.00	0.74
Hungary (S)	IBT	0.98	01.7	1.00	1.00	0.99
Rwanda (S)	IBT	0.35	87.2	0.40	1.00	0.87
India: average	State IBTs	0.70	21.0	0.89	1.02	0.77
India, Kerala	State IBTs	0.65	14.5	0.93	1.00	0.69
India, Andhra Pradesh	State IBTs	0.78	16.4	0.89	1.01	0.87
India, Tamil Nadu	State IBTs	0.53	15.3	0.91	1.01	0.58
India, Karnataka	State IBTs	0.74	18.6	0.88	1.01	0.83
India, Maharashtra	State IBTs	0.66	13.8	0.98	1.01	0.67
India, Madhya Pradesh	State IBTs	0.70	12.4	0.94	1.00	0.74
India, Gujarat	State IBTs	1.00	21.6	0.93	1.08	1.00

India, Orissa	State IBTs	0.71	40.1	0.80	1.01	0.87
India, Punjab	State IBTs	0.91	13.4	0.97	1.07	0.88
India, Haryana	State IBTs	0.66	15.4	0.94	1.02	0.69
India, Rajasthan	State IBTs	0.84	20.7	0.91	1.02	0.90
India, Delhi	State IBTs	0.57	9.1	0.98	1.01	0.58
India, Uttar Pradesh	State IBTs	0.66	25.8	0.87	1.00	0.76
India, West Bengal	State IBTs	0.62	30.5	0.84	1.01	0.73
India, Bihar	State IBTs	0.43	47.7	0.63	1.00	0.69
Water cases						
Nepal, Kathmandu	IBT	0.56	53.0	0.74	0.99	0.77
India, Bangalore	IBT	0.66	60.5	0.74	1.00	0.90
Sri Lanka	IBT	0.83	69.5	0.83	1.00	1.00
Cape Verde	IBT	0.24	89.7	0.39	1.00	0.63

Source: Authors' elaboration using data from appendixes B–E.

Note: In the case of price subsidies that are only for metered customers, the targeting ratio includes metering as well as targeting. The ratio reflects the percentage of connected poor households that are targeted and that have meters, divided by the percentage of all connected households that are targeted and have meters.

performance, confirming that beneficiary and benefit incidence of subsidies are closely linked. Reaching more poor households is one way of improving the benefit targeting performance of the subsidy.

The results are based on the assumption that 40 percent of households in each case are poor. By an absolute definition of poverty, more than 40 percent of households would be poor in some of the cases, and fewer than 40 percent in others. In Rwanda, for example, 60 percent of households have per capita incomes below the national poverty line. Changing the assumed poverty line has little effect on the results. Errors of exclusion fall as the percentage of households assumed to be poor increases. Nonetheless, even if 80 percent of households were poor, the benefit targeting performance indicator, Ω, would be less than 1.0 for all cases. Figure 5.2 shows how Ω changes as the poverty line changes for a sample of water and electricity cases. Existing quantity-targeted subsidies for water and electricity do a poor job of targeting benefits to the poor, no matter where the poverty line is drawn.

Given the poor targeting performance of the quantity-targeted subsidies, it is interesting to ask whether the benefit and beneficiary incidence of those subsidies is any improvement over general price subsidies delivered through uniform volumetric tariffs. A subsidized uniform volumetric tariff consists of one below-cost price for all units of water or electricity consumed. Unlike the IBT or VDT, all units consumed are subsidized at the same rate.

If one compares the existing water IBTs in Bangalore and in Kathmandu and a simulated uniform volumetric tariff that would produce the same revenue for the utility, that comparison indicates that quantity targeting does almost nothing to make the distribution of subsidy benefits more progressive. In Bangalore, the benefit targeting indicator, Ω, would go down only from 0.66 to 0.64 if the IBT were replaced with a uniform volumetric tariff. In Kathmandu, the same change would result in a reduction from 0.56 to 0.55. A similar comparison was done for the electricity sector in Rwanda, where electricity bills are currently based on a uniform volumetric tariff. This existing tariff is very regressive ($\Omega = 0.26$) and would improve only marginally with a simulated two-block IBT (to 0.35). Beneficiary incidence in these three examples remains virtually unchanged with the simulated tariff modification, because almost all eligible households (connected and metered households) currently receive subsidies. The IBTs do nothing to limit the number of nonpoor households receiving the subsidy.

The Access Handicap: Only Connected Households Are Potential Beneficiaries

From table 5.1, it is clear that access factors play a major role in producing a regressive distribution of subsidy benefits in the IBTs and VDTs studied here. Table 5.2 compares access rates and uptake rates among the poor and

Figure 5.2 Effect of Poverty Assumption on Benefit Targeting Performance Indicator Ω

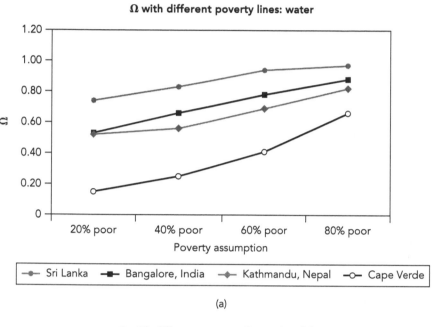

(a)

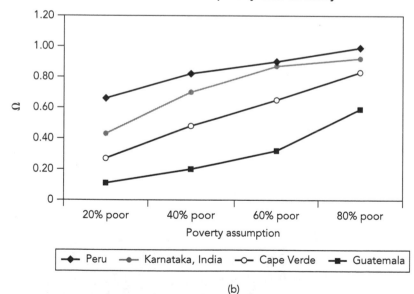

(b)

Source: Authors' elaboration.

Table 5.2 Detailed Decomposition of Factors That Contribute to Ω in the African Subsidy Cases

Country	Type of subsidy	Access factor			Subsidy design factors	
		Access to the network or grid (A)	Uptake of connections among those with access (U)	Targeting among those with access (T)	Rate of subsidization for those receiving the subsidy (R)	Quantity consumed among those receiving subsidy (Q)
Electricity cases						
Rwanda, urban (S)	IBT					
Poor households		0.78	0.16	1.00	0.25	60.56
All households		0.86	0.37	1.00	0.19	92.49
Ratio		0.90	0.44	1.00	1.33	0.65
Cape Verde	IBT					
Poor households		0.72	0.34	1.00	0.11	56.83
All households		0.82	0.54	1.00	0.06	111.72
Ratio		0.88	0.63	1.00	1.70	0.51
São Tomé and Principe	IBT					
Poor households		0.73	0.32	1.00	0.59	98.31
All households		0.85	0.49	1.00	0.51	153.43
Ratio		0.86	0.65	1.00	1.16	0.64
Water cases						
Cape Verde	IBT					
Poor households		0.52	0.20	1.00	0.40	3.36
All households		0.65	0.41	1.00	0.33	6.37
Ratio		0.79	0.49	1.00	1.19	0.53

Sources: Angel-Urdinola, Cosgrove-Davies, and Wodon 2005; Angel-Urdinola and Wodon 2005a, 2005b.
Note: S = simulated.

among all households in the African subsidy cases. In all cases, both access rates and uptake rates are lower for the poor than for the population as a whole. Access to the network is particularly low for water, but it is far from universal among the poor, even in electricity. Moreover, the percentage of households with access and that decide to connect is very low for both the poor and the nonpoor. This picture of low uptake rates may be partially influenced by the difficulty of accurately identifying from household survey data those households with access to the network or grid. This problem would tend to overestimate the percentage of households with access to the network and thus underestimate uptake rates. Nonetheless, the overall picture is clear: poor households are less likely than the population as a whole to have water and electricity connections in those African countries. Both the limited extension of water networks and electricity grids and the decisions by households not to connect when they have the choice contribute to this outcome.

Although it is not possible to decompose access and uptake for the other subsidy cases, connection rates among the poor are lower than for the population as a whole in all cases (see appendixes B.1 and C.1). There is sufficient evidence to suggest that low connection rates are not unique to the cases studied in this book. Komives, Whittington, and Wu (2001), for example, reached the same conclusion regarding the relative coverage rates of poor and nonpoor in their study of the relationship between income and infrastructure coverage in a different set of cases from around the world. The access handicap—and thus the gap between poor and nonpoor—is largest in cases of low coverage, which is more common for water services than for electricity services. This same result was found in an analysis of coverage in Latin American countries (World Bank 2004a).

This access handicap is a major hurdle for all utility consumption subsidies. Even in high coverage countries such as those of the former Soviet bloc, access factors, at best, have a neutral effect on benefit targeting performance. The ratio of access factors would equal 1 if coverage were universal. This ratio would be greater than 1 only for inferior goods, which the poor are more likely than the nonpoor to consume. Standard piped water and electricity service are not inferior goods.

Metering: A Necessary Condition for Quantity Targeting

To receive a quantity-targeted subsidy, households must have not only a connection but also a meter. Increasing block tariffs and VDTs depend on households having meters to measure water and electricity use. Subsidies delivered through quantity targeting, by definition, miss households that do not have meters.[1] Metering is less widespread in the water and sanitation sector than in the electricity sector. Most electricity connections are metered,

Table 5.3 Effect of Connection Rate and Metering Rate on Potential Beneficiaries of Quantity-Targeted Subsidies

Country, city	Year	Percentage of households with connections	Percentage of connections that are metered	Percentage of households that are potential beneficiaries of a price subsidy
Electricity cases				
Guatemala	2000	73.0	62.0	45.3
Water cases				
Santiago, Chile	1998	99.0	99.0	98.0
Lima, Peru	1991	75.0	30.0	22.5
Buenos Aires, Argentina	1992	70.0	2.0	1.4
Abidjan, Côte d'Ivoire	1987	60.0	96.0	57.6
Conakry, Guinea	1984	38.0	5.0	1.9
Kathmandu, Nepal	2001	65.5	27.9	18.3
Sri Lanka	2003	37.4	97.0	36.3

Sources: Foster and Araujo 2004; Noll, Shirley, and Cowan 2000; Pattanayak and Yang 2002; Pattanayak and others 2004.

whereas there are some unmetered water connections in almost all cities. Table 5.3 shows how metering can affect the potential beneficiaries of quantity-targeted water subsidies in a range of cities. At the time these data were collected, fewer than 2 percent of households in Conakry would be eligible for a quantity-targeted water subsidy, whereas nearly all households are eligible for water price subsidies in Santiago. Even in cities with similar coverage rates, differences in metering patterns can create huge differences in the pool of potential subsidy beneficiaries. Lima and Buenos Aires had water coverage rates of 75 and 70 percent, respectively. In Lima, 30 percent of connections were metered, compared with 2 percent in Buenos Aires. In the end, fewer than 2 percent of households in Buenos Aires stood to potentially benefit from a quantity-targeted subsidy, compared to 23 percent of households in Lima.

Because utilities often charge households for the installation and maintenance of a meter, one might expect to find that poor households with connections are less likely to have meters than richer households with connections. In Guatemala, for example, roughly one-quarter of all households in the poorest income quintile that have electricity connections do not have meters. By contrast, only 10 percent of the connected households in the richest quintile are missing meters (Foster and Araujo 2004). If this were true more generally, metering coverage patterns would accentuate coverage trends and would further increase the gap between poor and nonpoor potential subsidy beneficiaries. Unfortunately, information about the coverage of meters by income class is scarce, making it difficult to assess whether this finding from the Guatemala electricity sector extends to the water sector and to other cities and countries.

Targeting Potential: Do the Poor Consume Less Than the Rich?

The extension of networks, connection rates, and metering rates are factors over which subsidy designers have little immediate control. Most discussion of subsidy design, therefore, focuses on how to target households within the pool of potential beneficiaries. Quantity targeting is used to direct subsidies to particular households on the basis of the quantity of water or electricity that the households use. The premise behind quantity targeting is that subsidizing low-volume consumers is tantamount to subsidizing the poor because the poor consume less than the nonpoor. Testing this assumption, however, is not a simple matter (box 5.1), because information about the relationship between household income and water and electricity consumption is not regularly reported. There is, however, sufficient evidence to draw some preliminary conclusions about income and consumption patterns for water and electricity.

Electricity Consumption Patterns Differ between Poor and Rich, Less between Poor and Middle-Income Households

A recent study of the relationship between urban growth and fuel use (Barnes, Krutilla, and Hyde 2005) examines household fuel use in 45 cities in 12 countries on three continents using household surveys conducted under the auspices of the Energy Sector Management Assistance Programme (ESMAP) of the World Bank between 1984 and 2000.[2] The data from all cities were pooled, and the relationship between household per capita income and household fuel use was analyzed. As table 5.4 shows, the study found that per capita total energy use is essentially constant across income classes. However, households at higher income levels tend to use less lower-efficiency fuel such as wood and charcoal and more higher-energy-value modern fuels such as electricity and propane (also known as liquefied petroleum gas, or LPG).

Per capita electricity use among middle-income households in this study is roughly double that of low-income households. The gap between middle-income and rich households is even larger: the richest households consume

Box 5.1 The Challenge of Comparing Consumption Levels of the Rich and the Poor

Until quite recently, little information has been available about the relationship between income and the consumption of water and electricity. Information needed to compare consumption levels across income groups is rarely available. Consumption information is available only for metered households. It is costly to determine how much water or electricity unmetered households or households with nonfunctioning meters are using. This problem is particularly acute in the water sector, where low coverage of meters is common. A second problem is that available consumption information can rarely be associated with household income information. Most utilities know how much water or electricity metered households use but not whether the households are rich or poor.

In the absence of ideal data, analysts must make a number of assumptions in order to estimate the relationship between income and consumption in a particular case. Household surveys are used as the data source because they facilitate linking information on income with information on water and electricity bills. In those surveys, households are usually asked to report how much they spent on water or electricity in the previous month. They are also asked to show their bills, if available. The bills help ensure that households accurately report their expenditures and also give the enumerators a chance to record the exact quantities of water or electricity consumed by metered households. It is then possible to use the consumption information from metered households to predict water or electricity consumption levels for other households in the sample for which consumption information is not available. Analysts accomplish this goal with regression techniques that predict consumption as a function of income and other household characteristics (number of people in the household, presence of appliances, and so forth).

Some observers would question the usefulness of estimating current consumption patterns, even if accurate information on both income and consumption for all households were easily available. The observed relationship between the two variables is a function of the tariff structure in place. If the data reveal that poor households consume the same amount of electricity as the rich on average, is that because subsidies lower prices and thus encourage the poor to consume more? If prices were to rise to achieve cost recovery, would the consumption gap increase? There is every reason to expect that consumption by all customers would decrease if prices increased, but there is little evidence available to suggest whether the response of poor and nonpoor customers would be different.

Table 5.4 Relationship between Income and Energy Use in 45 Cities in 12 Developing Countries: Average KgOE per Capita per Month

Income class	Monthly income (US$ per capita)	Firewood	Charcoal	Coal	Kerosene	LPG	Electricity	Total
Low	8.59	3.63	3.28	2.38	1.33	0.15	0.60	11.59
Middle-lower	15.51	2.57	2.66	3.21	1.73	0.42	0.82	11.59
Middle	25.02	2.10	2.20	2.83	1.50	1.25	1.15	11.15
Middle-upper	41.94	2.62	2.54	0.67	1.14	2.09	1.77	10.82
High	116.95	1.66	1.79	0.00	0.60	3.70	4.15	11.62

Source: Reprinted by permission from Barnes, Krutilla, and Hyde 2002, table 3.2.

Note: KgOE = kilograms of oil equivalent; LPG = liquefied petroleum gas.

nearly four times as much electricity per capita as the middle class. If poor households are larger on average than rich households (which is generally the case in developing countries), the difference in household electricity use between the lowest and the highest income groups would be somewhat smaller than the per capita figures reflect.

Because this study pools data from 45 cities, it is not obvious whether this pattern would hold true for each city or utility service area. The relationship between income and consumption in a number of cases is depicted in figure 5.3, table 5.4, and appendix B.2.[3] The figure shows that electricity consumption rises with income, but the rate of increase differs across cases.

In the middle of the income distribution, most of the consumption curves are fairly flat: there is a 1 percent to 30 percent difference in average consumption between the second and third quintiles and between the third and the fourth quintiles. The gap between the richest quintile and the poorest varies more widely across cases. In Indian states, the gap between poor and rich differs from state to state. In Haryana, households in the richest quintile consume, on average, only 1.3 times more than those in the poorest quintile. In Maharashtra, the rich consume more than 4 times as much as the poorest. The Latin American cases have a similar spread, with the richest quintile in Uruguay consuming only 1.3 times more than the poorest versus a difference of 4.5 times in Guatemala. In the three African cases, the rich consume between 2.99 and 3.8 times more than the poorest quintile, on average. In Croatia, the difference is only 1.5 times.

Even where average consumption rises with income, that rise does not mean that all poor households consume small amounts of electricity and all rich households consume large quantities. In urban Colombia, for

Figure 5.3 Average Monthly Electricity Consumption per Household, by Quintile

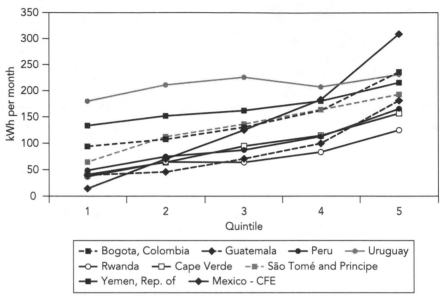

Source: Authors' elaboration from appendix B.2 data.

example, nearly 20 percent of households in the poorest quintile consume more than 200 kilowatt-hours per month (considered the subsistence level of consumption) and nearly 47 percent of the wealthiest households consume less than this threshold (Melendez 2005; Melendez, Casas, and Medina 2004). In Guatemala (figure 5.4), many nonpoor households also figure among the low-volume customers. Any subsidy directed to those consuming less than the subsistence level of consumption will reach many rich households and will exclude a substantial number of poor ones. Those cases suggest that, even though electricity use is generally positively correlated with income (and thus would seem at first glance to be a good proxy indicator to use for targeting), it is difficult to accurately isolate the poor from the nonpoor with quantity targeting.

The Relationship between Income and Water Consumption Is Weaker

Quantity targeting faces the same problem for water supply. In Colombia, more than half of households in all quintiles consume less than 20 cubic meters of water a month, the designated subsistence level of consumption

Figure 5.4 Electricity Consumption among Poor and Nonpoor Households in Guatemala

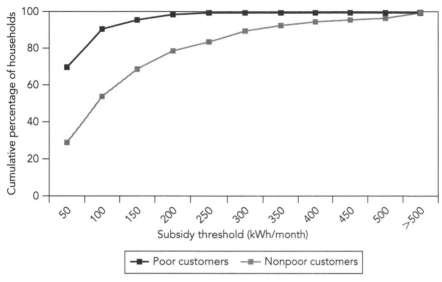

Source: Foster and Araujo 2004.

(Melendez 2005; Melendez, Casas, and Medina 2004). A recent study of IBTs in Niamey, Niger, and in Maturin, Républica Bolivariana de Venezuela (Komives, Prokopy, and Lauria 2004), found a similar situation. In Niamey, the cumulative frequency distributions of consumption among poor and nonpoor households are virtually identical, and in Maturin, poor households are only slightly less likely than nonpoor ones to consume small quantities of water. Because some poor households consume nearly as much as rich households in both places, the only way for an IBT to subsidize consumption for all poor households is to have a very large subsidized first block in the tariff. Increasing the size of the first block, however, also means that many nonpoor households receive the subsidy.

Figure 5.5 shows average water use by quintile for a range of water cases. In three of the Central American cases, average water use by the richest quintile is actually less than that by the poorest quintile. In the other cases, consumption by the richest is between 1.06 and 2.6 times that by the poorest. As with electricity, the middle of those curves is fairly flat, with small differences between consumption in the second, third, and fourth quintiles in most cases. The flatness of the curves suggests that there is no guarantee that, on average, the poorest utility customers will consume less water than middle-class or rich customers.

Figure 5.5 Average Water Consumption per Household by Quintile

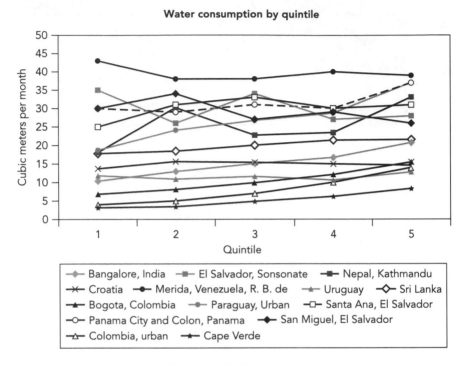

Source: Authors' elaboration from appendix C.2 data.

This information on water and electricity consumption patterns suggests that, on average, poor households consume less water and electricity than nonpoor households in most cases. The difference in consumption levels between the rich and the poor is much more marked in the electricity sector than in the water sector. At the same time, the consumption patterns among poor and nonpoor households often overlap, making it difficult to isolate the poor from the nonpoor using a consumption variable alone. A final important lesson is that the correlation between income and consumption can vary significantly from case to case.

Available evidence on income elasticity of demand for water and electricity corroborates those conclusions (table 5.5). A survey of the results of many studies of income elasticity found a positive correlation between income and consumption, with a stronger relationship in the electricity sector than in the water sector. The income elasticity data also show that there is a great variation between cases, with little or no income elasticity in some instances. There appears to be a stronger relationship between income

Table 5.5 Summary of Evidence on Income Elasticity of Demand for Water and Electricity

	Electricity	Water
Number of cases	22 countries and 38 observations	19 countries and 69 observations
Mean (and standard deviation): all cases	0.47 (0.45)	0.36 (0.22)
Mean (and standard deviation): developing country cases	0.40 (0.49)	0.21 (0.18)
Mean (and standard deviation): developed country cases	0.65 (0.26)	0.39 (0.21)

Source: Authors' elaboration based on a survey of existing studies.

and consumption in developed countries than in developing countries, indicating that the quantity consumed may be a weaker indicator of poverty in developing than in developed countries.

This evidence on the relationship between income and consumption suggests that there are important limitations on the use of quantity consumed as an income proxy. Nonetheless, to the extent that the poor do consume less water or electricity than the population as a whole, on average, in a particular case, quantity targeting could help target benefits to the poor in two ways: by excluding nonpoor households from the pool of subsidy recipients (reducing the error of inclusion), or by producing more subsidized bills for poor customers than for others. The first possibility—beneficiary targeting—is represented by the targeting ratio in the framework presented in chapter 4. The second possibility—manipulating the size of the subsidy that each recipient obtains—is a function of both the subsidy rate ratio and the quantity ratio.

Beneficiary Targeting in Practice: No One Is Excluded

In practice, the use of quantity targeting to restrict the pool of subsidy beneficiaries is limited, because IBTs and VDTs are often combined with general price subsidies for residential customers. In many instances, the price of every block in an IBT and the prices applied to all customer groups in a VDT are all less than average cost, which results in all residential customers receiving subsidies regardless of how much water they consume. Even when the top block of an IBT exceeds average cost, the structure of an IBT is such that all residential customers receive a subsidy over some units of consumption. A household ceases to be a net subsidy recipient only when the surcharge applied to the last units consumed is large enough to exceed the subsidy received on the first units consumed. Because the cost recovery threshold is usually set very high, this situation rarely occurs. In La Paz, Bolivia, in the late 1990s, for example, only 1 percent of households consumed enough water each month to reach the block in the IBT where the price was set at average cost (Komives 1999).

The problem is less pronounced with a VDT because this tariff structure can be designed so that households consuming more than a set threshold do not receive a subsidy on any units of consumption. For example, in a two-tariff structure, all units of electricity or water can be subsidized for households that consume less than a particular monthly threshold, with no unit subsidized for households that consume more than that. How high the threshold is set, however, determines whether the tariff structure will, in fact, exclude many households from the subsidies. In the cases of VDT subsidies studied here, the threshold is set high enough so that few households are relegated to the unsubsidized tariff.

Benefit Targeting in Practice: High-Volume Consumers Receive Larger Subsidies

Even if quantity targeting does not exclude most connected households from receiving subsidies, one might still expect it to have a progressive effect on the distribution of subsidy benefits to the poor. Table 5.1 shows that the opposite is true. Quantity-targeted subsidies provide smaller subsidies, on average, to the poor than to other subsidy recipients: the product of the subsidy rate ratio and quantity ratio is less than 1 in all cases. The following sections examine this issue in more depth.

Fixed Charges May Reduce or Eliminate the Discount for Small-Volume Consumers

First, the difference in rates of subsidization enjoyed by the poor and the nonpoor can be small either because the consumption gap between poor and nonpoor is small (particularly in the water sector) or because the presence of fixed charges in the tariff structure works against the lowest-volume consumers. Two forms of fixed charges are commonly added to IBTs or VDTs. One form of fixed charge is a minimum consumption rule, which charges households for some minimum level of consumption even if they use less. Alternatively, utilities require households to pay a fixed monthly charge on top of the volumetric IBT. At least half of the water and electricity utilities whose tariffs were reported in chapter 2 apply a minimum consumption rule, a fixed charge, or both.

Figure 5.6 Effect of Minimum Consumption Rules and Fixed Charges on Average Price Paid with an Increasing Block Tariff at Different Consumption Levels

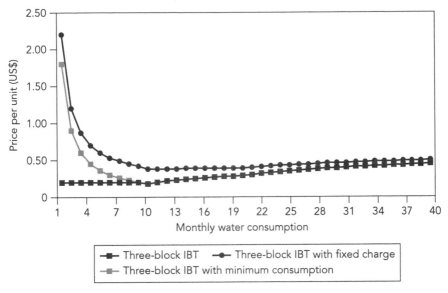

Source: Authors' elaboration.

Note: IBT = increasing block tariff.

Fixed charges and minimum consumption rules both have a dramatic effect on the prices paid by low-volume consumers. Figure 5.6 compares the average price per unit paid by households at different consumption levels under three hypothetical IBTs for water service: a straight IBT, an IBT with a fixed charge, and an IBT with a fixed charge and a minimum consumption level. Under the tariff structures with the fixed charge or minimum consumption levels, the highest prices per unit are paid by the customers with the lowest consumption levels. The fixed charge in effect erases—and may even reverse—any progressive effect of quantity targeting on subsidization rates.

Aside from the tariff structure itself, some utilities impose other fixed charges on households that can have a similar effect on the price per unit paid by low-volume customers. In Uruguay, for example, the water tariff includes fixed charges for system expansion, which are applied most heavily in areas of new expansion, where the poor are most likely to live. Similarly, the electricity tariff in that country includes two fixed charges: one to cover customer administration costs and one that differs according to the maximum kilowatt-hours supported by the contract (Ruggeri-Laderchi 2003).

It is, therefore, erroneous to conclude that quantity targeting necessarily results in lower unit prices for low-volume consumers, let alone for the poor. One must look at the entire tariff structure to determine whether a quantity-based tariff results in low-volume households paying less than high-volume households.

High-Volume Households Receive Subsidies
on More Units of Consumption

The second and greatest problem that plagues quantity-targeted consumption subsidies lies in the quantity ratio. This ratio is less than 1 in all of the African cases (table 5.2), which is consistent with the expectation that poor households are, on average, lower-volume consumers than other households. When nonpoor households consume more than poor households, they receive a subsidy on more total units of consumption. Unless the average rate of subsidization among the poor is much greater than that applied to the population as a whole, the average value of the subsidy accruing to a nonpoor household quickly becomes larger than that of the one received by a poor household. As one illustration, suppose average consumption among all subsidy recipients is three times greater than average consumption among the poor recipients. In that case, the rate of subsidization of the poor would have to be at least three times greater than that of the general population for the product of the subsidy rate ratio and the quantity ratio to equal or be greater than 1. In the African IBTs, this situation is never achieved: the difference in average consumption levels between poor and nonpoor is always larger than the difference in rates of subsidization.

The Combined Effect of Subsidy Design Factors
Is Unlikely to Be Progressive

If one considers the expected values of the targeting ratio, subsidy rate ratio, and quantity ratio, there appears to be little prospect for a significantly progressive distribution of subsidy benefits with quantity-targeted subsidies. This is true even when the base conditions for quantity targeting appear to be favorable—that is, when there is a strong correlation between income and consumption. Table 5.6 displays how the correlation between quantity consumed and income would affect the three ratios. If there is no correlation between income and quantity consumed, none of the ratios will have any effect on benefit incidence: the access factors alone will determine how the

Table 5.6 Expected Effect of Quantity Targeting on Determinants of Benefit Incidence, under Different Assumptions about the Correlation between Income and Consumption

Correlation between quantity and income	Targeting ratio (T)[a]	Subsidy rate ratio (R)	Quantity ratio (Q)
High positive correlation (more likely found in the case of electricity)	**Progressive:** Much > 1.0, or neutral if subsidy threshold is set too high	**Progressive:** Much > 1.0, but could be regressive in case of fixed charges	**Regressive:** Much < 1.0
Low positive correlation (more likely found in the case of water)	**Progressive:** Slightly > 1.0, or neutral if subsidy threshold is set too high	**Progressive:** Slightly > 1.0, but could be neutral or regressive in case of fixed charges	**Regressive** Slightly < 1.0
No correlation	**Neutral:** 1.0	**Neutral:** 1.0	**Neutral:** 1.0

Source: Authors' elaboration.

a. Assuming that metering rates are the same across quintiles.

benefit is distributed. When there is a positive correlation, the targeting and subsidy rate ratios may increase the progressiveness of the subsidy, but the quantity ratio will have the opposite effect. In the end, it is likely that the access factors will be the dominant determinants of subsidy performance, even where there is a strong positive correlation between income and consumption.

Summary

This chapter reviewed the importance of different access factors [access to the network (A) and connection uptake rate (U)] and subsidy design factors (targeting of beneficiaries (T), rate of subsidization (R), and consumption level (Q)) in explaining the targeting performance.

To depict the relationship between the two sets of factors, figure 5.7 plots the product of the access factor ratios ($A \times U$) against the product of the subsidy design factor ratios ($T \times R \times Q$). The product of the access factor ratios reflects the likelihood that a poor household will be connected to the network, versus any household. A value of 0.5, for example, indicates that poor households are only half as likely as households in general to be connected to the network. The product of the subsidy design factor ratios

Figure 5.7 Access Factors versus Subsidy Design Factors in Quantity-Targeted Subsidies

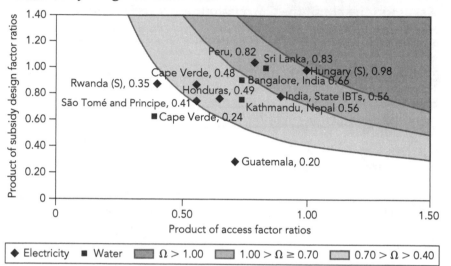

Source: Authors' elaboration.

Note: The product of access factor ratios is the product of the access ratio (A) and the uptake ratio (U). The product of the subsidy design factor ratios is the product of the targeting ratio (T), the subsidy rate ratio (R), and the quantity ratio (Q). IBTs = increasing block tariffs; S = simulated. The values following the case names are the benefit targeting performance indicator Ω for each case.

measures the average subsidy accruing to a connected poor household relative to the average value accruing to all connected households.[4]

The curves on the graph show the combinations of access and subsidy design factors that would produce an Ω of 1.0, 0.7, and 0.4. The poorer the subsidy model performs with respect to access, the more is demanded of the subsidy design factors, and vice versa. For example, if the product of the access factor ratios is 0.5, then the product of the subsidy design factor ratios would have to be greater than 2.0 to generate a progressive distribution of subsidy benefits. The analysis in this chapter suggests that low values of the access factor ratios are common, but values much greater than 1.0 for the ratio of the subsidy design factors would not be possible to achieve with a pure quantity-targeted subsidy. This is why all the quantity-targeted subsidies listed in table 5.1 have regressive distributions.

In short, the prospects for producing a progressive subsidy distribution with an IBT or a VDT are slim in cases where coverage is not universal. In countries with very low coverage rates, such as countries in Africa, the subsidies could even be highly regressive. Moreover, even where coverage is universal (and, therefore, the product of the access factor ratios is 1.0), the distribution of subsidy benefits could still be regressive and is never likely to do much better than achieving a neutral distribution.

Notes

1. Quantity-based subsidies might indirectly reduce bills for unmetered households if the fixed charges for unmetered households are calculated on the basis of the IBT or VDT and of an assumption that unmetered households are low-volume consumers. In this case, however, any subsidy received by unmetered households would be an implicit subsidy (see chapter 2), not an explicit quantity-targeted subsidy.

2. The countries in the study are Bolivia, Botswana, Burkina Faso, Cape Verde, Haiti, India, Indonesia, Mauritania, the Philippines, Thailand, the Republic of Yemen, Zambia, and Zimbabwe.

3. Appendix B.2 lists household consumption by quintile for the cases studied in this book.

4. Note that this is different from the product of the subsidy rate ratio and the quantity ratio, which measures the average subsidy to a poor subsidy recipient relative to the average subsidy to all subsidy recipients. Some connected households are not subsidy recipients; thus, the value of the subsidy they receive is 0.

6

Can the Targeting Performance of Consumption Subsidies Be Improved?

The poor performance of quantity-targeted subsidies may come as a surprise to some. For others, that performance confirms the growing perception in development circles that increasing block tariffs (IBTs) are ineffective tools for subsidizing the poor. It is increasingly common to hear development practitioners suggest that modifying the design of IBTs and volume-differentiated tariffs (VDTs) would improve the effectiveness of such subsidies. The most common remedy considered is to reduce the subsidy threshold. In an IBT, that means reducing the size of the first block of the tariff and limiting the subsidy to only that block. For a VDT, the threshold that defines who is eligible for the subsidized tariff can also be lowered. This chapter explores this strategy and other possible strategies for improving the benefit and beneficiary incidence of consumption subsidies.

Improvement of Subsidy Performance by Modifying Tariff Design?

Much of the critique of IBTs and VDTs as subsidy mechanisms stems from the fact that those tariffs tend to subsidize most residential customers over a large proportion of total consumption. In most cases, the IBTs have many subsidized consumption blocks, and the size of the first block (which receives the largest subsidy) is quite large.

The average first block of the water IBTs presented in table 2.4 ranges from 13 cubic meters per month in Asia to 24 cubic meters per month in Latin America. Twenty-four cubic meters of water per month exceed the average consumption of households in the richest quintile in half of the cases studied here (appendix C.2). In electricity, there is more variation in the size of the first block (table 2.6). The first block size ranges from only 10 kilowatt-hours per month in the Philippines to 300 kilowatt-hours per month in Zambia and República Bolivariana de Venezuela. Three hundred kilowatt-hours of electricity per month is greater than the average monthly consumption in the fifth quintile in all the cases included here (appendix B.2).

Volume-differentiated tariffs have similar problems. In Guatemala and Honduras, for example, the electricity VDTs use a threshold consumption level of 300 kilowatt-hours per month to differentiate between households that will receive a subsidy and those that will not. The result is that in Guatemala only 14 percent and in Honduras only 16 percent of connected customers do not receive a subsidy.

The failure to set subsidy thresholds at subsistence levels of consumption and the tendency to subsidize all residential consumers is generally attributed to political influence in rate setting. General residential subsidies and large subsidized blocks are politically popular precisely because they offer subsidies to many households. Thus, although IBTs are often justified in policy discussions as ways to keep service affordable for the poor, there could be other underlying and contradictory objectives that would favor poorly targeted subsidies.

Modifying the Tariff Can Improve Only Some Determinants of Subsidy Performance

The framework in chapter 4 can be applied to assess the extent to which changes in tariff structures could theoretically improve the targeting performance of IBTs and VDTs (table 6.1). Tariff modifications do not change the base coverage conditions that tend to make consumption subsidies

Table 6.1 Effects of Tariff Modifications on the Factors That Determine the Benefit Incidence of Quantity-Targeted Subsidies

	Reducing the first block of an IBT	*Moving from an IBT to a VDT, or reducing the subsidy threshold in a VDT*
Access ratio (A)	No effect	No effect
Uptake ratio (U)	No effect	No effect
Targeting ratio (T)	No effect unless the prices in subsequent blocks exceeds average cost	Will improve
Subsidy rate ratio (R)	Will improve	Will improve
Quantity ratio (Q)	Will remain < 1.00	Will remain < 1.00

Source: Authors' elaboration.

Note: Predictions assume that poor households consume less on average than nonpoor households.
IBT = increasing block tariff; VDT = volume-differentiated tariff.

regressive; they have no direct effect on access, uptake rates, or metering rates. Households that are ineligible for the subsidies because they do not have metered connections will remain excluded from the subsidy. The margin for improvement in performance is, therefore, more limited in low-coverage areas than in high-coverage areas.

Where tariff changes could potentially help is rather in altering the subsidy design factor ratios: subsidization rate ratio, targeting ratio, and quantity ratio. To the extent that poor households consume less than nonpoor households, lowering the subsidy threshold should increase the gap in the rate of subsidization between poor and nonpoor. The lower the subsidy threshold, the higher the percentage of total consumption at unsubsidized (or less subsidized) rates for the higher volume customers.

Whether or not modification of tariff structures will affect the targeting ratio is highly dependent on the type of tariff modification under consideration. Moving from an IBT to a VDT, or reducing the subsidy threshold of a VDT, should improve targeting as long as the change moves more nonpoor than poor households away from a subsidized tariff and into an unsubsidized tariff. The drawback of the change is that the error of exclusion will also increase, as some poor households are inadvertently shifted to the unsubsidized tariff.

Reducing the size of the first block in an IBT will not necessarily produce this type of targeting improvement. Even after the first block shrinks, all households that consume water or electricity continue to benefit from the admittedly smaller subsidy on their first units of consumption—they are all still subsidy recipients. Only if the prices in subsequent blocks are above average cost will this change turn some households into net cross-subsidizers. Because most IBTs subsidize virtually all blocks of consumption, modifying only the first block of a typical IBT will not change the targeting picture.

The final determinant of benefit targeting performance, the quantity ratio, will change if the pool of subsidy recipients changes or if households alter their consumption patterns in response to the tariff modification. Significant tariff modifications are likely to elicit a price response from poor and nonpoor households. Because the precise magnitude of response is uncertain, it is difficult to predict how the quantity ratio may change. Notwithstanding, this ratio will remain less than 1 as long as poor subsidy recipients consume less on average than nonpoor subsidy recipients, which means it will continue to work against progressivity of the subsidy distribution.

Change Brings Little Improvement, but Moving to a VDT Is More Effective Than Modifying an IBT

The conclusion is that moving from an IBT to a VDT or reducing the threshold in a VDT is more likely to produce an improvement in beneficiary and benefit targeting performance than changing the structure of an IBT. The scope for improvements arising from IBT modifications is limited unless prices exceed average cost in the upper blocks and a significant proportion of household consumption actually falls in those upper blocks. Moreover, if poor households do not actually consume less than nonpoor households, on average (as in some of the water cases examined in the last chapter), the impact of any tariff modifications on the poor would be either neutral or negative.

Empirical studies that simulate the distributional effect of changes in tariff structures support the conclusion above. Table 6.2 shows the predicted impact

Table 6.2 Targeting Performance of Simulated Improvements to IBT and VDT Design

Country, city	Benefit targeting performance indicator (Ω)	Error of exclusion (%)	Access factors — Product of access ratio and uptake ratio ($A \times U$)	Targeting ratio (T)	Subsidy design factors — Product of subsidy rate and quantity ratios ($R \times Q$)
Reducing the subsidy threshold for a VDT					
Electricity cases					
Guatemala					
Original: 300 kWh	0.20	55.4	0.71	1.00	0.28
Simulation: 100 kWh	0.48	58.7	0.71	1.23	0.56
Rwanda: national[a]					
Simulation: 50 kWh	0.01	100.0	0.02	1.58	0.36
Simulation: 20 kWh	0.14	100.0	0.02	10.58	0.77
Reducing the size of the first block of an IBT					
Electricity cases					
Rwanda: national[a]					
Simulation: 50 kWh	0.01	100	0.02	1.00	0.54
Simulation: 20 kWh	0.01	100	0.02	1.00	0.71
Water cases					
India, Bangalore					
Original: 25 m^3	0.66	60.5	0.74	0.99	0.90
Simulation: 18 m^3	0.67	60.0	0.74	1.00	0.91
Simulation: 6 m^3	0.81	60.0	0.74	1.00	1.10
Nepal, Kathmandu					
Original: 10 m^3	0.56	53.0	0.74	0.99	0.77
Simulation: 7 m^3	0.56	53.0	0.74	0.99	0.77

(Table continues on the following page)

Table 6.2 (*continued*)

Country, city	Benefit targeting performance indicator (Ω)	Error of exclusion (%)	Access factors Product of access ratio and uptake ratio ($A \times U$)	Targeting ratio (T)	Subsidy design factors Product of subsidy rate and quantity ratios ($R \times Q$)
Paraguay, urban					
Original: 15 m³	0.96	98.1	0.87	0.87	0.88
Simulation: 5 m³	1.67	96.6	0.87	1.93	1.00
Moving from an IBT to a VDT					
Electricity cases					
Cape Verde					
Original IBT: 40 kWh	0.48	75.6	0.55	1.00	0.87
Simulated VDT: 40 kWh	1.06	88.6	0.55	1.99	0.96
São Tomé and Principe[b]					
Original IBT: 300 kWh	0.41	76.8	0.56	1.00	0.74
Simulated VDT: 300 kWh	0.59	79.2	0.56	1.25	0.85
Rwanda, urban					
Original IBT: 40 kWh	0.35	87.2	0.40	1.00	0.87
Simulated VDT: 40 kWh	0.53	94.3	0.40	1.61	0.82
Water cases					
Cape Verde					
Original: 7 m³	0.24	89.7	0.39	1.00	0.63
Simulation: 7 m³	0.36	90.2	0.39	1.18	0.78

Source: Appendixes D–E.

Note:

a. Angel-Urdinola, Cosgrove-Davies, and Wodon (2005) use national poverty line, not the poorest 40 percent of households.

b. Three-block IBT.

c. IBT = increasing block tariff; VDT = volume-differentiated tariff.

on targeting performance of altering tariffs in a handful of cases in Africa, Asia, and Latin America. The ratios for access factors and metering rates remain unchanged after the modifications. The product of the subsidization ratio and quantity ratio improves in most cases. With one exception, the targeting ratio improves only for changes that involve a VDT. The exception is urban Paraguay, where reducing the size of the first block of the IBT to 5 cubic meters (and pricing the second block at average cost) significantly improves the targeting ratio of the subsidy. The result is an improvement in the benefit targeting performance indicator (Ω) in most cases but only a progressive subsidy distribution in two cases: the move from an IBT to a VDT for electricity in Cape Verde, and the IBT with the 5-cubic-meter first block in Paraguay. Increasing the size of the first block in Paraguay—even to just 10 cubic meters—would cause a reversion to a regressive distribution of benefits.

Foster and Araujo (2004) analyze how the distributional incidence of subsidies for the electricity in Guatemala would change if the lifeline in the VDT were reduced to 100 kilowatt-hours, from the current 300 kilowatt-hours per month. They found the change would significantly reduce the number of subsidy recipients, from 86 percent of connected households to 65 percent, and, as a result, would reduce the total cost of the subsidy program. The modification also leads to a slightly higher error of exclusion, but it does not produce any dramatic changes in the benefit incidence of the subsidy. The indicator Ω improves from 0.20 to 0.48; hence, the subsidy remains regressive. The same pattern emerges with simulated VDTs for electricity in Rwanda. In this case, the access handicap is so large (almost no poor households in the country have connections) that even a 10-fold improvement in the targeting ratio has no significant impact on Ω (Angel-Urdinola, Cosgrove-Davies, and Wodon 2005).

Four recent studies assessed the impact of changing the block structure in IBTs: water subsidies in Bangalore, India; in Kathmandu, Nepal; and in urban Paraguay, and electricity subsidies in Rwanda. All simulations involved reducing the size of the first block of the IBT either to the average consumption level of the poor or to a small subsistence level. With the exception of Paraguay, the only determinant of Ω that changes in those cases is the product of the subsidy rate and quantity ratios: there is no improvement in the targeting of beneficiaries.

Finally, the sample includes four simulated moves from an IBT to a VDT in Africa: water and electricity subsidies in Cape Verde, an electricity subsidy in São Tomé and Principe, and an electricity subsidy for urban Rwanda. Those moves produce an impressive improvement in the targeting ratio in each case and particularly in the case of electricity in Cape Verde. The product of the subsidy rate and quantity ratios also improves somewhat. Those changes are enough to produce a slightly progressive subsidy distribution in Cape Verde for electricity, but the benefit incidence remains very regressive in the other cases.

Other Quantity-Targeted Tariff Structures Are Possible

The discussion thus far has focused on the most common tariff structures. Other structures would also be possible. In Rwanda, for example, a tariff with the highest price block in the middle consumption range is under consideration. This structure ensures that households quickly begin to repay the subsidy they receive in the first subsidized block of the tariff and manages to avoid one major problem with VDTs, which assign households to one tariff or another on the basis of the total level of consumption. Consuming just 1 cubic meter or kilowatt-hour more than the threshold of a VDT would relegate a household to the unsubsidized tariff (and thus exclude the household from the lifeline block). The proposed Rwanda tariff provides for a more gradual transition from net subsidy recipient to net cross-subsidizer. However, for the tariff to produce a progressive distribution, nonpoor households would have to consume more on average than poor households, and the block structure would have to be such that a large proportion of households were net cross-subsidizers.

Beyond Quantity Targeting: Can Subsidy Performance Be Improved with Administrative Selection?

As discussed above, the potential for improving benefit and beneficiary targeting through changes in tariff structure is quite limited. One alternative is to use other targeting methods to improve the targeting ratio (by excluding nonpoor households and by including more of the poor) or to improve the subsidy rate ratio (by targeting larger subsidies to poorer households). This approach is found in practice in a number of utilities. In some cases, IBTs and VDTs are combined with various forms of administrative selection. In other cases, administrative selection alone is used to target consumption subsidies.

The targeting methods that fall under the category of administrative selection can be divided into two general groups: those that rely on a single variable (categorical targeting such as geographic location of residence or household composition), and those that use multivariate methods (which usually involve proxy means tests). The purpose of both forms of administrative selection is to identify households that are likely to be poor. Multivariate methods are likely to be more accurate, but they are more complex and costly to administer.

A handful of recent studies estimate the benefit and beneficiary incidence of consumption subsidies targeted through administrative selection or simulate the potential improvement in subsidy performance that adding administrative selection would generate. The results suggest that the prospects for a progressive subsidy distribution are much greater with administrative selection than with quantity targeting. For most of the simulated and existing subsidies that use administrative selection, Ω is greater than 1, but there are exceptions (table 6.3). As expected, where access rates among poor households are low, the poor benefit the least from using administrative selection to target consumption subsidies.

Table 6.3 Targeting Performance of Subsidy Models That Use Administrative Selection

Country, city	Benefit targeting performance (Ω)	Error of exclusion (%)	Access factor — Product of access ratio and uptake ratio (A × U)	Targeting ratio (T)	Subsidy design factors — Product of subsidy rate and quantity ratio (R × Q)
Geographic targeting					
Electricity cases					
Colombia, Bogota					
Original: geographically defined tariffs with IBT	1.10	3.7	1.00	1.17	0.95
Mexico					
Original: geographically defined tariffs with IBT	0.60	n/r	0.96	0.92	0.67
Water cases					
Nicaragua, Managua					
Original: IBT plus slum discount	1.18	5.0	0.98	1.00	1.21
Venezuela, R. B. de, Merida					
Original: IBT plus slum discount	1.09	0.0	1.00	1.00	1.09
Colombia, Bogota					
Original: geographically defined tariffs with IBT	1.09	1.9	0.99	1.08	1.02
Paraguay, urban					
Simulation: poorest 10% of neighborhoods	1.42	98.8	0.87	1.71	0.95
India, Bangalore					
Simulation: poorest 10% of neighborhoods	0.67	60.0	0.74	1.00	0.92

(Table continues on the following page)

Table 6.3 (*continued*)

Country, city	Benefit targeting performance (Ω)	Error of exclusion (%)	Access factors Product of access ratio and uptake ratio ($A \times U$)	Subsidy design factors Targeting ratio (T)	Subsidy design factors Product of subsidy rate and quantity ratio ($R \times Q$)
Nepal, Kathmandu					
Simulation: slum targeting (revenue neutral)	0.60	53.0	0.74	0.99	0.82
Simulation: slum targeting (charge others cost recovery price)	0.74	76.5	0.74	0.86	1.17
Means testing					
Electricity cases					
Argentina*					
Original: average of provincial means-tested subsidy	1.50	94.0	0.98	n/r	n/r
Georgia, Tiblisi					
Original: limited free allowance of electricity for targeted households	1.20	75.0	n/r	n/r	n/r
Colombia, Bogota					
Simulation: adding means test to geographic targeted subsidy	1.35	16.8	1.00	1.47	0.92
Cape Verde					
Simulation: means-tested subsidy on 40 kWh	1.46	93.3	0.55	3.56	0.74
Water cases					
Argentina*					
Original: average of provincial means-tested subsidy	1.23	76.0	0.95	n/r	n/r

Chile					
Original: discounts of 40–70% on 15 m^3 for targeted households	1.63	78.0	0.91	1.74	1.02
Paraguay, urban					
Original: discount on 15 m^3 for targeted households (means test based on housing characteristics)	1.64	93.1	0.87	1.89	1.00
Simulation: discount on 15 m^3 for targeted households (means test including household characteristics)	2.14	96.0	0.87	2.22	1.11
Colombia, Bogota					
Simulation: adding means test to geographically targeted subsidy	1.31	19.0	0.99	1.48	0.90
Cape Verde					
Simulation: means-tested subsidy on 10 m^3	1.39	98.0	0.39	4.69	0.76
Nepal, Kathmandu					
Simulation: Discount for means-tested households	0.65	52.1	0.74	1.00	0.89
Simulation: Discount for means-tested households (all others pay cost recovery)	0.90	73.1	0.74	1.07	1.07
India, Bangalore					
Simulation: Discount for means-tested households	0.66	60.0	0.74	1.00	0.90

Sources: Appendixes D–E.

Note: IBT = increasing block tariff; n/r = not reported.

*Analysis assumes all the eligible households that are receiving the subsidy.

Geographic Targeting Can Work If Poor and Nonpoor Households Live in Different Areas

Of the many forms of administrative selection, geographic targeting is most commonly found combined with an IBT or VDT. Geographic targeting involves identifying neighborhoods, cities, or regions where concentrations of poor households live and targeting subsidies to those areas. It works well where poverty is highly spatially correlated, such as where poor households live together and isolated from nonpoor households.

In the realm of utility subsidies, the use of geographic targeting may take a number of different forms. One approach is to use a poverty map created with census or household survey data to identify poorer neighborhoods. Another approach is to choose types of neighborhoods where high levels of poverty are expected, such as designated slum areas. The water tariffs in Panama City; in Merida, República Bolivariana de Venezuela; and in Managua, Nicaragua, for example, combine such a special tariff for slum areas with a general IBT for residential customers.

Colombia has a more complex and comprehensive national system of geographically targeted subsidies, for both water and electricity. All neighborhoods in the country are divided into six strata that are based on housing quality. The tariffs for both water and electricity are designed so that households in the first three strata receive subsidies (50 percent in the first stratum, 40 percent in the second, and 15 percent in the third).[1] Households in the fourth stratum pay the cost recovery price.[2] The fifth and sixth strata pay a surcharge of 20 percent. This geographically targeted tariff system is combined with quantity targeting. For water supply, the tariff for each group is a three-block IBT with a first block of 20 cubic meters per month. For electricity tariffs, subsidies for all strata are limited to 193 or 182 kilowatt-hours per month (depending on elevation).

For geographic targeting to improve targeting performance, location of the household must be a reliable proxy for income status. Figure 6.1 shows the relationship between geographic strata and income deciles in Bogota, Colombia. The majority of households in the top three strata (the cross-subsidizers in the subsidy scheme and those paying the cost recovery price) are indeed among the wealthiest. Very few of the poorest households are located in these strata. There are, nonetheless, a fair number of households from upper-income deciles who qualify for subsidies because they are in one of the three lowest strata. This pattern suggests that few very poor households live in the wealthiest neighborhoods of Bogota, but that the lower-income areas are populated by both poor and nonpoor households.

Table 6.3 (shown earlier) lists the performance indicators for the Central American water subsidies and for the water and electricity subsidies in Bogota. All four examples perform better than any of the pure quantity-targeted subsidies presented in the last chapter and better than most of the "improved"

Figure 6.1 Relationship between Strata (Assigned by Housing Quality) and Income Deciles in Bogota, Colombia

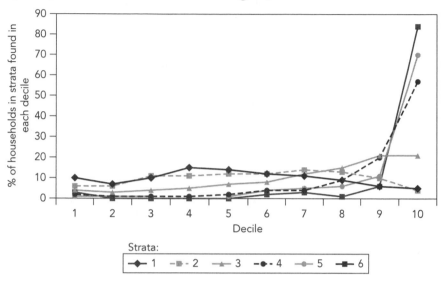

Source: Melendez 2005.

IBTs and VDTs discussed above. The factors contributing to achievement of those results is reflected in the decomposition of the determinants of Ω (table 6.3).

For Geographic Targeting to Improve Performance, Many Customers Must Pay Cost

The Central American water subsidies are general subsidies for residential customers: average prices are below cost for all metered and unmetered customers.[3] The geographic targeting of slum residents does not, therefore, affect the targeting ratio. The discounts for slums instead improve the subsidy rate ratio, the average subsidy per unit received by the poor relative to that received by the entire population.

In Bogota, by contrast, the subsidy scheme excludes some nonpoor households and achieves a targeting ratio greater than 1. Only 4 percent and 2 percent of poor households in the city fail to receive the electricity and water subsidy, respectively, meaning that most connected poor households are subsidy recipients. By contrast, nearly a quarter of nonpoor households are excluded from the electricity subsidy, and 12 percent do not receive the water subsidy.

The ability of the Colombia subsidy scheme to exclude the nonpoor is not only a consequence of the use of geographic targeting, but also results from the fact that not all residential consumers do benefit from general price subsidies (box 6.1). A recent World Bank study found that the surcharges on some residential customers in Colombia are very progressively distributed. Only 10–15 percent of subsidy resources are raised from the bottom 40 percent of the income distribution. The surcharges increase the progressiveness of the subsidy scheme (World Bank 2004a).

Simulations of the potential impact of implementing geographic targeting are available for Kathmandu, Bangalore, and urban Paraguay. For urban Paraguay, Robles (2001) simulated the effect of a VDT in which targeted households would receive a subsidy on the first 15 cubic meters of water used each month and unsubsidized households would receive no subsidy. Households targeted for this simulated subsidy were all in the poorest 10 percent of neighborhoods served by the utility (defined as neighborhoods in which the highest percentage of the population had at least one unsatisfied basic need). The distribution of this subsidy is clearly progressive ($\Omega = 1.42$).

The Kathmandu study (Pattanayak and Yang 2002) simulated a revenue-neutral change that would include free water for metered households in neighborhoods with at least a 60 percent poverty rate, as well as half-price fees for households in those neighborhoods that had unmetered connections. To pay for this subsidy, the second block of the IBT for unsubsidized households was increased. The Bangalore study (Prokopy 2002) looked at the potential of adjusting the existing IBT slightly to provide an extra subsidy for all slum residents (9 percent of the population), without increasing the subsidy budget. In both cases, the effect was only mildly progressive: Ω increased from 0.56 to 0.60 in Kathmandu and from 0.66 to 0.67 in Bangalore.

What explains the much poorer performance of geographic targeting in these two cases relative to the Latin American cases? One difference is the coverage rate: whereas almost all households in the Latin American cases have water or electricity connections, only 48 percent of the poor in Kathmandu and 40 percent of the poor in Bangalore have connections. Moreover, the simulations in Kathmandu and Bangalore are revenue-neutral modifications of a general residential subsidy. If unsubsidized households paid cost recovery prices instead of subsidized prices, geographic targeting in Kathmandu would result in a benefit targeting performance indicator (Ω) of 0.74—still regressive, but more of an improvement. Another difference between the Bogota case and Kathmandu and Bangalore could be that the spatial distribution of poverty in the cities differs, with more physical separation between the places of residence of poor and nonpoor in Bogota. Unfortunately, insufficient information about the residence patterns in Kathmandu and Bangalore make it impossible to verify this hypothesis.

Box 6.1 Funding Colombia's Geographically Targeted Subsidy Scheme

In theory, the facts (a) that the Colombian tariff structure includes two strata of residential customers who pay more than cost and (b) that surcharges are also imposed on industrial and residential customers make it possible to fund the Colombian subsidy model through cross-subsidies. In practice, however, neither water nor electricity subsidies have been able to break even on cross-subsidies alone. Both the water and electricity sectors suffer structural losses as a result of the subsidy scheme (equal to 12 percent of sector turnover in electricity and 20 percent of sector turnover in water), and it is necessary for the national government to step in and help cover those losses.

Part of the problem is that it is difficult to achieve the right balance between customers receiving cross-subsidies and those providing them in each service area. Because policy guidelines for the subsidy are set at the national level, localities have limited control over how many of their residential customers become subsidy recipients or cross-subsidizers. Upper-strata customers (as well as business and industrial customers) are overwhelmingly concentrated in larger cities, making the situation especially difficult for utilities that serve smaller cities and rural areas. Even Bogota has only 7 percent of its residential customers in strata 5 and 6. In this situation, transfers from the central government are an attractive and practical solution. This solution is not without its problems, however.

First, as of 2003, many water utilities had failed to raise prices to the levels indicated by the law. This failure was largely because tariffs in this sector had to increase significantly (more than four times for stratum 1, for example) to comply with the legally set targets for the tariff in each stratum. Given the likely political difficulties of raising tariffs to the appropriate levels, utilities put off the move as long as possible. During this transition period of gradual tariff increases, the losses from the subsidy scheme were larger than expected.

Second, the possibility of obtaining external support creates a disincentive for utilities. Not only must they raise their tariffs to appropriate levels but also they have to worry about finding an appropriate balance of cross-subsidizers and subsidy recipients. Under the current stratification system, local mayors have the ability—as well as the political incentive—to reclassify neighborhoods downward from high to low strata. Household survey evidence from the World Bank (2004a) shows (a) that the percentage of households classified in the lower strata has increased markedly during the past decade and (b) that the changes are not justified on the basis of changes in the poverty rate. From 1993 to 2003, there has been a 20 percent

(continued on the next page)

(continued from p. 105)

increase in the proportion of households eligible for the subsidy. The percentage of those classified as stratum 1 has tripled in this period. Moving households down a stratum is a roundabout way to avoid increasing tariffs as much as is required by the law.

Distortions in Socioeconomic Stratification over Time

	Percentage of households falling into			
	Stratum 1	*Stratum 2*	*Stratum 3*	*Strata 1–3*
1993	6.4	25.1	43.5	75.0
1997	12.6	42.3	32.7	87.5
2003	21.2	41.7	27.5	90.5

Sources: World Bank 2004a; Gomez-Lobo and Contreras 2003.

Other Forms of Categorical Targeting Are Used in the Utility Sectors

Geography is but one mechanism for administrative selection that relies on a single variable. Many others are possible. The challenge is to identify a categorical variable that is a good predictor of poverty.

In the countries of the former Soviet Union, the use of categorical targeting is quite common. There is a tradition of providing discounts that are based on household membership: discounts are often available for households that include pensioners, war veterans, students, or refugees. The original purpose of those schemes was rarely to target poor households but rather to provide discounts to individuals who were considered particularly worthy of additional state assistance. Whether those programs now can also serve to direct subsidies to the poor depends on the extent to which the categories are correlated with poverty in each particular location.

The sample of subsidy programs includes two group discount programs: one for water service in Odessa, Ukraine (Komives 1998), and one for electricity service in Tbilisi, Georgia (Lampietti and others 2003). The discount programs in Ukraine and Georgia operated slightly differently. In Odessa, pensioners, people with disabilities, students, and war veterans received discounts of between 15 and 100 percent on their municipal services bills. In Tbilisi, veterans and pensioners received a free allowance of electricity of between 35 and 70 kilowatt-hours per month.[4] There is insufficient information available on either case to disaggregate the determinants of subsidy distribution, but some indicators of subsidy performance illustrate how the subsidies work in practice.

In Odessa, the income distribution of subsidy recipients mirrored the income distribution of the survey sample as a whole. The recipients of group discounts in Tbilisi were likewise spread across all income groups: 10 percent of the poorest and 10 percent of households in the richest quintile in Tbilisi received discounts. Eighteen percent of households in the middle quintile qualified for the subsidies. In both cities, many poor households were excluded from the discounts. In Odessa, for example, only 37 percent of households under the poverty line qualified for a discount. In Tbilisi, only 13 percent of the poorest 40 percent of households were subsidy recipients. The evidence suggests that the categories chosen for the discount programs were not necessarily highly correlated with poverty. This finding is consistent with a recent study of the targeting effectiveness of transfer programs (Coady, Grosh, and Hoddinott 2003). That study concluded that programs that targeted the elderly were among the poorest performers with respect to targeting.

Household size is another proxy that is sometimes used for targeting utility subsidies, either targeting large or small families or providing larger discounts to larger families. If large households are more likely to be poor, using this variable could help increase the progressivity of the subsidy. In the late 1990s, Flanders, Belgium, introduced a free allowance for water. The free allowance is calculated on a per person basis: 15 cubic meters of water per person per year. The value of the subsidy thus increases with family size. In this case, family size was positively correlated with household income, which meant that the introduction of the scheme most benefited the wealthiest households (Van Humbeeck 2000).

Means-Tested Subsidies Outperform Other Existing Consumption Subsidies

Means testing offers an alternative to geographic and categorical targeting. Like those two methods, means testing may be used in combination with quantity targeting or may be the sole basis for identifying subsidy beneficiaries. The sample of means-tested subsidies includes five subsidy programs that rely on means testing alone to identify subsidy beneficiaries: an electricity subsidy in Georgia, water subsidies in Chile and Paraguay, and province-level means-tested subsidies for water and electricity in Argentina.

The Georgian Winter Heating Assistance Program (GWHAP) was put in place in 1998 as electricity prices were set to increase in Georgia because of sector reform. This scheme provides subsidy recipients with free electricity for a set number of kilowatt-hours per year. The free allowance varied each year of the program and was determined by the number of recipients and the annual subsidy budget (850 kilowatt-hours in 2000; 1,000 in 2001 and 2002; and 480 in 2003). Over its lifetime, the GWHAP has used several different approaches to choosing subsidy beneficiaries. When a poverty and social impact analysis study of electricity reform in Georgia examined this subsidy program, proxy means testing was the major form of targeting in use to identify beneficiaries. The study found that the means-tested subsidy performed better than the government's electricity discount program described earlier. Whereas 27 percent of households in the bottom quintile of the Tbilisi population received the GWHAP subsidy in 2001, only 14 percent of the top quintile did (Lampietti and others 2003). Thus, while 75 percent of poor households are excluded from the subsidy, the targeting performance indicator shows that the benefit incidence of the subsidy is progressive ($\Omega = 1.2$).

The Chilean water subsidy is another—and perhaps the most widely cited example of a—means-tested consumer utility subsidy. This subsidy program has been in place since 1990 and was introduced to soften the effect of increases in water prices. The program subsidizes between 40 and 70 percent of up to 15 cubic meters of water for poor households. Utilities apply this discount to the water bills of eligible households and are then reimbursed by the government.

To be eligible for the Chilean water subsidy, a household must apply for the subsidy at the municipality and must meet two criteria:[5] The household must not have any arrears with the water company (increasing the incentive for households to pay their bills), and it must be among the poorest 20 percent of households in the region, according to the means testing instrument used in the Chilean welfare system, the *ficha CAS* (box 6.2). The Chilean subsidy model reaches only 19 percent of poor households, leaving many households in the first two quintiles without this assistance. However, poor households make up the bulk of the beneficiaries and fully 65 percent of subsidy benefits accrue to the poorest 40 percent of households in the country. As a result, the benefit incidence of the subsidy is highly progressive, with a targeting performance indicator of 1.63. Poor households in Chile as a group receive more than 1.5 times as large a share of the subsidy benefits as they would under a random allocation.

The means-tested water subsidy in urban Paraguay performs equally well ($\Omega = 1.64$). To qualify for a water subsidy in Paraguay, households must live in a dwelling that has four characteristics of a "precarious dwelling," or *vivienda precaria*. Households that qualify are offered 15 cubic meters of water at a subsidized price. Simulations indicate that, if household characteristics were added to the means-test formula, this subsidy program would do an even better job of directing benefits to the poorest: $\Omega = 2.14$.

In Argentina, the average performance of provincial means-tested subsidies for water and electricity services was recently evaluated (Foster 2004). Both the electricity and water programs are progressive, on average, but the bulk of poor households are excluded from receiving subsidies in both cases.

Box 6.2 Chile's *ficha CAS*, Reducing the Cost of Means Testing

Chile's *ficha CAS* (Caracterisación Social) is a two-page form that is used for determining the eligibility of households for a wide range of government programs, ranging from water subsidies to cash transfers and access to low-income housing and childcare centers. The form collects detailed information on the housing conditions of each dwelling unit in which households live, the material assets of each household, and the members of each household (their occupations, educational levels, dates of birth, and incomes). Points are allocated to households on the basis of the information provided, with the number of points fluctuating between 380 and 770 points. Households receiving fewer than 500 points are considered extremely poor, and those between 500 and 540 points are considered poor. The *ficha* for each household is updated every three years.

The Ministry of Planning (MIDEPLAN) is responsible for the design of the *ficha CAS*. Municipal employees administer the form but are trained by the Ministry. To avoid abuse, municipalities usually separate the activities of data collection and data entry from those of needs assessment.

The various national programs that are targeted using the *CAS* scoring system use the system in different ways. National income transfer programs apply the formula in a strict manner: the score obtained by a household automatically and exclusively prevails, so that eligibility depends only on the number of points obtained. The *ficha* is also used for targeting locally financed safety nets, but in that case, social workers and other professionals can often give some weight to other eligibility criteria, such as the presence of a chronic illness, the civil status of household members, and their actual financial resources at the time of request.

One of the advantages of using the *ficha* for many different programs is that doing so reduces the cost of means testing. The cost of a *CAS* interview is about US$8.65 per household. Because the fixed administrative costs of targeting are spread across several programs, the *CAS* is very cost-effective. In 1996, administrative costs represented a mere 1.2 percent of the benefits distributed using the *CAS* system. If the administrative costs of the *CAS* system were to be borne by water subsidies alone, for example, they would represent 17.8 percent of the value of the subsidies.

Sources: Clert and Wodon 2001; Gomez-Lobo and Contreras 2003.

Simulations Confirm the Potential Power of Means Testing

These examples clearly point to the potential benefits of using means testing to identify recipient households. Simulations of adding means testing to water and electricity subsidy programs in Colombia and Uruguay also suggest that means testing could improve subsidy performance.

In Bogota, Colombia, one factor that works against the progressivity of the geographically targeted subsidy described earlier is that the third stratum, which is eligible for a 15 percent subsidy, contains many nonpoor households (see figure 6.1). Melendez, Casas, and Medina (2004), therefore, simulated how the benefit incidence of the subsidies would change if a proxy means test were used to determine which households in the third stratum would receive the subsidy and which would not. To qualify as poor, households had to have three indicators of poverty. The water simulation also raised tariffs in all strata to the level permitted by the law, and the electricity subsidy simulation reduced the lifeline for all subsidized strata to 120 kilowatt-hours (from more than 160). Those changes were found to have a significant effect on the benefit incidence of the subsidies, particularly in the water sector: for the electricity subsidy, Ω increased from 1.10 to 1.35, and for water it increased from 1.09 to 1.31.[6]

Ruggeri-Laderchi (2003) also experimented with innovative uses of multivariate means testing to try to enhance the progressiveness of water and electricity expenditures in Uruguay, where fixed charges in the tariffs weigh heavily against the poor. She simulated the effect of using means testing to selectively exclude poor households from fixed charges and then recovering that lost revenue through a higher volumetric charge. The result was a more progressive distribution of expenditures on water and electricity services.

The previous examples all point to the power of multivariate means testing. Means-tested subsidies appear to do a better job of targeting subsidy benefits than either quantity-targeted subsidies or subsidies that use single-variable approaches to administrative selection. However, the simulations all consider the use of means testing in high-coverage areas. The predicted results of using means testing in low-coverage areas are more mixed.

In Cape Verde, a means-tested discount on 10 cubic meters of water or 40 kilowatt-hours of electricity produces a progressive subsidy distribution ($\Omega = 1.39$ and $\Omega = 1.46$, respectively). The effect of using means testing on water subsidies in Kathmandu and in Bangalore, by contrast, is less impressive. Revenue-neutral simulations of means-tested discounts plus IBTs in the two cities do little to improve the regressive distribution of the existing IBTs. Part of the problem is that all residential customers in the two cities are subsidized. If the IBT were eliminated and if all unsubsidized households paid cost recovery prices, the performance indicator for a means-tested subsidy in Kathmandu would reach 0.90, nearly a neutral distribution.

But Means Testing Also Increases Administrative Costs and the Error of Exclusion

Targeting does have costs, however. First, means testing can have high administrative costs. If the cost of implementing a targeting program is greater than the savings it generates by excluding the nonpoor, it is worth reconsidering the value of targeting. Second, targeting can be costly to some poor households. As more nonpoor households are excluded from the subsidy, some poor households will also lose their benefits. For example, the poverty proxy developed for the Uruguay study correctly classified only 75 percent of the sample as either poor or nonpoor. Forty-four percent of the poor were incorrectly identified as nonpoor and thus excluded from receiving the subsidy in the simulations. There can be thus a trade-off between an increase in the value of the benefit targeting performance indicator (Ω) and the share of poor households receiving the subsidy. As figures 6.2a and 6.2b show, however, it is not the case that all subsidies with a progressive distribution of benefits exclude large numbers of the poor.

Figure 6.2a Benefit and Beneficiary Incidence of Water Consumption Subsidies

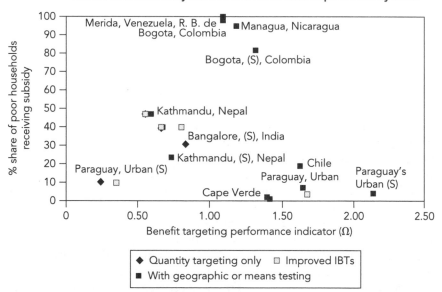

Sources: Appendixes D.1 and D.6.

Note: IBT = increasing block tariff; S = simulation.

Figure 6.2b Benefit and Beneficiary Incidence of Electricity Consumption Subsidies

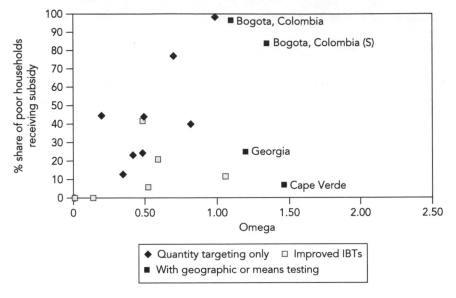

Benefit and beneficiary incidence in electricity consumption subsidy cases

Sources: Appendixes E.1 and E.6.

Note: IBT = increasing block tariff; S = simulation.

How a Means-Testing Program Is Implemented Can Affect Subsidy Performance

Another problem with means testing, which is not immediately obvious from the subsidy analysis, is implementation. Implementation problems can arise on both the side of the subsidy provider and the side of the benefit recipient. The subsidy provider must have the administrative capacity and budget necessary to conduct means tests in a timely manner and then link results with households' utility bills. The systems that need to be in place for accurate and cost-effective means testing are not built overnight. The Chilean means-testing system is more than 15 years old. Likewise, the means-testing instrument used for the Georgian electricity subsidy has been modified each year of the six-year-old program.

For the benefit recipient, most means-test programs require an application. Households must know about the subsidy and must make the effort to apply. This requirement introduces an element of self-selection into most means-tested subsidies. If truly poor households are more likely than others to apply, then the application requirement would tend to increase the progressiveness of the subsidy. If the opposite is true (for example, because poorer households are not as well informed), then the application requirement can increase the error of exclusion. The simulated subsidies presented here do not consider this potential problem. The Chilean water subsidy example does offer one potential solution, however. After take-up of the means-tested subsidy was low in the first year of the program, water companies were temporarily authorized to apply for the subsidy on behalf of the clients.

Access Factors Limit the Effect of Improved Targeting on Performance

Well-targeted or not, all subsidies on consumption from private water taps and electricity connections are affected by the base coverage and metering conditions in the utility service area. Few subsidy models of any kind are able to overcome severe access handicaps to produce progressive subsidy distributions. Most of the progressive consumption subsidies (shown in the dark gray zone of figures 6.3a and 6.3b) are high-coverage cases.

Figure 6.3a Water: Access Factors versus Subsidy Design Factors in Modified IBTs and Subsidies Using Administrative Selection

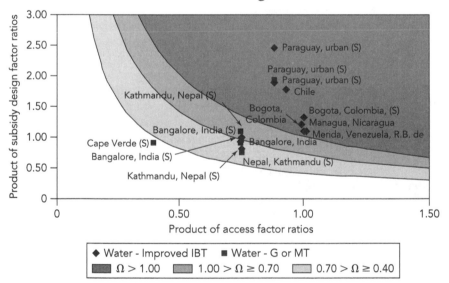

Source: Authors' elaboration.
Note: G = geographic targeting; IBT = increasing block tariff; MT = means testing; S = simulations.
The product of the access factor ratios is the product of the access ratio (A) and the uptake ratio (U). The product of the subsidy design factor ratios is the product of the targeting ratio (T), the subsidy rate ratio (R), and the quantity ratio (Q).

Figure 6.3b Electricity: Access Factors versus Subsidy Design Factors in Modified IBTs and Subsidies Using Administrative Selection

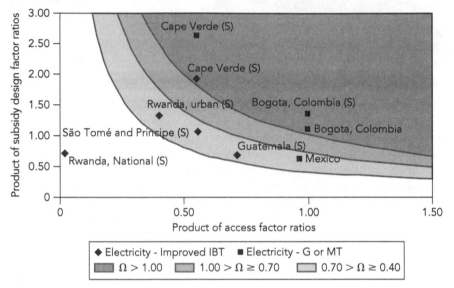

Sources: Tables 6.2 and 6.3.

Note: G = geographic targeting; IBT = increasing block tariff; MT = means testing; S = simulations.

The product of the access factor ratios is the product of the access ratio (A) and the uptake ratio (U). The product of the subsidy design factor ratios is the product of the targeting ratio (T), the subsidy rate ratio (R), and the quantity ratio (Q).

This conclusion makes the connection subsidies discussed in the next chapter an attractive alternative form of utility subsidy for low-coverage environments. When service expansion is slow or not feasible, even expanding the coverage of metering can dramatically improve the performance of consumer utility subsidies. The study of water subsidies in Kathmandu found that expanding metering would significantly improve the targeting performance of the existing IBT and also of the simulated subsidies that relied on geographic targeting and means testing to identify subsidy beneficiaries (box 6.3).

Beyond Private Connections: How Do Alternative Forms of Consumption Subsidies Perform?

All the subsidy models described so far are subsidies on private water or electricity connections. The subsidies, even at their best, are delivered only to customers with private connections. The final section of this chapter

Box 6.3 Metering and Water Subsidy Performance in Kathmandu

In Kathmandu, one-third of all households lack connections to the water system. Of households with connections, only 40 percent have functioning meters that could be used to enable volumetric water pricing. Households without functioning meters pay fixed charges for their water consumption.

Among the poor, only half have connections, and 38 percent of those connected households have functioning meters. Thus, only 32 percent of poor households are even potentially eligible for a subsidy delivered through volumetric pricing. Unmetered households could also be subsidized, but, because fixed charges are the only pricing option for those households, the fixed charge would have to be very low in order to provide a subsidy to the lowest-volume customers. In practice, the low-volume users with unmetered connections are often paying more than cost, while high-volume users are subsidized.

To test the effect of the low metering rates on subsidy performance, the Kathmandu analysis compares the benefit incidence and errors of exclusion of simulated subsidies on private connections under two scenarios: (a) using the current coverage of metering and (b) projecting rates if 100 percent of connected households were metered. The table shown in this box presents the results of various simulations in which the tariffs charged to households that do not qualify for the subsidy are raised to cost recovery levels.[1]

Simulation	Benefit Targeting Performance Indicator (Ω)	Error of exclusion (%)
Quantity-targeting: IBT with lifeline of 7 m³		
With current metering coverage	0.56	75
With 100% metering	0.73	52
Geographic targeting: free water for metered households in poor areas and uniform volumetric pricing elsewhere		
With current metering coverage	0.74	77
With 100% metering	1.3	82
Means testing: free water for metered households that are poor and uniform volumetric price for others		
With current metering coverage	0.9	73
With 100% metering	1.28	64

Whether water subsidies are allocated through quantity targeting, geographic targeting, or means testing, the progressiveness of the benefit incidence increases dramatically when metering is extended to all

(continued on next page)

(*continued from p. 115*)
households. Without metering, nonpoor households that use large
volumes of water retain a large percentage of the total subsidy. They are
charged a flat fee for service, but the cost of the service they receive is
much higher. Through the metering expansion, more households gain
access to the subsidized prices offered to metered customers, and those
implicit subsidies to high-volume, unmetered customers are eliminated.

Source: Authors' elaboration based on Pattanayak and Yang 2002.

Note: All scenarios assume that unsubsidized households pay average cost.
IBT = increasing block tariff.

considers two alternative forms of consumption subsidies, each of which
has the potential to address those weaknesses of standard consumption
subsidies.

Service-Level Targeting Is Promising, Especially for Water Subsidies

The benefit incidence of the subsidy models discussed so far is a function of
administrative decisions about subsidy design and household consumption
decisions. An alternative approach to targeting is to allow households to
self-select into a subsidy scheme by choosing a particular level of water, sanitation, or electricity service. These service-level-targeted subsidy models
provide subsidies only for inferior service levels, which would presumably
be unattractive to wealthier households. Those levels could include lower-
quality, less-reliable, or less-convenient services, such as a public water tap
or a low-voltage electricity service. The expectation is that poor households
are more likely than rich households to choose the subsidized service because
they are more concerned about cost than about quality and convenience. To
the extent that this expectation is true, service-level targeting can be an effective approach to excluding nonpoor households from utility subsidies.

Service-level targeting is a particularly interesting alternative to consider
in low-coverage situations where the pace of expansion of traditional water
or electricity services is slow. Many of those lower-level services actually cost
less to install and operate than a network system with private connections.
Lower costs make it possible to serve more customers for the same cost and
to spread any available subsidy budget across more households. As with
other forms of subsidy, the financial value of a service-level-targeted subsidy
is the difference between the cost of service provision and the payment the
household makes to receive that service. Because the cost of those services
is lower, the absolute value of the consumption subsidies per cubic meter
or kilowatt-hour can also be lower.

This lower financial cost, however, has to be weighed against the implications of providing households with a lower quality of service. The benefits associated with using water from a private connection, for example, are clearly superior to the benefits of using water from a public tap. Not only do connected households consume more water, but also they avoid the risk of contamination that comes with collecting water in containers that are not always clean and the physical and time costs of carrying water. Thus, even if the financial value of subsidies from two different service levels is the same, the welfare benefit of the subsidies could be quite different.

Targeting subsidies by service level is still fairly rare in the utility sectors, but those subsidies are more common in the water sector than in the electricity sector. Most urban areas in developing countries have at least two types of water service (private connections and public taps), whereas multiple service levels are not always feasible in the electricity sector. Even in the water sector, some alternative technology options can be implemented only if a whole neighborhood agrees to use that technology. Condominial sewer and water systems, described in more detail in chapter 9, are one example. It is possible to apply a subsidy to those technologies, but the targeting method is then more accurately described as neighborhood-selection rather than self-selection.

Unfortunately, there are still very few studies of the distributional effect of service-level-targeted subsidies in the literature. One exception is the analysis of subsidies for public taps in Bangalore and in Kathmandu, where water from public taps is provided free of charge (Pattanayak and Yang 2002; Prokopy 2002). In Bangalore, 24 percent of the population obtains water from public taps: 44 percent of the poor households and only 10 percent of the non-poor. Poor households are four times more likely than nonpoor households to use public taps. Likewise, in Kathmandu, half of poor households and only one-quarter of nonpoor households use public taps. That is good news for public tap subsidies, because a greater share of poor households than of nonpoor households have opted to take advantage of this subsidy. The resulting benefit targeting performance indicators reflect this choice. For public tap subsidies in Kathmandu, Ω is 1.54. In Bangalore, it is 2.14—the best-performing subsidy in the group of subsidy cases. The errors of exclusion of the subsidies are, nonetheless, high: 72 percent of poor households do not receive this subsidy in Kathmandu, and 61 percent do not receive it in Bangalore.

The Performance of Multisectoral "Burden Limit" Subsidies Is Varied

Another approach to subsidizing consumption comes from Eastern Europe and the countries of the former Soviet Union. A number of those countries have implemented cash transfer programs that are especially designed to try to help households pay for utility service in the context of sector reform and rising prices. Because coverage levels in urban areas in those countries are very high, the principal policy challenge is not to connect unserved households but rather to ensure that households can continue to use the services as the highly subsidized prices rise toward cost recovery. Unlike standard consumption subsidies, which address only the problem of affordability in one service sector, the "burden limit" programs in those countries are designed to protect households in an environment of across-the-board price increases. The cash transfers are targeted to households for which expenditures on utility bills (and sometimes housing) constitute what policy makers perceive to be an unacceptably high proportion of household income.

Recent studies have examined the targeting effectiveness of two of the burden limit programs, in Odessa, Ukraine (Komives 1998), and in Riga, Latvia (Shkaratan 2005). The burden limit was defined as 15 percent in Ukraine and 30 percent in Latvia: households qualified for the subsidy if their monthly municipal services or utilities bill and their housing expenditures exceeded the defined percentage of household income. In Ukraine, the limit was subsequently raised to 20 percent (Lovei and others 2000).

The burden limit programs, by definition, support households with high expenditures on housing and utility services relative to income. The expectation is that implementing the burden limit program will help preserve consumption and connection levels by assisting those who have the most difficult time paying their bills. This expectation, however, is based on the assumption that households would choose to use their cash transfer to pay utility bills and that inability to pay bills would result either in disconnection or in reduced consumption. That assumption does not hold when utility bills are not assessed on the basis of metered consumption (as is often the case with water in those countries) or when there is no strict policy on disconnecting those who do not pay. In an attempt to ensure that subsidy recipients would pay their utility bills, Ukraine reserved the burden limit subsidy only for households that owed no debt to the utility or that had reached agreement with the utility on a payment schedule. That move helps provide an incentive for those households to use the cash transfer to pay utility bills, but it is also a possible reason why poor households might choose not to apply for the subsidy (Lovei and others 2000).

The targeting performance of the subsidies depends on the strength of the relationship between income and expenditure on utility bills and housing. In Odessa in 1996, 80 percent of poor households and 64.9 percent of nonpoor households had municipal services bills that exceeded 15 percent of household income. Although municipal services bills took up on average a higher percentage of income for poor than nonpoor households, they were high for both groups. Table 6.4 shows how the eligibility of poor and nonpoor households would have changed if the burden limit changed.

Table 6.4 Percentage of Households That Qualify for Burden Limit Subsidy as Burden Limit Changes

If services bills account for more than . . . percent of household income	Odessa, Ukraine				Riga, Latvia	
	Poor (Poor = 27% of households)	Nonpoor	Poor (Poor = 40% of households)	Nonpoor	Poorest 20% of households	Richest 20% of households
15	80	64	91	91	88	86
20	75	30	—	—	—	—
30	55	15	59	62	61	51
45	—	—	35	32	31	31

Sources: Komives 1998; Shkaratan 2005.

Note: — = not available.

For example, in Ukraine, if the threshold for the burden limit were increased from 15 percent to 30 percent of household income, 55 percent of poor households would still qualify but only 15 percent of nonpoor households would qualify. Raising the burden limit reduces the error of inclusion, but this improvement comes at the cost of excluding some poor households as well.

In Riga, Latvia, expenditures on rent and utility services as a percentage of income vary little between rich and poor households. Changing the burden limit does not, therefore, perceptibly change the targeting performance of the subsidy. The burden limit subsidy model faces a problem quite similar to that of quantity-targeted subsidies: there is much overlap in the expenditure patterns of poor and nonpoor households, which makes it very hard to use expenditure to isolate only the poor households.

With only two cases to study, it is not possible to draw conclusions about whether burden limit programs would, on average, be more progressive than the consumer utility subsidies studied in previous chapters. In Odessa, at the actual registration levels in the scheme in 1996, poor households received 70 percent more of the value of the subsidy than they would receive from a neutral subsidy program ($\Omega = 1.7$). In Riga, no information is available on the actual recipients of the subsidy. However, if all households that qualified for the subsidy were receiving it, the subsidy for a 30 percent burden limit would be regressive (Ω would be 0.78). In sum, the targeting performance of burden limit programs, like other consumption subsidies, can vary tremendously depending on the criteria set for inclusion in the subsidy program, the local patterns of expenditure on housing and utility services, and the profile of households who choose to register for the subsidy.

Summary

This chapter has examined approaches to improving the performance of existing quantity-targeted consumption subsidies or replacing them with alternative forms of subsidizing consumption. The analysis reveals that modifying existing quantity-targeted tariffs will not necessarily have a great effect on subsidy performance. The most promising modifications involve moving from an IBT (in which some consumption of all customers is subsidized) to a VDT (where only households consuming below a certain threshold are subsidized). It is also important to ensure that the threshold of the VDT is low enough to exclude a substantial number of households from the subsidized tariff. Those modifications are likely to have more effect in the electricity sector than in the water sector because there is more overlap in water consumption levels between poor and nonpoor households.

More promising than modifying tariff design is introducing elements of administrative selection into the subsidy mechanism. Of the types of administrative selection considered here, means testing, if well implemented, generated the most impressive improvement in simulated subsidy performance. The means-tested subsidies in the sample also have among the most progressive benefit incidence. The downside of means testing, or any other targeting method, is that errors of exclusion also increase as targeting of benefits improves. Some poor households are inevitably incorrectly classified as nonpoor or fail to apply for the subsidy.

Although few examples are available, service-level targeting also appears to be a promising avenue to explore if the primary policy goal is to target subsidy benefits to poor households. Results of the burden limit programs for Eastern European countries are mixed, with a high Ω in Odessa and a low Ω in Riga.

Notes

1. The subsidy for the third group is not automatic. A regulatory commission determines whether to grant the subsidy to this group (Gomez-Lobo and Contreras 2003).

2. In practice, subsidies in both sectors tended to exceed the guidelines set out in the law. That conclusion has been corrected in the electricity sector, but in the water sector it is still common to find that subsidies exceed those limits.

3. The subsidy analysis for this city analyzes the subsidy provided to both metered and unmetered households. Metering is, therefore, not a barrier to receiving a subsidy in those cases.

4. It was subsequently increased to 240 kilowatt-hours per month in the winter and 120 in the summer.

5. When the subsidy was originally introduced, in 1990, the eligibility requirements included both an income means test and a maximum consumption level. Only households with overall monthly consumption below 20 cubic meters were eligible for the subsidy. Households lacking meters and households sharing connections were also excluded. The take-up rate for the subsidy when it was introduced was only 5.1 percent. As a result, one year later, the consumption limit and the restriction on type of connection were eliminated.

6. Given that means testing was not the only change in the simulations, it is not possible to conclude that this result is due entirely to the introduction of means testing.

7

The Targeting Performance of Connection Subsidies

One overriding weakness of the consumption subsidies studied in the previous two chapters is that they are unable to deliver benefits to unconnected households. Those unconnected households are the potential beneficiaries of connection subsidies. Thus, the access factors that plagued consumption subsidies work in favor of using connection subsidies to target benefits to the poor. This chapter compares the targeting performance of connection subsidies for water, sewer, and electricity services with the consumption subsidies studied in previous chapters.

Comparing connection and consumption subsidies solely on their targeting performance, however, overlooks the fact that the two models operate in very different ways and have different effects on recipient households and on water and electricity use and coverage patterns. From the perspective of households, consumption subsidies are a continuous benefit, whereas connection subsidies are a one-time benefit. Nonetheless, the long-term effect of connection subsidies—providing households with access to utility services—may far exceed the benefit of the subsidy itself. Connecting to the water or electricity network gives households the opportunity to tap into lower water and energy prices and also into any available consumption subsidies. The combination of subsidies and of fuel and water source substitution either generates a reduction in household spending on water and energy or gives households the opportunity to consume more energy or water for the same budget. This stream of benefits from lower-cost water or electricity is a large part of the welfare gain that households receive from a connection subsidy (Ajwad and Wodon 2003).

Two examples illustrate this point. In a study of energy use in Guatemala, Foster and Araujo (2004) found that those with electricity connections paid US$0.08 per kilowatt-hour for energy, while the unconnected poor paid US$5.87 per kilowatt-hour equivalent for kerosene lamps, or US$13.00 per kilowatt-hour equivalent to illuminate with candles. Unconnected households consumed the equivalent of 2 kilowatt-hours per month on average for lighting and appliances. Kerosene users who connected to the utility network could save nearly US$139 over a year on these 2 kilowatt-hours of consumption. The net present value of the savings alone (not to mention the value to the household of consuming more than 2 kilowatt-hours of energy) would dwarf the electricity connection fee and thus would also exceed the financial value of the connection subsidy in this case. Bardasi and Wodon (forthcoming) did a similar comparison of the cost savings associated with connection to the water network in Niamey, Niger. They found that the poor would save about US$0.75–$1.00 per cubic meter by connecting to the water system. The yearly savings for a household consuming 10 cubic meters a month is equal to between one-quarter and more than one-half the fee charged to obtain a connection, depending on the definition of poverty adopted in the analysis. Again in this case, the net present value of these cost savings quickly exceeds the cost of connection.

On the basis of these examples, it is clear that considering the connection cost alone underestimates the value of the connection. Moreover, the future value of the stream of benefits that arises from a connection will vary across households, depending on what the households' current water, sanitation, or fuel situation is. The analysis of targeting performance in this chapter does not capture those effects, but it rather examines what the distribution of benefits across households would be if the benefit received by each subsidy recipient were the same.

Few examples of existing connection subsidies have been studied in the literature. In fact, in many countries, there are no such explicit connection subsidies, although it could be argued that connections have been subsidized to the extent that households often do not have to pay for their connection, or must pay very little. A survey found that water connection charges ranged from only US$2 to US$450 (table 7.1). Sewer connections in Latin American ranged from just US$20 to US$400. No systematic source

Table 7.1 Connection Charges for Water and Sewerage (US$)

	Water				Sewer
	Global	East Asia and Pacific	South Asia	Latin America and the Caribbean	Latin American and the Caribbean
High	450.00	450.00	129.00	387.20	400.00
Low	2.00	10.00	2.00	20.00	20.00
Average	92.22	100.81	41.67	128.23	155.68
Median	83.00	83.00	35.14	125.00	133.00
Observations	66	22	18	21	19

Source: Authors' elaboration based on Karinki and Schwartz (2005).
Note: Observations = number of cases.

of data on electricity connection charges was found. There is no universal rule about which costs associated with connecting a household a connection charge should cover. Nonetheless, the connection charges at the lowest end of this scale are clearly less than a reasonable estimate of the cost of a connection. Given that we have available insufficient data to identify who actually benefits from implicit connection subsidies and there are few explicit cases of connection subsidies, this chapter relies heavily on simulations to examine the potential performance of connection subsidies.

Universal Connection Subsidies: Subsidy Performance If All Who Could Benefit Actually Did

The simplest way to think about a connection subsidy is to assume that all unconnected households are offered and do accept subsidized connections. If we recall the framework in chapter 4, the benefit targeting performance indicator Ω^C is the product of the access factor ratios (in this case, the share of unconnected poor households relative to the share of all unconnected households) and of subsidy design factor ratios. There are three subsidy design factor ratios: the targeting ratio, the future uptake ratio, and the subsidy rate ratio. If all unconnected households received and accepted a subsidized connection, then the targeting and future uptake ratios in this equation would become 1. If, in addition, all households received the same value of subsidy (for example, all households receive free connections instead of paying the US$100 connection fee), then the subsidy rate ratio would also equal 1. The indicator Ω is reduced to the ratio of the share of poor unconnected households to the share of all unconnected households, and the distribution of subsidy benefits across quintiles is equal to the distribution of subsidy beneficiaries across income groups. This change enables analysis of the distributional incidence of simulated subsidies without knowing what the precise value of a connection subsidy in any given case would be.

With data on coverage of water, sewer, and electricity connections, it is possible to estimate the benefit and beneficiary incidence for this form of universal connection subsidy. Figure 7.1 graphs the relationship between the share of poor households receiving the subsidy and the targeting performance indicator Ω for the simulated subsidies. The distribution of the benefits of connection subsidies is nearly always progressive: Ω is greater than 1.0 in virtually all cases. The exceptions are Azerbaijan and Belarus.

This analysis is consistent with the results of an interesting trio of recent studies that tested the hypothesis that an expansion of access to basic services would be pro-poor, or at least more pro-poor than the current distribution of access to services. In Sri Lanka, Bolivia, and Paraguay, Ajwad and Wodon (2001) calculated the marginal benefit incidence of expanding various

Figure 7.1 Performance of Simulated Universal Connection Subsidies

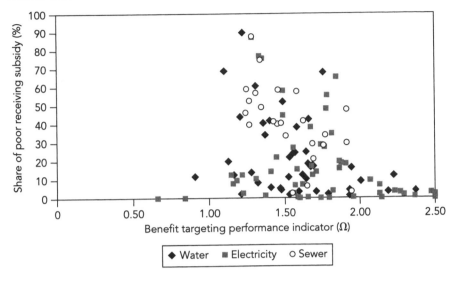

Source: Authors' elaboration with data from appendixes B.1 and C.1.

different types of services. They conclude that the marginal benefit incidence for a wide range of services is more pro-poor than the current distribution of access to those services, especially when the access rates to the services are already relatively high (and thus a large percentage of the nonpoor already have the service).

This finding has a potentially interesting implication for consumption subsidies as well: being unconnected is a good proxy for poverty in most cases (some countries of Eastern Europe would be the exception). Consumption subsidies targeted only to newly connected households are likely to be well targeted.

Targeted Connection Subsidies: Can Performance Be Improved?

The earlier analysis assumes that no attempt is made to target the connection subsidies. The next question is to what extent targeting could be used to further improve targeting performance. A number of recent studies have simulated the targeting performance of targeted connection subsidies for water and for sewer. In all cases, the future uptake ratio and the subsidy rate ratio were assumed to be 1: all targeted households were assumed to

Table 7.2 Performance Indicators for Simulated Targeted Connection Subsidies

Country, city	Benefit targeting performance indicator (Ω)	Unconnected households ratio $(1 - A \times U)$	Targeting ratio (T^C)	Future uptake ratio (U^C)	Subsidy rate ratio (R^C)
Water cases					
Nepal, Kathmandu					
Water universal					
connection	1.50	1.50	1.00	1.00	1.00
Geographic targeting	1.51	1.50	1.01	1.00	1.00
Mean tested	2.10	1.50	1.40	1.00	1.00
India, Bangalore					
Water universal					
connection	1.31	1.31	1.00	1.00	1.00
Geographic targeting	1.94	1.31	1.20	1.00	1.00
Means tested	1.57	1.31	1.48	1.00	1.00
Paraguay					
Water universal					
connection	1.25	1.25	1.00	1.00	1.00
Geographic targeting	0.82	1.25	0.66	1.00	1.00
Mean tested	1.10	1.25	0.88	1.00	1.00
Argentina					
Water universal					
connection	1.75	1.75	1.00	1.00	1.00
Water mean tested	1.85	1.75	1.06	1.00	1.00
Sewer cases					
Argentina					
Sewer universal					
connection	1.27	1.27	1.20	1.00	1.00
Sewer means tested	1.55	1.27	1.48	1.00	1.00

Source: Authors' elaboration from data from appendixes B, C, and F6.

choose to connect, and all households would receive the same value of subsidy. Table 7.2 presents the decomposition of the benefit targeting performance indicators for those simulated subsidies.

As with consumption subsidies, means testing clearly helps improve the targeting performance of the connection subsidies. Geographic targeting has more mixed results. In Bangalore, it does help improve targeting performance to a greater degree than does means testing. In Paraguay, a geographically targeted connection subsidy (identified through a criterion of unsatisfied basic needs) actually performs more poorly than the untargeted subsidy. This discovery is surprising because the same criteria, when applied to households with connections for a consumption subsidy, did improve the benefit distribution of the subsidy.

Assumptions in the Simulations: Will They Hold in Practice?

A major weakness of all of the simulations presented thus far is that they assume that all potential or targeted beneficiaries could and would eventually be connected. There are two scenarios under which this connection would not be the case: (a) when not all eligible households choose to connect and (b) when a connection is not offered at all.

Future Uptake Rates: Will All Households Really Connect?

The first scenario is when the future uptake rate is less than 100 percent—some households without connections might choose not to connect if offered the chance. If this were true, errors of exclusion would increase, and Ω could fall (if the future uptake rate among the poor were lower than for the population as a whole). Conventional wisdom is that high connection fees are a major barrier to entry for all households and for poor households in particular. Low connection fees should help encourage connection (connection credits, discussed in chapter 9, could also do so). But there are a number of reasons to expect that lowering connection fees will not, by itself, result in all unconnected households choosing to connect to the network.

Connection fees are not, in fact, the only cost that households face if they want to use network water, sanitation, or electricity services. The connection itself is worth little without some basic installations in the home to make use of the services: toilets, bathrooms, faucets, and lighting. The cost of such fixtures could dissuade households from connecting, even if the connection fee were free. Households will also consider the quality and reliability of water, electricity, or sewer service, as well as the tariff or fees they would have to pay in deciding whether it makes sense for them to connect. Another important factor in household decisions would be the cost and quality of alternatives to network water, electricity, and sewer connections. At existing prices, many households would save money by connecting to the official networks. In cases where there are good low-cost alternatives or where tariffs for network service are high, however, the incentive to connect will be lower, regardless of the connection fee.

Those problems suggest that if one is to evaluate the likely effectiveness of connection subsidies in reaching the poor and connecting the poor, it is

Figure 7.2 Performance of Connection Subsidies If 50 Percent of Poor Households Choose Not to Connect

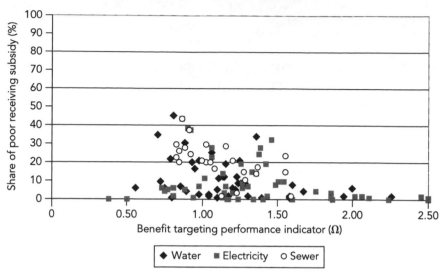

Source: Authors' elaboration with data from appendixes B.1 and C.1.

important to know the extent of undercoverage in the service areas and to understand why many households are not connected. The answers to such questions will vary from place to place, creating variation in the effectiveness of connection subsidies.

The problems also indicate that the assumption in the simulations that all unconnected households will connect when offered a connection subsidy is unrealistic. Changing the assumptions about the future uptake rate of connections can produce a dramatic drop in the performance of connection subsidies. Figure 7.2, for example, graphs the benefit targeting share of poor households who receive the universal subsidy simulation presented above, but assumes that 50 percent of the poorest households choose not to connect, despite the subsidy. Errors of exclusion predictably increase, and targeting performance drops in many cases to less than 1.0, indicating that poor households receive a smaller share of the benefits than their share of the population. In other cases, the subsidies remain progressive, but the targeting performance indicator declines.

This example shows that one cannot conclude a priori that connection subsidies will necessarily produce a progressive distribution of subsidy benefits. However, even when only 50 percent of the poor connect, the targeting performance of the universal connection subsidies is better than that of many of the consumption subsidies studied in previous chapters.

Will All Unconnected Households Be Offered Connections?

A second scenario under which not all unconnected households would receive connection subsidies is when the utility does not offer connections to all. The basic framework presented in chapter 4 assumes that all unconnected households are potential beneficiaries. That would be the case if the entire service area were covered with a distribution network or grid or if the utility had plans to rapidly make this expansion. A more common scenario in developing countries is to find two different kinds of unconnected households: those that have access to the network but have chosen not to connect, and those that do not yet have a network in the neighborhood. For the latter group of households, connection is currently impossible.

The failure of networks and grids to reach all households is often the result of financial constraints faced by the utilities. However, other factors also contribute to the problem. Water or power shortages may make the extension of service unwise, because the current supply cannot serve even the existing customer base. Insecure tenure also contributes to this problem. Homeowners without secure title to their land are often barred from connecting to services—especially water and sewer services, which have higher network expansion costs. Those factors can mean that, in practice, many unconnected households will not receive the opportunity to connect to water or electricity services in the foreseeable future. The result can be the exclusion of some of the poorest households from the benefits of a connection subsidy. For example, a recent study of social water connections in Abidjan and Dakar (Lauria and Hopkins 2004) concluded that the social connection program excludes many of the poorest households by requiring that subsidy recipients have tenure to the land and that an existing house be located on the property where service is installed.

None of the connection subsidy simulations examined so far considers the fact that some unconnected households are likely to not have the opportunity to connect. If those that are excluded from taking advantage of the connection subsidy are indeed among the poorest, then this problem could significantly reduce the progressiveness of a connection subsidy.

As a demonstration of this point, consider the benefit targeting performance of a connection subsidy under two different scenarios. The first scenario is the case in which the utility will rapidly expand access to all households and in which new connection subsidies are randomly distributed among all households that currently do not have connections. In the second scenario, a financially constrained utility is unable to extend service; the only households that could benefit from the connection subsidy are those that have access to the network in the neighborhood but have for some reason chosen not to connect. As a point of reference, the targeting performance under the two scenarios can be compared with a third scenario

Table 7.3 Benefit Targeting Performance of Connection Subsidies under Three Scenarios

	Scenario 1: All unconnected households receive subsidy $(1 - A_H \times U_{H\mid A})$	Scenario 2: Only households with access but no connection receive subsidy $[(A_H \times (1 - U_{H\mid A})]$	Scenario 3: Distribution of connection subsidies mirrors distribution of existing connections $(A_H \times U_{H\mid A})$
	Ω	Ω	Ω
Water			
Cape Verde	1.22	1.08	0.39
Electricity			
Cape Verde	1.35	1.25	0.55
Rwanda, urban	1.28	1.20	0.40
São Tomé and Principe	1.32	1.16	0.56

Source: Authors' elaboration based on Angel-Urdinola and Wodon (2005a).

in which new connections are distributed to a population that mirrors the existing customer base of the utility. The comparison reveals whether the distribution of new connections under scenario 1 or 2 would be more progressive than the existing customer profile.

Table 7.3 estimates the benefit targeting indicator (Ω) for the three scenarios for four African cases: (a) water and electricity connection subsidies in Cape Verde, (b) urban electricity connection subsidies in Rwanda, and (c) electricity subsidies in São Tomé and Principe. The formulas used to estimate Ω in the three scenarios are described in box 7.1. All simulations assume that the subsidy ratio ($R^C_{P\mid T} / R^C_{H\mid T}$) equals 1—that the rate of subsidization is the same for the poor as for other households.

As expected, Ω^{C1} is greater than Ω^{C2}: the more unconnected households that are truly subsidy beneficiaries, the better is the benefit targeting performance of the subsidies. The performance of connection subsidies could be less progressive than expected in cases where many poor households are excluded from receiving connection subsidies, either because they do not have and will not rapidly gain access to the network or grid, or because other barriers (such as tenure status) prevent them from connecting. However, whether all unconnected households or only those that currently have access receive the subsidy, the distribution of benefits from a connection subsidy is more progressive than if new connections were allocated to mirror the current distribution of connections.

Box 7.1 Determinants of Targeting Performance

Consider three options for how connections are provided by the utility. In the first scenario, new connection subsidies are randomly distributed among all households that currently do not have connections. In the second scenario, connection are provided only to households that currently have access to the network in the neighborhood but have for some reason chosen not to connect (for example, the utility does not expand the network or grid). In the third scenario, new connections would be distributed in the same way as existing connections: the profile of newly connected households would mirror the profile of households that are already connected.

Recalling the framework from chapter 4 (and assuming that all households offered the subsidy choose to connect, that the targeting ratio $= 1$), the distributional outcome in the first scenario would be

$$\Omega^{C1} = \frac{1 - A_P \times U_{P|A}}{1 - A_H \times U_{H|A}} \times \frac{R^C_{P|T}}{R^C_{H|T}}, \tag{7.1}$$

where $(1 - A_P \times U_{P|A})$ is the percentage of poor households without connections and $(1 - A_H \times U_{H|A})$ is the share of all households without connections.

The distributional outcome in the second scenario would be

$$\Omega^{C2} = \frac{A_P}{A_H} \times \frac{1 - U_{P|A}}{1 - U_{H|A}} \times \frac{R^C_{P|T}}{R^C_{H|T}} \tag{7.2}$$

where $A_P \times (1 - U_{P|A})$ is equal to the share of poor households that have access but no connection, and $A_H \times (1 - U_{H|A})$ is the share of all households in that situation.

Because the expectation in most cases is that poor households are less likely to have connections and to have access to networks or to the grid than nonpoor households, one would expect Ω^{C1} to be greater than Ω^{C2}. Both distributional outcomes should be more progressive than the third scenario, in which new connections would be distributed in the same way as existing connections. This third scenario is a somewhat pessimistic assumption from a distributional point of view because it tends to favor better-off households, but it could be the case if access rates to the network are still very low and thus the profile of the unconnected population is very similar to that of the connected population. In this

(continued on the next page)

(continued from p. 131)

third case, the distributional outcome would be

$$\Omega^{C3} = \frac{B_P}{B_H} \times \frac{R^C_{P|T}}{R^C_{H|T}} \tag{7.3}$$

where, following the framework from chapter 4, B_P is the share of poor households that are currently subsidy beneficiaries and B_H is the share of all households that receive the subsidy. In most cases, one would expect $\Omega^{C1} > \Omega^{C2} > \Omega^{C3}$.

Source: Angel-Urdinola and Wodon 2005a.

Subsidy Funding and Implementation: How Do They Affect Distributional Incidence?

The discussion of connection subsidies has so far abstracted from methods of funding and implementation. However, these methods can have a significant impact on the ultimate performance of this subsidy mechanism.

Funding Mechanisms Can Increase or Decrease the Progressiveness of Subsidies

Lauria and Hopkins (2004), in their study of the social water connections, discuss how the funding mechanism for the social connection programs affects the distribution of net subsidy benefits in Côte d'Ivoire. Social connections there are paid for out of a Water Development Fund, which is capitalized through a surcharge on water tariffs. The resulting subsidy is poorly targeted, with nearly 90 percent of all connections in Abidjan qualifying for the subsidy. One perverse effect of financing a poorly targeted or untargeted connection subsidy scheme in this way is that some of the connected households that pay for this surcharge are, in fact, poorer than many of the households receiving the new social connections. This problem arises in Abidjan because many nonpoor households still lack water connections and are not excluded from the social connection program.

A study of a similar financing mechanism in Buenos Aires, Argentina, reached different conclusions (Foster 2004). A fixed charge of US$3.31 every two months has been applied to water bills in this metropolitan area since 1997. This charge (*Cargo Servicio Universal y Medio-Ambiente*, or Cargo SUMA)

Figure 7.3 Distributive Effect of the Cargo SUMA

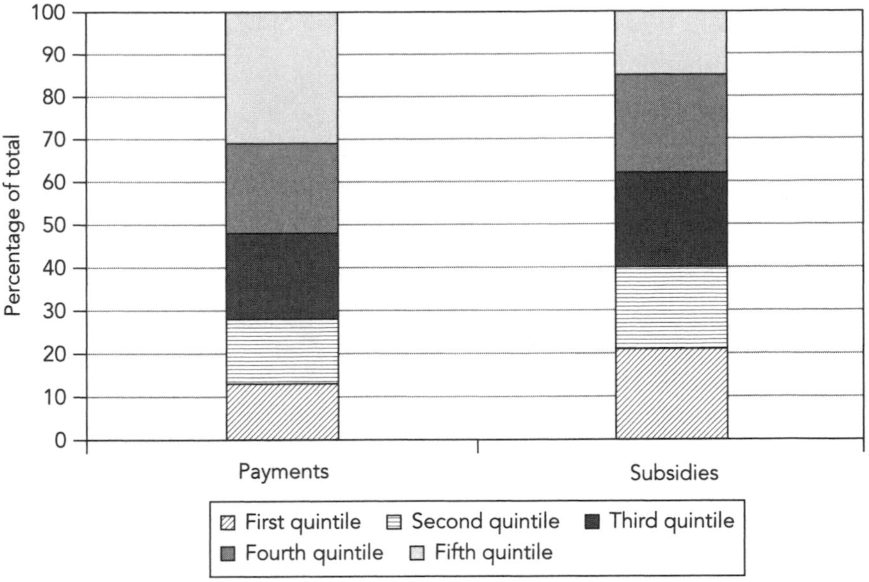

Source: Foster 2004.

Note: SUMA = Servicio Universal y Medio-Ambiente.

is used to fund new connections and wastewater treatment. Foster simulated the net distributional effect of using the portion of the charge dedicated to fund water and sewer connections over a five-year period. Her simulation takes into account that households that are currently unconnected will, once connected, have to begin paying the Cargo SUMA. Figure 7.3 compares the distribution of payments into this fund with subsidies received from the fund. Foster found that the charge itself is mildly progressive. Using the Cargo SUMA funds for water subsidies would be highly progressive because only poor households are left without water connections in the city at this stage. Using the funds for sewer connections is almost distributionally neutral, because there are many households of all income levels who lack sewer connections.

A simulation of subsidy models for water service in Uruguay also examined the possible effect of using a fixed surcharge on water service to fund connections, this time looking at connections to the sewer system (Ruggeri-Laderchi 2003). The simulation attempted to make the net subsidy distribution more progressive by imposing the extra fixed charge only on nonpoor households. In practice, however, the targeting method applied to differentiate poor from nonpoor was not precise enough—some poor households were improperly classified as nonpoor and thus were required to pay the surcharge on their water bills. This imprecision reduced the progressiveness of the subsidy model design.

The Implementation of Subsidies Can Have Important Effects on Utility Behavior

In addition to the funding mechanism, how a connection subsidy program is implemented can also affect the distribution of benefits, as Lauria and Hopkins (2004) point out in their analysis of the social connections program in Côte d'Ivoire. The private water system operator, SODECI, carries out this program. SODECI is reimbursed a flat fee for each social connection it installs. This arrangement potentially creates a perverse effect, giving the concessionaire an incentive to maximize the number of social connections (even at the cost of poor targeting) and to install connections in neighborhoods where high levels of consumption are expected and where connection costs are low. The wealthier unconnected neighborhoods are more likely than the poorest to be attractive in this way to the water operator. Lauria and Hopkins hypothesize that installing too many social connections may actually lengthen the time the neediest households (living in informal settlements) have to wait before getting a connection.

More generally, utilities concerned with cost recovery will want to expand service into areas where they can rapidly recover their costs of expansion. To the extent that poor households are not covering the cost of the service they receive (either the cost of the connection or the cost of consumption) and that those subsidies are not reimbursed through government transfers, utilities have little incentive to expand into such areas (Komives 1999). This problem is important to consider in the design of consumer utility subsidies, so as to avoid delaying access to services for the poorest household.

Summary

The benefit targeting performance of connection subsidies provided to unconnected households could be more impressive than that of consumption subsidies to connected households, particularly in low-coverage environments. The lack of connections to the water or electricity networks are good proxies for poverty in many cases.

However, many of the potential beneficiaries of connection subsidies may not in actuality be able to take advantage of this subsidy, either because they do not meet the requirement for connection or because there is no network or grid in their neighborhood to which they can connect. Such problems can prevent connection subsidies from living up to their potential. At the same time, a number of measures can be taken to improve the performance of connection subsidies. Examples discussed in this chapter include targeting and the use of surcharges on the nonpoor to finance new connections. Both of those strategies require targeting mechanisms that are able to accurately differentiate poor from nonpoor.

8

Consumer Utility Subsidies as Instruments of Social Policy

Chapter 3 explained that consumer utility subsidies are generally justified for one of two reasons. First, they can be understood as a component of social policy because they provide a mechanism for delivering assistance to the poor. Second, they can be regarded as part of a sectoral strategy to ensure that most households can afford utility services, particularly as prices for services rise with sector reform. This chapter takes up the question of consumer subsidies as social policy: what does the empirical evidence show about the prospects of using consumer utility subsidies as an instrument of social policy?

Previous chapters have demonstrated that the benefit targeting incidence of the most common form of consumer utility subsidy—quantity-targeted subsidies—is quite poor. Other subsidy models are able to improve targeting performance, but a progressive distribution is by no means guaranteed, and the errors of exclusion of many of the subsidies remain high in many cases. Does this observation then mean that consumer utility subsidies make poor instruments of social policy? To answer this question, four aspects of subsidy performance are reviewed in this chapter: (a) the benefit targeting performance of consumer utility subsidies relative to other social policy instruments, (b) the distributional incidence of subsidies relative to the income distribution in the case area, (c) the materiality of the subsidies—how significant they are for poor households, and, finally, (d) the potential effect on poverty levels of adding or removing consumption subsidies.

What Is the Benefit Targeting Performance of Utility Subsidies Relative to Other Transfer Mechanisms?

From a social policy perspective, consumer utility subsidies are just one of a wide range of possible mechanisms for delivering assistance to the poor. If the goal is to raise disposable incomes of poor households, the objective is to find the mechanism that can achieve this goal most efficiently. The higher benefit targeting performance indicator, Ω, the lower is the leakage of subsidy benefits to the nonpoor, which, in turn, means more benefit for the poor per dollar spent on the subsidy program. The Ω values for the most common type of consumer utility subsidies—quantity-targeted subsidies—are not very impressive. Connection subsidies, by contrast, produce a progressive distribution of subsidy benefits. What is unclear from this analysis is how this performance compares with other social policy instruments. Would resources spent on consumer utility subsidies be better applied to other programs if social policy objectives were the only objectives under consideration?

To answer this question, one will find it useful to compare the targeting performance of consumer utility subsidies with the results of a study of the targeting performance of a wide range of social programs (Coady, Grosh, and Hoddinott 2003), including cash transfers, food subsidies, and social funds. Table 8.1 compares the benefit targeting performance indicator for existing utility subsidies described in previous chapters with that of the sample of other social programs.

Table 8.1 Targeting Performance of Utility Subsidies Relative to Other Social Policy Instruments

Type of transfer (and number of cases)	Mean (median) Ω	Range of Ω	Percentage of cases with progressive distribution ($\Omega > 1$)
Existing utility consumption subsidies			
Water consumption subsidies: private water connections (33)	0.96 (0.90)	0.24 to 2.14	39
Water consumption subsidies: public taps (2)	1.84 (1.84)	1.54 to 2.14	100
Electricity consumption subsidies (37)	0.76 (0.66)	0.20 to 1.50	22
Other social policy instruments			
Cash transfers (28)	1.53 (1.40)	0.40 to 3.47	82
Near cash transfers (16)	1.26 (1.28)	0.58 to 1.63	94
Public works (4)	2.30 (1.96)	1.48 to 4.00	100
Social funds (6)	1.13 (1.10)	0.93 to 1.30	83
Food subsidy (15)	0.84 (0.93)	0.28 to 1.23	27

Source: Authors' elaboration based on Coady, Grosh, and Hoddinott (2003) and appendixes D.6 and E.6.

Consumption Subsidies Perform Poorly in Comparison with Other Transfer Mechanisms

Table 8.1 indicates that many existing water and electricity consumption subsidies are poor performers when compared with many other models of social policy instruments. Whereas most of the social policy instruments in the Coady study generate a progressive distribution of benefits, half of the existing subsidies on private water taps and the vast majority of the existing electricity subsidies are regressive.

In terms of performance and type of subsidy, food subsidies can be categorized as the social policy instrument that most resembles water and electricity subsidies. Like water and electricity subsidies, food subsidies are consumption subsidies. The poor performance of all three groups of subsidies would suggest that it is in general very difficult to use consumption subsidies of any sort to target the poor effectively.

The model presented in chapter 4 helps explain why consumption subsidies of any type have a hard time targeting the poor. The first hurdle for any consumption subsidy to overcome is access to that good—how many poor households can and do use the good that is a candidate for subsidization? Goods with universal reach (such as staple foods) would not have this access problem, but, in most sectors, finding goods that all households consume is very difficult. Even in the case of electricity, which generally has high coverage in urban areas, the excluded households were found to be disproportionately poor.

Even better than a good used by all is something consumed by all poor households, but not by the nonpoor. Quality differentiation of goods is one way to try to achieve this separation. Public taps are an example of quality differentiation from the water sector, and those subsidies are among the best-performing water subsidies in the sample. It is, however, difficult to find candidate goods for which access factors would tend to tilt the distribution of beneficiaries and benefits toward the poor and away from the nonpoor.

A second problem with consumption subsidies stems from the consumption patterns of those households that use a subsidized good. Poor households may spend a greater percentage of income on water, electricity, or food than richer households, but the total expenditure of the richest households on those goods is, on average, likely to be higher than that of the poor. As chapter 5 showed, if a consumption subsidy is provided for each unit consumed, the richer households will, on average, receive a greater total subsidy than the poor. Unless a highly effective targeting mechanism can be used to completely exclude the nonpoor from receiving the subsidy, the value of subsidies accruing to nonpoor households will be larger than the value delivered to poor households.

Quantity Targeting Is Inferior to Administrative Selection for All Types of Subsidies

The general difficulties with consumption subsidies help explain the poor targeting performance of most water and electricity subsidies in relation to other social policy instruments. Most of the existing water and electricity subsidies are consumption subsidies that rely on quantity targeting alone to allocate benefits. However, chapter 6 demonstrated that the targeting performance of water and electricity subsidies can improve significantly if alternative targeting methods are used—means testing, in particular. When water and electricity subsidies and other social policy instruments that use the same targeting method are compared, there is less difference between them (table 8.2).

The average value of Ω for subsidy programs using means testing to allocate benefits is greater than 1 for water subsidies, electricity subsidies, and other social policy instruments. Those subsidies that are targeted on the basis of consumption (or quantity) are the poorest performers in all three groups. Geographic targeting falls in between, producing progressive distributions on average for water subsidies and other instruments, but not for electricity subsidies. In short, much of the poor performance of consumer utility subsidies in relation to other existing transfer mechanisms can be explained by the targeting methods used in the samples. Administrative selection of

Table 8.2 Median Targeting Performance, Ω, by Targeting Method: Consumer Utility Subsidies versus Other Social Policy Instruments

	Consumption (quantity targeting)	Geographic targeting	Means testing (individual assessment)	Self-selection (service level, workfare)
Water subsidies				
Existing consumption	0.60	1.05	1.36	1.84
Simulated consumption	0.78	0.86	1.19	—
Simulated connection	—	1.30	1.71	—
Electricity subsidies				
Existing consumption	0.63	0.90	1.23	—
Simulated consumption	0.64	—	1.39	—
Other social policy instruments	1.00	1.33	1.4	1.78

Source: Authors' elaboration based on Coady, Grosh, and Hoddinott (2003) and appendixes D.6., E.6, and F.6.

Note: — = not available.

any type (but particularly means testing) is far superior to consumption- or quantity-based targeting.

This conclusion is bad news for those who advocate for quantity-targeted water and electricity subsidies as an important alternative transfer mechanism in countries or areas with weak administrative structures, where the implementation of a means-tested subsidy program would be difficult. Subsidies on water and electricity service delivered without any form of administrative selection are highly unlikely to be progressive.

The exception to this rule would be service-level-targeted subsidies where poor households are more likely than other households to self-select into the program (as with the subsidies on public taps). Beyond public tap subsidies, this type of subsidy is still relatively rare in the water and electricity sectors. There are some technical constraints to service differentiation, particular with electricity and sewer services, but this option clearly deserves more attention from policy makers.

Connection subsidies are also a promising option. The median targeting performance of the simulated targeted connection subsidies rivals that of other social policy instruments. Even the untargeted universal subsidies perform as well as many other social policy programs. The challenge for the connection subsidy programs is to ensure that having the subsidy in place actually leads to poor households connecting to the service. If poor households fail to connect, then the targeting performance of the subsidies will decline.

What Is the Distribution of Subsidy Benefits Relative to Income?

Another way to evaluate the benefit targeting performance of consumer utility subsidies is to compare the distribution of subsidy benefits with the distribution of income in the case area. This comparison can be done using Lorenz curves and Gini coefficients. A Lorenz curve is created by ranking the total population from richest to poorest, and then plotting a curve that shows the percentage of income or of the subsidy that is captured by the poorest X percent of the population. The shape of the Lorenz curve can be summarized with a single indicator known as a Gini coefficient, or a quasi-Gini when used to examine the distribution of subsidy benefits rather than income (box 8.1). A quasi-Gini coefficient can range from −1 (very pro-poor distribution) to 1 (a very pro-rich distribution).

In every case where data were available, the distribution of subsidy benefits is less unequal (more pro-poor) than the distribution of income in the case area. Figure 8.1 demonstrates this result for the Indian state electricity

Box 8.1 An Introduction to Gini Coefficients

One way to understand the overall pattern of subsidy incidence across the full spectrum of rich and poor is to rank the total population from richest to poorest, and then to plot a Lorenz curve, which shows the percentage of subsidy that is captured by the poorest X percent of the population.

Regressive distribution. The first Lorenz curve plotted in the diagram (LC_1) represents a situation where the poorest 20 percent of the population receives only 5 percent of the total subsidy, while the poorest 50 percent receives only 15 percent of the total subsidy. As a result, the Lorenz curve bows down below the 45-degree line, indicating that the distribution is regressive.

Progressive distribution. The second Lorenz curve plotted in the diagram (LC_2) represents a situation where the poorest 20 percent of the population receives 60 percent of the total subsidy, while the poorest 50 percent receives 90 percent of the total subsidy. As a result, the Lorenz curve bows up above the 45-degree line, indicating that the distribution is progressive.

For convenience, it is typical to summarize the shape of the Lorenz curve in a single indicator known as a quasi-Gini coefficient (QGC). The quasi-Gini coefficient is defined as the area underneath the 45-degree line down as far as the Lorenz curve, divided by the whole area of the triangle under the 45-degree line. Thus, for the first Lorenz curve (LC_1), the quasi-Gini coefficient is defined as $QGC = A_1/T$. When the Lorenz curve bows up above the 45-degree line, the area between the Lorenz curve and the 45-degree line is deemed to be negative. Hence, for the second Lorenz curve (LC_2), the quasi-Gini coefficient is defined as $QGC = -A_2/T$.

The quasi-Gini coefficient is bounded between -1 and $+1$, with an intermediate value of zero. A quasi-Gini of zero essentially indicates that the Lorenz curve lies right on top of the 45-degree line. A quasi-Gini close to $+1$ means that the distribution of the subsidy is very pro-rich, so that the Lorenz curve is bowing out almost to the edges of the triangle and almost 100 percent of the subsidy is going to the richest few people in the society. A quasi-Gini close to -1 means that the distribution of the subsidy is very pro-poor, so that the Lorenz curve is bowing out to make almost a triangle above the 45-degree line and almost 100 percent of the subsidy is going to the poorest few people in the society.

(*continued on the next page*)

(continued from p. 141)

Gini coefficients are also commonly used to measure the distribution of income in a society. In that case, they can take values only between 0 and +1, because it is (by definition) impossible for the poorest 20 percent of the population to have more than 20 percent of the income.

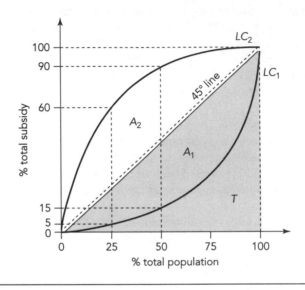

Figure 8.1 Inequality in the Distribution of Income versus the Distribution of the Electricity Subsidy in Indian States

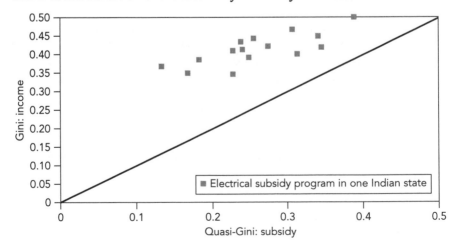

Source: Appendix D.6.

subsidies. Although those subsidies all have a regressive distribution, they are less regressive than the distribution of income in the states. This finding indicates that the subsidies contribute to reducing inequality, even when the distribution of subsidy benefits is regressive.

Do Subsidies Provide Material Benefits for Poor Recipients?

Ultimately, from a social policy perspective, the goal of transfer mechanisms is to reduce poverty levels. Both benefit and beneficiary incidence are important determinants of how well any subsidy or transfer program will reduce the poverty headcount. Subsidy models with high benefit targeting performance and low errors of exclusion have the best potential to reduce poverty because they deliver a large percentage of each subsidy dollar to poor households and because a large percentage of poor households receive the subsidy.

In addition to benefit and beneficiary incidence, a third dimension of subsidy performance, which has not yet been addressed in the book, is also important in explaining the relationship between utility subsidies and poverty levels: the materiality of the subsidy. Materiality is how significant the value of the subsidy is to the household that receives it. A subsidy that reaches all poor households but delivers a tiny benefit will have little effect on household disposable income or on poverty indicators, despite its accurate targeting performance.

Consumer utility subsidies (as well as other forms of consumption subsidies) have one important limitation as transfer mechanisms. Unlike cash transfer programs, there is a cap on the value of the subsidy provided to any household through a utility subsidy. The maximum value of the subsidy is the cost of the water or electricity service that the household consumes or of the connection that the household receives. Where the cost is a significant portion of household income, utility subsidies have the potential to significantly affect disposable household income. Where cost relative to income is low or where water or electricity consumption is very low, even a full subsidy will have only a limited effect. The public tap subsidies in Kathmandu and Bangalore are good examples. Those well-targeted subsidy programs provide water free of charge at public taps. Nonetheless, because households using public taps use very little water, the average financial value of the subsidy that each household receives is equal to only 0.3 percent of the average household income among the poor in Bangalore, and 1.3 percent of the average household income among the poor in Kathmandu.

Figure 8.2 Average Consumption Subsidy to the Poor as a Percentage of Average Income of the Poor

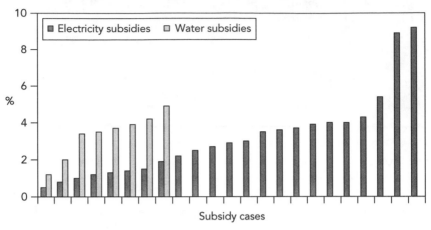

Source: Authors' elaboration from appendixes D.3 and E.3.

Most of the Existing Utility Subsidies Are of Significant Size Relative to Income

Nonetheless, in most of the cases of existing subsidies, the value of the water and of the electricity subsidies provided to poor households is fairly large relative to income. Figure 8.2 shows the average financial value of existing water and electricity subsidies relative to the income of poor households for the subsidy cases. Among the sample of subsidies from private water connections, the most significant one is in Bangalore, where the subsidy is nearly 5 percent of income for the poor. Most of the other water subsidies are, on average, equivalent to 3–4 percent of the income of poor households. Among the electricity subsidies, the range is greater. Those subsidies range from 1 to 3 percent of the average income of poor households in many Indian states to nearly 9 percent of income in Delhi and in São Tomé and Principe. A number of cases in the middle range from 2.5 to 5 percent of the income of the poor.

It is important to recall, however, the distinction between the financial value of a subsidy and the cash value of a subsidy, which was introduced in chapter 4. Few residential customers are paying the full cost of water and electricity service. As a result, even if the financial value of a subsidy is quite large relative to household income, such value does not mean that the effect of the subsidy on household disposable income will be that large. The most a subsidy can do (directly) to raise disposable incomes is to completely eliminate a water or electricity charge, raising disposable income by the amount that the household would otherwise have paid. When current charges for service are very low, the cash value of the consumer utility subsidy will be very small. This problem arises in a number of the cases studied in this book, making the average financial value of the subsidy exceed the average expenditure on water or electricity services. If prices were set at cost recovery levels, this distinction would disappear.

To What Extent Do Subsidies Contribute to Poverty Reduction?

The cases with the best potential for reducing poverty are those with high benefit targeting performance, low errors of exclusion, and high value relative to income. Few of the subsidies fit those criteria. The electricity volume-differentiated tariff in Honduras is one example of a typical consumption subsidy: half of all poor households are excluded from electricity subsidies, and the targeting performance indicator for the electricity subsidy is only 0.49. A recent study of the poverty reduction effect of this electricity subsidy found very little change in poverty levels as a result of the subsidy (box 8.2). The results do not bode well for other similar consumption subsidies.

Table 8.3 presents some rough simulations of the effect of increases in household expenditure on utility services on the poverty headcount and the extreme poverty headcount in a variety of cases. Increases of 10 percent, 50 percent, 100 percent, and 300 percent in expenditure on water, on electricity, and on both services are simulated. The simulations assume that connection rates do not change, so only households that currently have connections are affected by the increases. The results can be interpreted either as the increase in poverty that could result from eliminating subsidies (and thus raising prices) or as the reduction in poverty levels that is made possible by preserving existing subsidies.

In either case, the results suggest that the effect on poverty levels of changes in expenditure would be greater for electricity than for water and would be greatest for the case in which prices of both services would rise. Doubling expenditure on water would, on average, produce a 1.1 percent increase in the poverty headcount, whereas doubling electricity expenditure would increase this poverty indicator by 3 percent. This result is not surprising, given that household expenditure on electricity generally exceeds expenditure on water and that coverage of electricity is much more extensive among the poor than is coverage of water.

The rough estimates of subsidies' effects on poverty are quite large, considering that water and electricity utilities in many countries would need to more than double prices in order to recover operation, maintenance, and capital costs (chapter 2). Some water utilities would need to increase prices 10-fold to reach cost recovery. As one interprets those results, however, it

Box 8.2 Poverty Reduction Effect of the Honduran Electricity Subsidy

In the late 1990s, Honduras had an electricity subsidy that was delivered through a volume-differentiated tariff, with a lifeline of 300 kilowatt-hours. Households consuming less than 300 kilowatt-hours all received a subsidy. The government reimbursed the electrical utility for the cost of those subsidies. In 1998, the cost of the electricity subsidies to the government of Honduras totaled US$17 million a year.

To assess the effect of this subsidy on poverty levels, Wodon, Ajwad, and Siaens (2003) combine administrative information provided by the utility with household survey data. The merged data set reveals that only 16.5 percent of households consume more than 300 kilowatt-hours. The vast majority of utility customers, rich or poor, are subsidized. It is, therefore, no surprise to learn that 80 percent of the benefits of the subsidy go to nonpoor households. Moreover, because nearly 50 percent of poor households lack electricity connections, errors of exclusion are high.

The table in this box is reproduced from Wodon, Ajwad, and Siaens and shows that the changes in poverty levels that could arise with the elimination of the subsidy are very small. This finding is robust to changes in the poverty line. The methodology used for the estimation did not take into account any substitution effects of the imposition or elimination of the subsidy; thus, if anything, the changes in poverty levels associated with eliminating the subsidy are likely to be overestimated.

Effect of the Electricity Subsidy on Poverty, Honduras, 1999

	Without subsidy			With subsidy		
KWh consumed	Headcount	Poverty gap	Poverty gap squared	Headcount	Poverty gap	Poverty gap squared
Poverty line at L 400 per person per month						
0–20	44.93	12.42	5.99	44.93	12.29	5.92
20–100	36.00	10.45	4.26	35.66	10.19	4.11
100–150	20.57	6.06	2.61	16.82	5.60	2.35
150–200	10.98	2.67	0.93	10.98	2.24	0.72
200–250	15.64	5.32	2.00	15.64	4.56	1.51
250–300	17.09	3.06	1.02	17.09	2.38	0.79
300+	10.15	2.70	1.12	10.15	2.19	0.87

(continued on the next page)

(Continued)

	Without subsidy			With subsidy		
KWh consumed	Headcount	Poverty gap	Poverty gap squared	Headcount	Poverty gap	Poverty gap squared
Poverty line at L 600 per person per month						
0–20	71.01	29.00	14.56	71.01	28.85	14.44
20–100	63.47	23.70	11.60	63.47	23.36	11.36
100–150	44.74	13.97	6.75	43.39	13.29	6.34
150–200	31.26	8.19	3.35	27.45	7.47	2.95
200–250	35.80	13.15	6.05	34.16	11.88	5.21
250–300	29.15	10.41	4.37	29.15	9.36	3.73
300+	17.97	6.33	3.03	17.97	5.65	2.60

Source: Wodon, Ajwad, and Siaens 2003.

is important to remember that doubling expenditure is not equivalent to doubling prices. One would expect households to be sensitive to price changes and thus to reduce their consumption as a result of a price increase. In that case, it would take more than a 100 percent increase in water or electricity prices to make households double their expenditures on those services. Given median estimates of price elasticity of demand for water and electricity (table 2.2), a price increase of about 150 percent or 450 percent would be needed to increase expenditure by 100 percent or 300 percent, respectively. Large increases in prices might also push some households off the utility system altogether, because higher prices for utility services would make other alternatives like wells and generators more attractive. Table 8.3, thus, is likely to overstate the effect on poverty levels of changes in subsidy levels.

Summary

The preceding findings send three clear messages to subsidy designers. First, the most common forms of consumer utility subsidies are poor transfer instruments in comparison with other social transfer programs. The poor performance of utility subsidies comes largely from their use of quantity targeting. When more sophisticated targeting methods are used for utility subsidies, their targeting performance improves in line with other social welfare programs. Connection subsidies and well-targeted consumption

Table 8.3 Poverty Effect of X Percent Changes in Water and Electricity Expenditures, If Consumption Levels Do Not Change

Country, state, or city	Survey year	Poverty headcount				Extreme poverty headcount			
		10% change	50% change	100% change	300% change	10% change	50% change	100% change	300% change
Electricity									
India	2001–2	0.3	1.6	3.2	9.6	0.2	1.2	2.6	8.1
India, Kerala	2001–2	0.1	0.7	1.4	4.4	0.1	0.5	1.0	3.2
India, Andhra Pradesh	2001–2	0.3	1.3	2.6	8.2	0.2	1.0	2.1	6.8
India, Tamil Nadu	2001–2	0.2	1.0	2.0	6.2	0.2	0.7	1.5	4.8
India, Karnataka	2001–2	0.3	1.3	2.6	8.4	0.2	0.8	1.6	5.4
India, Maharashtra	2001–2	0.2	1.2	2.4	7.9	0.2	0.9	1.8	6.0
India, Madhya Pradesh	2001–2	0.3	1.7	3.4	2.2	0.3	1.4	2.9	2.2
India, Gujarat	2001–2	0.5	2.3	4.7	15.3	0.0	1.4	3.4	12.7
India, Orissa	2001–2	0.3	1.6	3.2	9.7	0.3	1.5	3.0	9.5
India, Punjab	2001–2	0.5	2.4	5.0	16.2	0.3	1.8	3.8	13.4
India, Haryana	2001–2	0.5	2.5	5.2	16.6	0.4	2.1	4.3	15.0
India, Rajasthan	2001–2	0.5	2.3	4.7	15.6	0.4	1.8	3.7	13.0
India, Delhi	2001–2	0.3	1.4	2.8	8.8	0.2	1.2	2.4	7.7
India, Uttar Pradesh	2001–2	0.3	1.4	2.8	8.7	0.3	1.3	2.6	8.4
India, West Bengal	2001–2	0.2	1.2	2.5	7.8	0.2	1.0	2.0	6.4
India, Bihar	2001–2	0.3	1.4	2.8	8.6	0.2	1.2	2.5	7.9
Croatia	1998	0.2	1.1	2.1	6.3	0.2	0.9	1.9	5.9

	Year								
Hungary	1997	0.5	2.4	4.9	14.9	0.4	2.0	4.2	13.9
Latvia, Riga	1997	0.1	0.6	1.2	3.6	0.1	0.4	0.8	2.7
Cape Verde	2001–2	0.3	1.3	2.7	8.7	0.2	1.1	2.3	7.5
Rwanda	2000–1	0.2	1.0	2.0	6.1	0.2	1.0	1.9	6.1
São Tomé and Principe	2000–1	0.5	2.4	4.9	16.5	0.3	1.5	3.3	12.6
Guatemala	2000	0.0	0.2	0.5	1.5	0.1	0.3	0.7	2.0
Average		0.3	1.5	3.0	9.2	0.2	1.2	2.4	7.9
Water									
Croatia	1998	0.1	0.5	0.9	2.8	0.1	0.4	0.9	2.6
Latvia, Riga	1997	0.2	0.9	1.7	5.1	0.1	0.7	1.4	4.3
Cape Verde	2001–2	0.2	0.8	1.7	5.2	0.2	0.8	1.5	4.8
Nepal, Kathmandu	2001	0.1	0.6	1.2	3.5	0.1	0.6	1.2	3.7
India, Bangalore	2001	0.1	0.3	0.6	1.8	0.1	0.3	0.6	1.7
Sri Lanka	2003	0.1	0.3	0.7	2.0	0.0	0.2	0.5	1.4
Average		0.1	0.6	1.1	3.4	0.1	0.5	1.0	3.1
Water and electricity									
Croatia	1998	0.3	1.5	3.0	9.2	0.3	1.4	2.8	8.8
Latvia, Riga	1997	0.3	1.4	2.9	8.8	0.2	1.1	2.3	7.3
Cape Verde	2001–2	0.4	2.2	4.5	14.8	0.4	1.9	3.9	13.7
Average		0.3	1.7	3.5	10.9	0.3	1.5	3.0	9.9

Source: Authors' elaboration based on data from appendixes B and C.

subsidies could be reasonable substitutes for other transfer mechanisms, provided that the magnitude of the desired transfer is not larger than the cost of utility service.

Second, the typical value of existing utility subsidies as a proportion of household income is significant—at about 3–5 percent in the cases surveyed. Third, households could spend 10–50 percent more on water and electricity without major effects on poverty levels, but in many countries, much larger price increases are needed to reach cost recovery. Raising expenditures by 100 percent (by raising prices by approximately 150 percent) would, on average, increase the poverty headcount by 3 percent. Substantial price increases in multiple sectors at the same time could quickly affect poverty levels, or living standards, if households decided that they could no longer afford utility services.

9
Beyond Subsidies—Other Means of Achieving Sectoral Goals

Chapter 8 reviewed the available evidence regarding the extent to which utility subsidies contribute to social policy objectives. This chapter turns to the sectoral objectives of promoting universal access and affordability to water supply and electricity services. Table 9.1 summarizes how consumer utility subsidies could be expected to support these sectoral objectives.

Regarding affordability of service, the key findings of this study have been as follows. First, the low values of Ω [typically in the range 0.3 to 0.6 for most increasing block tariff (IBT) structures] indicate that utility subsidies are not a very cost-effective way of increasing affordability to the poor. Every dollar of benefits to the poor entails two to three dollars of subsidy expenditure. Second, relatively high errors of exclusion (typically in the range of 60 percent to 80 percent for most IBT structures) demonstrate that utility subsidies do not reach a substantial proportion of poor households; hence, their impact on affordability is severely circumscribed. Third, for the minority of the poor who receive utility subsidies, the reduction in household expenditure is modest but significant, given that the value of utility subsidies is typically between 3 and 5 percent of household income. Therefore, utility consumption subsidies as currently practiced are a relatively expensive way of making services more affordable for a small minority of the poor. More sophisticated targeting techniques offer the potential to improve the cost-effectiveness of utility subsidies, although that gain may sometimes come at the expense of increasing errors of exclusion.

As regards increasing access to service, the evidence indicates that connection subsidies have the potential to be much better targeted to poor households than do consumption subsidies and, thus, could promote greater access among the poor. Moreover, the stream of cost savings that many unconnected households experience by connecting can exceed the magnitude of the connection subsidy itself manyfold. Nevertheless, connection subsidies address only one of many possible barriers to connection, namely that associated with unaffordable connection charges. Even if connection charges are kept to a minimum, households may still face difficulties in financing complementary investments in their dwellings or may be precluded from connecting as a result of a lack of legal tenure or by physical distance to the

**Table 9.1 Effect of Utility Subsidies on Achievement
of Sectoral Goals**

	Access to network	Connection to network	Consumption of service
Consumption subsidy	Possible negative effect, if consumption subsidy dilutes incentive to serve corresponding communities	No direct effect, but may make connection more attractive	Positive effect, decreasing unit price of water for qualifying households
Connection subsidy	Possible negative effect, if subsidy leaves utility underfunded to finance expansion	Positive effect, decreasing price of connection for qualifying households, but may not address other constraints	No effect

Source: Authors' elaboration.

network. Furthermore, the presence of consumption subsidies may, of itself, undermine access objectives, insofar as it reduces the commercial incentive for utilities to expand the network into low-income areas.

Given those concerns, it is worth asking whether consumer utility subsidies are really necessary or sufficient to reach sectoral policy objectives, or whether there are other alternative or complementary approaches that could be more successful. This reflection is particularly important because the potential benefits of utility subsidies are accompanied by many risks, such as risks to financial health of the utility, the departures from efficient consumption behavior, and the creation of perverse incentives for the utilities to serve the poor.

This chapter examines some alternative approaches to achieving the goals of increasing affordability and coverage of water and electricity services. Those approaches may be regarded as substitutes or complements to consumer utility subsidies, depending on the context. The approaches include reducing the cost of service provision, adapting payment systems, and removing legal barriers.

Cost Reduction Measures: Bringing Down the Cost Recovery Threshold?

Subsidies are not the only way to lower consumer prices and to promote affordability. Reducing costs could be equally effective and could be accomplished by improving the efficiency of the service provision or by increasing revenue collection so that existing costs are spread across the full customer base. Nevertheless, it is important to recognize that cost reductions will not always necessarily be passed on to consumers. This conclusion is so for several reasons. First, if average utility prices are well below efficient cost recovery levels, then lower operating costs may simply increase the amount available for funding the requisite level of capital maintenance (recall the discussion of underpricing in chapter 2). Second, lower costs in one area of service may simply be absorbed by greater inefficiency elsewhere or may be retained in the form of higher profits (Ugaz and Waddams Price 2002). Third, as was the case in Argentina, lower utility costs may be offset by an increasing burden of indirect taxation so that the government effectively captures the efficiency gain and so there is no positive impact on final consumer prices (Estache 2002).

Increasing Operating Efficiency May Be Helpful to a Limited Extent

Many water and electricity utilities in developing countries and transition economies have very high cost levels because of inefficiencies in operations. Those inefficiencies include underutilization of existing capacity in water treatment or power plants, poorly designed plants, excessively high losses in distribution and transmission networks, and overstaffing. For example, distribution losses of 10 percent to 30 percent for power and 40 percent to 60 percent for water are by no means uncommon. Fixing any of those problems would bring down the average cost of service and would make it possible for the utility to charge lower rates to all consumers. Reforms such as privatization, competition, and regulation may contribute to the achievement of efficiency savings.

Estimates of potential savings for individual utilities are hard to come by, but a few recent studies serve to illustrate the point. Estache, Rossi, and Ruzzier (2004) found that electric utilities in Latin America could achieve efficiency gains of about 5–7 percent per year. A recent Latin American study of the impact of private sector participation in water and electricity distribution found that both labor productivity and distribution losses improved significantly, particularly during the transition period from public to private management. Thus, during the transition for electricity, labor productivity grew by 6 percent per year and distribution losses fell by 3 percent overall. In the case of the water sector, labor productivity grew by 5 percent per year during the transition, while distribution losses under private management fell by 1 percent per year faster than under public management (Andres, Foster, and Guasch forthcoming).

One issue that has been studied in greater detail is the potential for reducing power consumption in water service provision. Studies of utilities in China and Central Asia have found that electricity can account for up to

50 percent of operating costs for water utilities (Ijjaz 2003; Levin 2003). Moreover, reductions of 25 percent to 50 percent in electricity usage can be achieved by measures such as repairing pumping systems and controlling distribution losses (ESMAP 2004; James, Godlove, and Campbell 2003).

Nevertheless, improvements in operating efficiency are not always easy to obtain. Moreover, given the capital intensity of utility services, even large gains in operating efficiency have relatively small impacts on the total cost of service. Operating costs account for about one-third of water supply costs and one-half of electricity supply costs. Thus, achieving a challenging 25 percent reduction in operating costs would reduce the total cost of service provision by only about 10 percent.

Reducing Capital Costs Could Have a Larger Impact

Reductions in capital costs have a much greater potential for reducing costs, or at least for limiting the extent of future cost increases as services are expanded and upgraded. Options for reducing capital costs include improvements in the planning, design, and execution of capital projects, as well as efforts to manage and contain the overall demand for the service.

Improving the process of planning, designing, and executing capital projects could result in significant savings. For political reasons, utilities sometimes embark on the construction of large-scale capital projects that are not optimal for sustaining service provision. Moreover, there is a tendency to overengineer projects, without due regard for either the potential cost savings in choice of materials or the trade-offs between investment costs and service reliability. In addition, procurement costs for capital works may often be unnecessarily high because of the lack of competition, as well as the presence of paybacks to corrupt officials.

Capital costs are strongly linked to consumption levels: both average and, in particular, peak consumption. Taking measures to slow the growth of demand can, therefore, substantially postpone the need for new investments. So-called demand-side management was developed in the 1970s as an alternative to traditional supply-driven planning in response to the oil price shocks of that period. The idea was that actively managing demand could be much more cost-effective than forecasting demand on the basis of past trends and then building projects to meet those forecasts. The concept has since been institutionalized in the electricity and natural gas sectors with the emergence of a comprehensive planning approach called integrated resource planning (Charles River Associates 2004), but the concept has been much slower to catch on in the water sector.

Demand-side management encompasses a wide range of measures and includes reducing network losses as well as metering and economic pricing (including peak and seasonally differentiated tariffs). Public education on efficient use of the service is also an important tool. It is sometimes combined with grants or tax write-offs to install more efficient appliances in households and businesses (such as low-flow toilets or efficient light bulbs). For example, the water utility serving Soweto in South Africa offered one-time free repair of plumbing fixtures as a prelude to meter installation (Smith 1999).

In Lima, Peru, a program to raise metering from 4 percent to 67 percent, to reduce distribution losses from 31 percent to 22 percent, and simultaneously to increase the tariff closer to cost recovery levels, made it possible to increase coverage from 75 percent to 88 percent, while improving continuity of service from 11.5 to 20.4 hours per day (World Bank forthcoming a). Such consumer-based, demand-side management initiatives bring a dual benefit: not only do they reduce the overall costs of service provision to the utility, but also they serve to reduce the monthly bill to the customer, thereby having a direct impact on affordability at the household level.

Improving Revenue Collection Often Represents a "Quick Win"

Many water and electricity utilities do not receive revenue for all units of water or electricity delivered to customers. Even after technical losses are accounted for, commercial losses from uncollected bills and malfunctioning meters further reduce the number of revenue-producing units produced and sold. In the former socialist countries, revenue collection rates for electric utilities range from 16 percent in Azerbaijan to 98 percent in Bosnia and Poland (World Bank forthcoming b). Reducing commercial losses allows costs to be spread across a larger number of customers, thereby reducing the average unit price that must be charged in order to reach cost recovery goals. For example, to recover all costs through tariff revenue, the average tariff in Azerbaijan would need to be nearly five times larger than in Bosnia or Poland (assuming total costs were the same), just because of the differences in revenue collection. Reducing commercial losses is, therefore, an important target for utilities to generate revenues to maintain and expand service without having to resort to disproportionate increases in average tariffs. For utilities with very low collection rates, improvements in this area could almost certainly have an immediate and more significant positive impact on the financial position of the utility than could efforts to reduce operating and maintenance costs.

Billing and Payment Systems: Matching the Cash Flow of the Poor?

The cost of utility services can sometimes be made more manageable for low-income customers by providing flexible billing and payment arrangements. Low-income households often face cash flow problems and lack financial reserves or access to credit from which to cover large bills. In this sense, utility services that are provided on credit and that entail periodic bills covering relatively long service periods are ill-suited to the financial condition of the poor, which can be contrasted to the traditional alternatives to utility services, such as vendor water or candles. Although such services are much more expensive overall, they do provide the flexibility of purchasing small amounts on a daily basis and, as such, may appear to be more affordable to low-income households. In comparison with providers of other goods and services, utilities tend to be very conservative in their approach to commercial policy; they rarely attempt to differentiate their products in commercial terms. This reluctance becomes evident when they are contrasted with the cellular telephony sector, which has been very innovative in designing service packages with different payment schemes that cater to a wide variety of customer needs. This section identifies a number of ways in which utilities could make their commercial policy more socially accessible.

More Frequent Billing Makes Payments More Manageable

Changing billing and payment methods and options can help low-income households spread the cost of their utility bills. Most utilities in developing countries bill monthly or bimonthly, while utilities in industrialized countries may bill as little as two to four times per year. Nevertheless, even monthly bills can be difficult for low-income households to absorb, and it may be desirable to allow more frequent payment. This approach adds significantly to the administrative costs of the utility, but the cost impact can be minimized by allowing a single monthly bill to be paid in a number of smaller installments, or by using remote meter reading technology. This process is facilitated by developing a dense network of payment points in collaboration with banks, supermarkets, post offices, or other local retailers. An alternative approach for periurban slums may be to subcontract billing to a small-scale operator or local community representative who becomes responsible for collecting and paying the bills for the entire settlement.

Microfinance Facilities Help to Spread Costs of Capital Charges

Even more than monthly utility charges, connection charges that frequently take the form of one-time, up-front capital payments can represent a major financial barrier for low-income households. Typical connection charges amount to US$70 for water, US$130 for sanitation, and US$110 for electricity though they vary widely. Moreover, in the case of services such as sanitation and natural gas, the cost of the in-house upgrades required to make full use of the network service can, in many cases, exceed the cost of the connection itself. Such costs can be prohibitive for poor households. One possible solution is for the utility to allow connection costs to be paid in installments over a medium-term period. This practice is relatively common. Regarding costs that households incur to install service within their dwellings or to connect to the network, utilities may build partnerships with local microfinance institutions that provide credit for housing improvements.

In the case of El Alto, Bolivia, for example, Foster (2002) estimated that the cost of installing a basic bathroom was roughly double the cost of the sewer and water connections. Nongovernmental organizations in the city worked in collaboration with the local water utility to provide microcredit for both connection and fixture costs. To help ensure repayment and thus make it possible to offer a lower interest rate, the water utility collected the loan payments with the water bills.

Consumption-Limiting Devices May Help to Control Expenditures

Utilities may also use measures to help households to control the amount of water and electricity they use and thus to have better control over their bills. One measure is metering. Metered households have more control over their bills, as their tariffs reflect their actual consumption. To reduce their bills, they can reduce their consumption.

Prepayment systems are an alternative method of helping customers manage their spending on utility services. Those systems allow households to buy a token or a card in advance, which they insert into the meter at home. The value of the token or card determines how much water or electricity can be used. Once the value purchased is reached, the system shuts off.

One problem with prepayment meters is that the hardware involved is still relatively expensive (though costs will likely decline over time). The prepayment meters entail a significant investment on the part of the utility, raising questions as to whether the additional costs should be recovered directly from the customers who adopt this payment approach. Thus far, prepayment meters have been more widely applied in industrialized than in developing country contexts. The prepayment approach effectively allows households to voluntarily disconnect themselves from the service during periods of financial adversity. Such a hidden disconnect may raise social concerns, particularly for services closely associated with public health.

An alternative approach is to install devices that physically limit the amount of service that the household obtains. In the case of electricity, load limiters restrict the number of appliances that can be used simultaneously. In the case of water, such devices are rarer—and more problematic because they may prevent basic hygienic use—but can take the form of plates that restrict the diameter of the supply pipe and, hence, the flow of water in the network. The devices prevent households from using larger amounts of the service than they can afford, and the devices are often associated with a fixed monthly charge that makes payment much more predictable. In Argentina, some utilities use such flow restrictors as an alternative to outright disconnection, which permits nonpaying households to meet their most basic needs (Foster 2003a, 2003b).

Legal and Administrative Barriers: What Removing Nonprice Obstacles Does to Serving the Poor

The cost reduction measures and modifications to billing and payment systems discussed previously in this chapter all represent efforts that utilities, of their own initiative, can make to facilitate access to and use of service by poor households. Unfortunately, utilities and other potential service providers often face legal and administrative barriers that constrain opportunities to make other changes that would help expand access to the poor.

Alternative Technologies Offer Major Cost-Reduction Potential

Most utilities in the developing world strive to provide a single standard of service, whose costs are dictated by engineering standards that have often been lifted directly from industrialized countries. Two sets of standards are relevant in driving costs. The first set relates to the quality of the service provided (including chemical and bacteriological standards for water and wastewater, as well as reliability standards for service continuity and voltage levels). The second set relates to the inputs and procedures used to construct infrastructure networks, including regulations governing quality of materials, design dimensions, and public works procedures. Parameters currently used in industrialized countries are often inappropriate for developing country contexts, either because they do not reflect an appropriate balance between cost and quality of service for lower-income countries or because they reflect climatic or geographic conditions typical of temperate zones. One example of this latter point is the typical requirement for deep burial of water mains to avoid seasonal freezing.

When the standards in place raise costs to the degree that service is considered unaffordable for the poor, it is worth asking whether an alternative service level could be as appropriate or more appropriate for some households or neighborhoods. Lower-cost service levels offer to poor households who are unable to—or choose not to—use standard utility service an alternative avenue to obtain water and electricity service, without requiring the utility to provide a subsidy—or as large a subsidy.

Although differentiated services levels do exist in electricity to some degree (for example, low-voltage systems), they are much more common in rural areas than in urban areas. The water and sanitation sector has made more progress in the area of offering different unsubsidized service levels to urban customers, largely because of the characteristics of the service: the water and sanitation sector does not have to cope with the dynamic instability challenges—which require narrow technical specifications—that the physics of electricity demand.

The cost implications of inappropriate engineering standards can be very substantial. An example of adapting conventional standards, along with the resulting cost savings, is in rural electrification. Growing use of photovoltaic systems to provide electricity service in rural areas may provide cost savings of up to 75 percent relative to grid extensions, depending on how far grid extension has already proceeded in any particular case (Reiche, Martinot, and Covarrubias 2000).

In Latin America, condominial systems have been developed as an alternative approach to providing household water and sewer services at lower costs. First introduced in Brazilian shantytowns (*favelas*), the systems reduce the length, diameter, and depth of the network by routing pipes under or along sidewalks or in backyards. The systems sometimes use community labor for civil works. They have since been applied in Bolivia and Peru. In El Alto, Bolivia, the condominial system reduced the pipe needs by 10–20 percent and the volume of earth that must be moved for burying the pipes by 45–75 percent. Total cost savings for network expansion were in the neighborhood of 40 percent for water and 25 percent for sewer (Foster 2002). This set of figures compares with cost savings on the order of 20 percent found in Brazil.

A few water utilities in South Africa have experimented with other low-cost delivery systems for water distribution. In Durban, for example, a flow restrictor meter is used in combination with a semipressure system, shallow networks, and individual ground tanks to provide low-income households with 200 liters of water a day (Brocklehurst 2001). This volume of water is provided free (although households contribute to the cost of connection) under South Africa's policy of free basic water service, but, in principle, households using this technology could be charged the actual, reduced cost of this level of water service quality.

The principal barrier to technological innovations of this kind is often legal or administrative. Many utilities are precluded from implementing and experimenting with alternative construction and service quality standards because national laws, regulations, construction codes, or contracts restrict technology choice. Revising such technical standards to provide operators with greater flexibility could, therefore, have a major impact on access to the poor—at minimum monetary cost. Beyond legal and administrative barriers, there are often significant cultural norms that are within the engineering profession and that work against departing from time-honored practices or providing infrastructure and services that meet less-rigorous standards. The standards also need to be addressed for low-cost technologies to be more widely applied.

Small-Scale Providers Are an Important, but Neglected, Part of the Solution

In areas where utility services are either unavailable to low-income households or prohibitively expensive, small-scale providers often step into the breach, providing a wide range of alternative services. Those services vary enormously, from resale of network water or electricity between neighbors, to sale of network substitutes (such as kerosene or water cylinders), or even to development of informal networks that are independent of the local utility. In Latin America, for example, some small-scale providers in Asuncion (Paraguay), Barranquilla (Colombia), Cordoba (Argentina), and Guatemala City have been able to provide service at lower cost than the water utilities by using smaller-scale and lower-cost delivery systems (Solo 1999).

In some cities, partnerships have developed between incumbent utilities and small-scale providers, with the former acting as bulk suppliers and the latter acting as local distributors and retailers. For example, in Accra (Ghana), many households rely on tanker water, which is traditionally of high cost and dubious quality. In the 1990s, a contract was signed between the tankers' association and the incumbent utility. According to the terms of the agreement, the utility would provide the tankers with metered public supply of potable water at designated stations throughout the service area. In return, tankers would submit their vehicles to hygiene inspections and would agree to charge no more than the regulated tariff. This agreement has led to substantial improvements in tanker service (Kariuki and Acolor 2000). Unfortunately, such arrangements are not the norm. More often, incumbent utilities and small-scale providers operate in parallel universes with little interaction and, hence, no attempt to exploit the potential complementarities.

Moreover, utility legislation and contracts often include restrictions on alternative service providers within the utility's service area. This restriction gives utilities the right (a) to prevent households from installing wells or using generators, (b) to restrict activities of small-scale service providers (whether private or community based), (c) to stop households from buying power and water from each other, and (d) to eliminate their own alternative service options (such as public taps) as soon as network service becomes available. All those actions are designed to increase demand for water and electricity service from the dominant network provider under the theory that households with few viable alternatives are more likely to purchase a connection to newly expanded distribution lines. However, while potentially beneficial for the utilities, such policies can undermine the objective of providing households with access to water and electricity services (Estache, Foster, and Wodon 2002; Komives 1999).

Lack of Legal Tenure Is Often a Major Obstacle to Access

Another major barrier to expanding utility services into low-income urban areas is the issue of legal tenure for housing. Many periurban communities in the developing world were formed as a result of unplanned invasions of public or privately owned land. The process of regularizing the ownership of the land and, hence, of securing legal tenure for residents can be a very slow and controversial one. Municipalities are often reluctant to provide utility services to communities located on land that they do not own—or on public land that is planned for another use—for fear that the services imply an acceptance of the unauthorized settlements. Hence, tenure insecurity effectively excludes households from receiving network services. In Lima, Peru, for example, despite a major public program to legalize tenure in the periurban belt, the local water utility estimates that approximately half of the unserved households in its service area still lack legal titles (Noth forthcoming).

One solution is to legalize the settlements by providing land titles to households occupying the land. A problem with this approach is that, once legalized, the land becomes more attractive to higher-income households. The lower-income occupants may then sell their land and move to another settlement without city services. The lower-income households benefit financially from this transaction, but this initial benefit only transfers the problem of unserved poor households to another location.

An alternative approach is to find ways to adapt municipality connection policies to permit utilities to serve untitled areas. In Dhaka, Bangladesh, nongovernmental organizations have negotiated on behalf of communities for the provision of time-limited municipal services (for example, with a service guarantee of only five years) (Water Aid 2001). In Manila, the government provided a moratorium on demolition of some slum areas, which was sufficient to give the operators time to recover the costs of the system expansion. This approach is more feasible with services that are not costly. The investment required for extending conventional water and sewer service is high enough that a five-year service contract may not be attractive to the water utility. Alternative technologies and arrangements between utilities and smaller-scale providers can provide solutions to this problem.

Summary

This chapter began with the observation that consumer utility subsidies on their own are typically not sufficient to ensure that poor households gain access to affordable utility services. This conclusion is based on the limitations in financial resources available to provide subsidies, the deficiencies in the targeting of such subsidies, and the fact that additional bottlenecks may prevent such subsidies from reaching the poor.

The measures reviewed in this chapter fall under three broad headings, and their anticipated impact is summarized in table 9.2. The first category is associated with reducing the costs of service, whether by achieving efficiencies in operating and capital expenditures or by improving revenue collection.

The second category is adapting billing systems to the needs of low-income households where affordability constraints are linked to cash flow problems faced by the household, as opposed to an absolute inability to pay. Options included increasing the frequency of billing, allowing financing of connection costs, and providing devices that assist households in controlling their consumption.

The third category is relieving legal restrictions that work against the expansion of services to the poor. These restrictions include technical norms that oblige utilities to use inappropriate high-cost technologies, legal tenure regulations that prevent services from being extended to periurban neighborhoods, and regulations restricting the services provided by small-scale providers.

It is relevant to reflect on how the different approaches interact with consumer utility subsidies. In most cases, they can be regarded as complements rather than outright substitutes. The commercial policy measures, for example, will reduce the need for a subsidy but are unlikely to eliminate it altogether. Similarly, efficiency measures may substantially reduce the cost of subsidization but will not always be enough to eliminate it altogether. Measures such as addressing legal tenure issues and providing microfinance for connection costs are essential complements to any policy on connection subsidies, because they address other barriers to connecting. When combined with the adoption of low-cost technologies, they may even be enough to substitute for connection subsidies entirely.

Although all of the approaches reviewed have a contribution to make, the potential materiality of that contribution varies substantially in each case. Those measures potentially likely to have the largest effect on access and affordability are those associated with legal changes. Adoption of new technologies, in particular, has been shown to lead to substantial cost reductions, even though experimentation has been relatively limited to date.

Table 9.2 Potential Effects of Different Policy Instruments on Use of Water and Electricity Services

	Access to network	Connection to network	Consumption of service
Reducing costs			
Reducing operating costs	Could increase expansion rate if improves financial health of utility	Has no direct effect, but may make connection more attractive	Lowers price per unit, if cost reductions are translated into lower tariffs
Reducing capital costs	Could have possibility of greater expansion with lower capital costs	Has no direct effect, but may make connection more attractive	Lowers price per unit, if cost reductions are translated into lower tariffs
Improving revenue collection	Could increase expansion rate if improves financial health of utility	Has no direct effect, but may make connection more attractive	Lowers price per unit, if cost reductions are translated into lower tariffs
Adapting payment systems			
Billing methods	Have no effect	Have no direct effect, but may make connection more attractive	Facilitate consumption
Microfinance facilities	Have no effect	Reduces financial barrier to connection	Have no effect
Consumption limiters	Have no effect	May increase connection cost	Give households more control over consumption
Removing barriers			
Alternative technologies	Could have possibility of greater expansion with lower cost technology	May lower connection cost and thus connection fee	May lower operating costs and thus consumption charge, but this is not necessarily the case
Small-scale providers	Have option for households outside the reach of conventional service	May lower connection cost and thus connection fee	May lower operating costs and thus consumption charge, but this is not necessarily the case
Legal tenure	Opens possibility for utilities to serve these areas	Has no effect	Has no effect

Source: Authors' elaboration.

In countries with low revenue collection or with inflated capital costs, improving efficiency in those areas could also have quite a material effect on costs. However, as noted above, given the low starting point of utility tariffs, efficiency gains do not necessarily translate into immediate price reductions for consumers. Nevertheless, they do serve to reduce the cost of providing a subsidy to the utility, the cross-subsidizers, or the government (depending on who is ultimately responsible for subsidy finance). Moreover, financially healthy utilities are in a much better position to expand service and to offer a quality of service that is attractive to potential new customers.

10
Conclusions

During the 1990s, there was a general tendency to advocate for full-cost recovery in water and electricity services, to help reduce the need for external subsidies, and to improve the financial viability of utilities. There are good reasons for this policy position. Financially strapped utilities tend to provide low-quality services and to lag behind in expanding networks, while soft budget constraints undermine incentives for efficient management.

In practice, achievement of full-cost recovery has proved elusive even in those countries that have had the political will to embrace this goal. In many parts of Asia and Africa, tariffs would have to increase between twofold and tenfold (especially in the water sector) in order to have residential consumers pay the cost of the service they receive. Tariff increases of this magnitude would push about half of households in Africa and South Asia, as well as about a third of households in East Asia, to devote more than 5 percent of their total monthly expenditure or income to water or electricity service, or to reduce their consumption of those services below subsistence norms. Such tariff increases also would have unpredictable effects on demand for utility services and nonpayment rates.

Beyond those social concerns, attaining full-cost recovery has also proved politically difficult. Given that utility subsidies currently benefit such a broad swathe of the population, it is often possible to form a large coalition against any measures to reduce or eliminate them.

Subsidies are, therefore, likely to remain an important component of utility service pricing over the medium term. The relevant policy questions thus concern how to improve the performance of utility subsidies, keep them as small as is practically possible, limit the extent to which they undermine the performance of the sector, and decide when there may be other (perhaps more effective) means of achieving policy objectives. This book has focused on one particular—but central—aspect of subsidy performance: the extent to which subsidies succeed in targeting the poor.

How Prevalent Are Utility Subsidies?

Consumer utility subsidies are a ubiquitous feature of water and electricity services in the developing world, and even in many industrialized countries. Global tariff surveys indicate that the majority of electricity and (particularly) water utilities charge tariffs substantially below levels commensurate with full cost recovery. A significant proportion of utilities charge tariffs that do not even cover operating and maintenance costs. There is a strong relationship between average residential tariffs and country income level. Average water tariffs in low-income countries stand at about a tenth of the level applied in high-income countries, while average electricity tariffs in low-income countries stand at about half of that level. Moreover, differential pricing of industrial and residential customers remains commonplace, being practiced by 90 percent of water utilities surveyed and 40 percent of electric utilities. In the case of water utilities, those tariff differentials can be as large as twofold to fivefold, potentially driving industrial consumers to seek alternative sources of supply.

How Do Standard Quantity-Targeted Utility Subsidies Perform?

The most widespread form of consumer utility subsidies is the quantity-targeted subsidy, practiced by about 80 percent of water and electric utilities surveyed. This type of subsidy often takes the form of an increasing block tariff (IBT), whereby all consumers face higher unit prices on successive increments of consumption. Another common variant is the volume-differentiated tariff (VDT), whereby all those consuming beyond a certain threshold pay a higher tariff on the entirety of their consumption. Although in both cases tariffs rise with the level of consumption, even the highest consumption blocks are typically charged rates that produce income significantly below full-cost recovery levels.

A central finding of the analysis is that standard, quantity-targeted utility subsidies are invariably regressive. Indeed, the average value of the benefit targeting performance indicator (Ω) is no more than 0.62 for quantity-targeted subsidies. The parameter Ω measures the share of subsidies received by the poor relative to the share of the poor in the overall population. Hence, this result means that poor households capture only half as much of the value of the subsidy as they would under a random subsidy distribution across the entire population. Although use of IBTs is often justified on social grounds, the available evidence suggests that they are rarely much more effective at targeting resources to the poor than a straightforward, subsidized, linear volumetric tariff would be.

In general, quantity-based subsidies tend to perform better in situations where a higher percentage of poor households are connected to the utility network. Nevertheless, even with universal service coverage, subsidies delivered through IBTs rarely achieve much more than distributional neutrality (Ω equal to 1), which is akin to random distribution of subsidies among the population.

Why Do Quantity-Targeted Utility Subsidies Perform So Poorly?

Several factors explain the poor performance of quantity-based utility subsidies. The first and most fundamental reason is that the access rate of poor households is typically much lower than the access rate of nonpoor households. Households that do not have access to the service are clearly unable to benefit from any subsidy, and this lack of access creates an automatic handicap that the optimization of subsidy design can never fully overcome. Moreover, in cases where meter coverage is less than universal, unmetered households are excluded from subsidies delivered through quantity targeting.

The second reason is that the differences in consumption between the poor and the nonpoor—particularly between the poor and the middle class—are less than is often assumed. Even though average consumption does tend to increase somewhat with income, there is huge variation around that average. Thus, a significant proportion of poor households consume large amounts of utility services, while a significant proportion of nonpoor households consume small amounts of utility services. The lack of strong, consistent correlation between consumption and household income, particularly for water supply, severely restricts the scope for quantity targeting.

The third reason is that—even when the poor do consume less than the nonpoor—various common features of tariff structures often preclude smaller consumers from benefiting from such subsidies. High fixed charges mean that households that consume very small quantities may face a much higher unit price than larger consumers. Moreover, failure to apply full cost recovery tariffs to those households consuming at higher levels means that even large consumers benefit from subsidization to a substantial degree. Thus, even when quantity-based tariff structures do manage to deliver greater per unit subsidies to low-consuming poor households, they still result in larger total subsidies going to high-consuming nonpoor households—because the larger volume they consume more than offsets the differential subsidy per unit consumed.

Do Quantity-Targeted Subsidies Perform Differently for Water and Electricity?

Quantity-targeted subsidies are found to be equally prevalent in both water and electricity services. Targeting performance was found to be equally deficient in both sectors, although for different reasons. On the one hand, electricity service has a number of characteristics that favor the targeting performance of quantity-based subsidies, including higher metering rates and better tariff designs (involving smaller subsistence blocks and price gradients that rise more rapidly toward cost recovery levels). On the other hand, consumption differentials between poor and nonpoor are larger for electricity than for water service, allowing the nonpoor to capture a larger absolute value of subsidies. Those two factors offset each other so that ultimate targeting performance is quite similar.

Is It Possible to Improve the Design of Quantity-Targeted Subsidies?

It is sometimes argued that the poor performance of quantity-based targeting could be quite easily reversed by improving the design of tariff structures. The evidence presented earlier indicates that adjusting the size of consumption blocks is unlikely to measurably improve the distributional incidence of subsidies. The deficiencies of quantity-based targeting have as much to do with large access differentials and similar consumption patterns between poor and nonpoor as they do with tariff structures. Evidence presented from seven case study simulations lends support to the view that tinkering with tariff structures does little to improve targeting performance.

For example, lowering the subsistence threshold for quantity-targeted subsidies—and thereby addressing one of the most commonly perceived design failures—has only a minimal effect on targeting performance. Switching from an IBT to a VDT has a somewhat larger effect on subsidy performance, particularly if the VDT obliges all those households consuming beyond a certain amount to pay a full-cost recovery tariff on their entire consumption. Nevertheless, even this modification is typically not enough to turn a regressive subsidy system into a progressive one.

Are the Alternatives to Quantity Targeting Any Better?

Quantity targeting is, of course, not the only mechanism to deliver consumption subsidies for utility services. Alternatives include geographic targeting, which attempts to identify low-income areas, and means testing, which evaluates the economic situation of individual households. In addition, subsidies can be focused on lower service levels (such as public standposts), thus allowing consumers to select their preferred cost and quality combination. The available evidence suggests that these alternative forms of targeting can contribute to a significant improvement in targeting performance, whether they are used as the sole targeting mechanism or used in combination with quantity targeting. The only exception is categorical targeting (for example, discounts for pensioners or veterans), which proved to be regressive in all cases considered.

Use of geographical targeting mechanisms raises Ω on average to 0.99. While this rise is a substantial improvement on the performance of quantity-based targeting alone (with an Ω of 0.62), it represents only a neutral distribution across households and, hence, is no better than a random distribution of subsidies. The efficacy of geographic targeting is circumscribed by the limited extent of spatial clustering of poverty in many urban environments.

Across the cases studied, use of means testing has a much greater effect on improving targeting performance, with Ω taking a strongly progressive average value of 1.31 when subsidies use means testing. However, this greater targeting accuracy comes at the cost of a substantial increase in the errors of exclusion, which rise from about 30 percent on average for geographic targeting to 60 percent on average in the case of means testing (comparable to typical errors of exclusion under quantity-based targeting). Furthermore, significant transaction costs may be associated with administering such subsidies if means-testing systems are otherwise absent in the locality in question. Households also face transaction costs in applying for such subsidies on the part of households.

The two available cases of service-level targeting through public standposts for water service suggest that this approach to targeting subsidies performs well in distributional terms, with an average Ω of 1.84. However, the value of the subsidy is relatively small, and significant welfare losses may be associated with the lower quality of service provided.

It is important to recognize that those alternatives to quantity-based subsidies work by improving subsidy design factors, but they do nothing to address the underlying access differential between the poor and nonpoor. Hence, there is a limit on the extent to which overall targeting performance can be improved through such approaches, particularly in countries where a sizable portion of the population does not have access to the service.

Do Connection Subsidies Perform Better Than Consumption Subsidies?

The performance deficiencies of consumption subsidies that have been identified, together with the major access differential between poor and nonpoor, suggest that connection subsidies may be a more effective approach to reaching the poor.

Unfortunately, virtually no case studies evaluate the distributional incidence of existing connection subsidy schemes. However, some inferences can be made by simulating connection subsidies using coverage data from existing case studies. Given low coverage rates among the poor, even untargeted connection subsidies have the potential to be quite progressive, with Ω greater than 1 in all cases considered. If connection subsidies are further combined with geographic targeting or means testing, simulations suggest that Ω could be raised to 1.30 or 1.71, on average respectively.

However, the results of those simulations are based on the bold assumption that, in introducing connection subsidies, unconnected households in each income decile would connect at the same rate. In practice, this assumption is unlikely to hold. For one thing, utilities may face many other constraints in expanding their networks into all the relevant geographic areas. Furthermore, even where networks are already present, poor households may face nonfinancial obstacles to connecting (such as the absence of legal tenure). Both of those considerations may substantially reduce the targeting performance of connection subsidies. For example, if only half of poor households are able to connect to the network when it is present in their neighborhood, the associated subsidies become regressive in some cases.

Do These Conclusions Vary across Geographical Regions?

It is difficult to draw firm conclusions about systematic differences in results across regions of the world. The number of fully documented subsidy cases available for consideration in this book was already relatively small. Moreover, some regions of the world have been more widely studied than others, with 12 cases from Latin America, 7 from Eastern Europe, 4 from South Asia, and 4 from Sub-Saharan Africa. No case study material at all was available for East Asia or the Middle East.

Nevertheless, one basic conclusion does emerge quite clearly. Given the importance of access factors in driving the ultimate performance of subsidies, differences in access rates across regions drive differences in targeting performance across regions.

Therefore, in regions with low access rates such as Sub-Saharan Africa, it is very difficult to achieve progressivity through consumption subsidies. Although the findings appear to point in favor of connection subsidies for Sub-Saharan Africa, another important result is that (notwithstanding sizable consumption subsidies) only 20–30 percent of poor households in the four African case studies examined here connect to utility networks even when networks are available. Unless those rates can be substantially improved, even connection subsidies are unlikely to be progressive in Sub-Saharan Africa.

The other extreme is Eastern Europe, where access is almost universal and where targeting performance is entirely related to subsidy design and consumption factors. Latin America and South Asia lie somewhere in between in terms of access factors. However, Latin American countries have gone further in experimenting with alternatives to quantity-based targeting and have, therefore, tended to achieve a better performance overall.

Are Utility Subsidies as Effective as Other Measures of Social Protection?

Utility subsidies are often regarded as an important component of a country's overall social safety net. For countries that lack sophisticated welfare systems, subsidizing essential utility services may represent a practical, second-best approach to social protection.

It is, therefore, instructive to compare the targeting performance of utility subsidies with other social protection programs. The results show that standard quantity-based utility subsidies tend to perform poorly in relation to a wide range of social programs. Whereas the vast majority of utility subsidies practiced today are regressive, most other social programs (including cash transfers, social funds, and workfare schemes) are progressive.

Much of this difference in targeting performance has to do with more widespread use of administrative targeting in other social programs than for utility subsidies. Controlling for the targeting method used, the performances of utility subsidies and other social programs are not so far apart. Moreover, the few cases of means-targeted and service-level-targeted utility subsidies (with Ω of 1.30 and 1.84, respectively) perform at least as well as other social programs, on average. The same would also be true of targeted connection subsidies if potential uptake problems could be overcome.

Do Utility Subsidies Have a Material Impact on Disposable Incomes?

In absolute terms, the value of most of the utility subsidies studied in this book amounts to about 3–4 percent of the total expenditures or income of the poorest households that receive them, with the value of electricity subsidies typically somewhat higher than that of water subsidies. As such, their effect on the spending power of the poor is modest but not immaterial. Moreover, although most utility subsidies currently practiced were found to be regressive in their distributional effect, they are still less regressive than the overall income distribution in the countries where they are practiced. Their effect on inequality is, therefore, mildly favorable.

Are There Viable Alternatives to Utility Subsidies?

At most, connection subsidies can help encourage poor households with access to the network to connect, and consumption subsidies will make ongoing service more affordable for the poor. But connection and consumption subsidies address only one of the many problems that may explain why poor households currently do not use utility services. Moreover, they are not the only instruments available for meeting social policy objectives in the provision of basic infrastructure services. Utility subsidies are, therefore, best seen as a potential part of a package of policy measures to help ensure access to utility services for the poor. Alternative measures may not do away with the need for utility subsidies altogether, but they are certainly complements that may help to contain the magnitude of utility subsidies and to address bottlenecks that could otherwise undermine their targeting performance.

The need for utility subsidies can be reduced—if not entirely eliminated—by measures that reduce the cost of providing network services or that improve the ability of poor households to pay for service at a given cost. Costs can be reduced by improving operating and capital efficiency, raising revenue collection, and revising technical norms to allow the adoption of lower-cost service delivery systems. Affordability of utility services can be enhanced through modifications of utility commercial policies, such as more frequent billing or prepayment of services. These reforms help reduce the cash flow difficulties that sometimes lie behind the inability of low-income households to pay for utility services, even without any reduction in tariffs.

The efficacy of utility subsidies can sometimes be enhanced by the adoption of additional policy measures. Perhaps the clearest example is the need to address legal tenure issues in order for connection subsidies to be able to work effectively.

Moreover, given that even well-targeted utility subsidies will probably continue to miss a substantial percentage of the poorest for the foreseeable future, measures relating to the legalization and improvement of alternatives to network supply of services are an essential complement in any strategy to improve water and energy supply for the poorest.

Appendixes

Appendix A: Case Background

Appendix A.1 Consumption Subsidy Cases: Electricity

Country, city	Type of subsidy	Year	Targeting method	Base study for subsidy analysis	Households assigned to quintiles by	Cost of service estimated as...	Assumption on price elasticity in simulation
Latin America							
Guatemala (E)	VDT with 300 kWh threshold	2000	Q	Foster and Araujo 2004	PCC	Average cost	n.a.
Guatemala (S)	VDT with 100 kWh threshold	2000	Q	Foster and Araujo 2004	PCC	Average cost	0
Honduras (E)	VDT with 300 kWh threshold	1999	Q	Wodon, Ajwad, and Siaens 2003	kWh	Undiscounted bill	n.a.
Peru (E)	IBT	2003	Q	OSINERG 2005	PCC	Undiscounted bill	0
Colombia, Bogota (E)	Geographically defined tariffs with IBTs	2003	Q, G	Melendez and others 2004; Melendez 2005	HI	Average cost	n.a.
Colombia, Bogota (S)	Geographically defined tariffs with IBTs and limited use of means testing	2003	Q, G, M	Melendez and others 2004; Melendez 2005	HI	Average cost	−0.5
Colombia, Urban (E)	Geographically defined tariffs with IBTs	2003	Q, G	Melendez and others 2004; Melendez 2005	HI	Average cost	n.a.
Mexico (E)[a]	Geographically defined tariffs with IBTs	2002	Q, G	World Bank 2004	kWh/PCI	Average cost	0
Argentina (E*)	Average of provincial means-tested subsidy	2002	M	Foster 2004	HI	Undiscounted bill	n.a.
Argentina (S)	Discount for means-tested households	2002	M	Foster 2004	HI	Undiscounted bill	0

174

Sub-Saharan Africa

Cape Verde (E)	IBT with 40 kWh first block	2001–2	Q	Angel-Urdinola and Wodon 2005a	PCE	Top block of IBT[*]	n.a.
Cape Verde (S)	VDT with 40 kWh first block	2001–2	Q	Angel-Urdinola and Wodon 2005a	PCE	Top block of IBT	0
Cape Verde (S)	Means-tested discount: housing and region	2001–2	M	Angel-Urdinola and Wodon 2005a	PCE	Top block of IBT	0
Rwanda, National (S)	VDT with 50 kWh threshold	2000–1	Q	Angel-Urdinola and others 2005	PCE	Top block of IBT	0
Rwanda, National (S)	VDT with 20 kWh threshold	2000–1	Q	Angel-Urdinola and others 2005	PCE	Top block of IBT	0
Rwanda, National (S)	IBT with 50 KWh first block	2000–1	Q	Angel-Urdinola and others 2005	PCE	Top block of IBT	0
Rwanda, National (S)	IBT with 20 kWh first block	2000–1	Q	Angel-Urdinola and others 2005	PCE	Top block of IBT	0
Rwanda, Urban (E)	Uniform volumetric tariff	2000–1	Q	Angel-Urdinola and others 2005	PCE	Top block of IBT	n.a.
Rwanda, Urban (S)	IBT with 40 kWh first block	2000–1	Q	Angel-Urdinola and others 2005	PCE	Top block of IBT	0
Rwanda, Urban (S)	VDT with 40 kWh threshold	2000–1	Q	Angel-Urdinola and others 2005	PCE	Top block of IBT	0
Saõ Tomé and Principe (E)	IBT with 300 kWh first block	2000–1	Q	Angel-Urdinola and Wodon 2005b	PCE	Top block of IBT	n.a.
Saõ Tomé and Principe (S)	VDT with 300 kWh threshold	2000–1	Q	Angel-Urdinola and Wodon 2005b	PCE	Top block of IBT	0
Saõ Tomé and Principe (S)	IBT with 200 kWh first block	2000–1	Q	Angel-Urdinola and Wodon 2005b	PCE	Top block of IBT	0

(Table continues on the following page.)

175

Appendix A.1 (continued)

Country, city	Type of subsidy	Year	Targeting method	Base study for subsidy analysis	Households assigned to quintiles by	Cost of service estimated as...	Assumption on price elasticity in simulation
Eastern and Central Europe							
Croatia (E)	Uniform volumetric tariff	1998	Q	Shkaratan 2005	PCE	Average cost	n.a.
Georgia, Tbilisi (E)	Winter heating allowance	2001	M	Lampietti and others 2003, Lampietti 2004	n/r	Average cost	n.a.
Georgia, Tbilisi (E)	Discount on bill for targeted households	2001	O	Lampietti and others 2003, Lampietti 2004	n/r	Average cost	n.a.
Hungary (S)	IBT	1997	Q	Shkaratan 2005	PCE	Top block of IBT	0
South Asia							
India: State, Urban (E)							
Andhra Pradesh	State IBTs	2001–2	Q	Santhakumar 2004a	PCE	Average cost	n.a.
Bihar	State IBTs	2001–2	Q	Santhakumar 2004a	PCE	Average cost	n.a.
Delhi	State IBTs	2001–2	Q	Santhakumar 2004a	PCE	Average cost	n.a.
Gujarat	State IBTs	2001–2	Q	Santhakumar 2004a	PCE	Average cost	n.a.
Haryana	State IBTs	2001–2	Q	Santhakumar 2004a	PCE	Average cost	n.a.
Karnataka	State IBTs	2001–2	Q	Santhakumar 2004a	PCE	Average cost	n.a.

Kerala	State IBTs	2001–2	Q	Santhakumar 2004a	PCE	Average cost	n.a.
Madhya Pradesh	State IBTs	2001–2	Q	Santhakumar 2004a	PCE	Average cost	n.a.
Maharashtra	State IBTs	2001–2	Q	Santhakumar 2004a	PCE	Average cost	n.a.
Orissa	State IBTs	2001–2	Q	Santhakumar 2004a	PCE	Average cost	n.a.
Punjab	State IBTs	2001–2	Q	Santhakumar 2004a	PCE	Average cost	n.a.
Rajasthan	State IBTs	2001–2	Q	Santhakumar 2004a	PCE	Average cost	n.a.
Tamil Nadu	State IBTs	2001–2	Q	Santhakumar 2004a	PCE	Average cost	n.a.
Uttar Pradesh	State IBTs	2001–2	Q	Santhakumar 2004a	PCE	Average cost	n.a.
West Bengal	State IBTs	2001–2	Q	Santhakumar 2004a	PCE	Average cost	n.a.

Note: Data from the sources were reanalyzed in many cases in order to create comparable analysis across cases. Thus, the results reported in the base study will not necessarily mirror the results reported in this book. E = existing subsidy, S = simulation, * = analysis assumes all the eligible households are receiving the subsidy.

Type of subsidy: IBT = increasing block tariff; VDT = volume differentiated tariff; n.a. = not applicable.

Targeting method: Q = quantity, G = geography, M = means testing, O = other.

Quintiles: PCC = per capita consumption, HI = household income, PCE = per capita expenditure, kWh = electricity consumption,
a. Two data sources were used to create the Mexico case data. One source, (listed as CFE in subsequent appendices), places households in quintiles by kWh of consumption. The second source, (identified as ENIGH in subsequent appendices), creates quintiles on the basis of per capita income (PCI).

Appendix A.2 Consumption Subsidy Cases: Water

Country, city	Type of subsidy	Year	Targeting method	Base study for subsidy analysis	Households assigned to quintiles by	Cost of service estimated as...	Assumption on price elasticity in simulation
Latin America							
Paraguay, Urban (E)	Discount for means tested households (housing characteristics)	2001	M	Robles 2001	PCI	Undiscounted bill	n.a.
Paraguay, Urban (S)	IBT with 15 m³ first block	2001	Q	Robles 2001	PCI	Undiscounted bill	0
Paraguay, Urban (S)	IBT with 5 m³ first block	2001	Q	Robles 2001	PCI	Undiscounted bill	0
Paraguay, Urban (S)	Discount for households in targeted areas	2001	G	Robles 2001	PCI	Undiscounted bill	0
Paraguay, Urban (S)	Discount for means-tested households (housing + household characteristics)	2001	M	Robles 2001	PCI	Undiscounted bill	0
Colombia, Bogota (E)	Geographically defined tariffs with IBTs	2003	Q, G	Melendez and others 2004; Melendez 2005	HI	Average cost	n.a.
Colombia, Bogota (S)	Geographically defined tariffs with IBTs and limited use of means testing	2003	Q, G, M	Melendez and others 2004; Melendez 2005	HI	Average cost	0
Colombia, Urban (E)	Geographically defined tariffs with IBTs	2003	Q, G	Melendez and others 2004; Melendez 2005	HI	Average cost	n.a.

Nicaragua, Managua (E)	IBT with slum discount	1995	Q, G	Walker and others 2000	PCI	Average cost	n.a.
Venezuela, R. B. de, Merida (E)	IBT with slum discount	1996	Q, G	Walker and others 2000	PCI	Average cost	n.a.
Panama, Panama City and Colon (E)	IBT with slum and pensioner discount	1998	Q, G	Walker and others 2000	PCI	Average cost	n.a.
Chile (E)	Discounts of 40–70% on lifeline block for means tested recipients	1998	Q, M	Gomez-Lobo and Contreras 2000; Gomez-Lobo and Contreras 2003	PCI	Average cost	n.a.
Argentina (E*)	Average of provincial means-tested subsidy	2002	M	Foster 2004	HI	Undiscounted bill	n.a.
Argentina, Buenos Aires (E*)	Average of provincial means-tested subsidy	2002	M	Foster 2004	HI	Undiscounted bill	n.a.
Argentina (S)	Discount for means-tested households	2002	M	Foster 2004	HI	Undiscounted bill	0
Sub-Saharan Africa							
Cape Verde (E)	IBT with 7 m^3 first block	2001–2	Q	Angel-Urdinola and Wodon 2005a	PCE	Top block of IBT	0
Cape Verde (S)	VDT with 7 m^3 threshold	2001–2	Q	Angel-Urdinola and Wodon 2005a	PCE	Top block of IBT	0
Cape Verde (S)	Means-tested discount on 10 m^3	2001–2	M	Angel-Urdinola and Wodon 2005a	PCE	Top block of IBT	0
Eastern and Central Europe							
Ukraine, Odessa (E)	Discount for pensioners and veterans	1998	O	Komives 1998	PCI	Undiscounted bill	n.a.
Croatia (E)	Uniform volumetric tariff	1998	Q	Shkaratan 2005	PCC	Top block of IBT	n.a.

(Table continues on the following page.)

Appendix A.2 *(continued)*

Country, city	Type of subsidy	Year	Targeting method	Base study for subsidy analysis	Households assigned to quintiles by	Cost of service estimated as...	Assumption on price elasticity in simulation
South Asia							
Nepal, Kathmandu (E)	Subsidy on public taps	2001	O	Pattanayak and Yang 2002; Pattanayak and others 2001	HI	Average cost	n.a.
Nepal, Kathmandu (E)	IBT with 10 m³ first block	2001	Q	Pattanayak and Yang 2002; Pattanayak and others 2001	HI	Average cost	n.a.
Nepal, Kathmandu (S)	Uniform volumetric tariff	2001	Q	Pattanayak and Yang 2002; Pattanayak and others 2001	HI	Average cost	−0.5
Nepal, Kathmandu (S)	IBT with 7 m³ first block	2001	Q	Pattanayak and Yang 2002; Pattanayak and others 2001	HI	Average cost	−0.5
Nepal, Kathmandu (S)	Discount for slums (revenue neutral)	2001	G	Pattanayak and Yang 2002; Pattanayak and others 2001	HI	Average cost	−0.5
Nepal, Kathmandu (S)	Discount for means-tested households	2001	M	Pattanayak and Yang 2002; Pattanayak and others 2001	HI	Average cost	−0.5
Nepal, Kathmandu (S)	Discount for slums (all others pay cost recovery price)	2001	G	Pattanayak and Yang 2002; Pattanayak and others 2001	HI	Average cost	−0.5
Nepal, Kathmandu (S)	Discount for means-tested households (all others pay cost recovery)	2001	M	Pattanayak and Yang 2002; Pattanayak and others 2001	HI	Average cost	−0.5

India, Bangalore (E)	Subsidy on public taps	2001	O	Prokopy 2002	HE	Average cost	n.a.
India, Bangalore (E)	IBT with 25 m³ first block	2001	Q	Prokopy 2002	HE	Average cost	−0.5
India, Bangalore (S)	Uniform volumetric tariff	2001	Q	Prokopy 2002	HE	Average cost	−0.5
India, Bangalore (S)	IBT with 18 m³ first block	2001	Q	Prokopy 2002	HE	Average cost	−0.5
India, Bangalore (S)	Discounts for households in poor areas	2001	G	Prokopy 2002	HE	Average cost	−0.5
India, Bangalore (S)	Discount for means-tested households	2001	M	Prokopy 2002	HE	Average cost	−0.5
India, Bangalore (S)	IBT with 6 m³ first block	2001	Q	Prokopy 2002	HE	Average cost	−0.5
Sri Lanka (E)	IBT	2003	Q	Pattanayak and Yang 2005; Pattanayak and others 2004; Brocklehurst 2004	PCC	Average cost	n.a.

Note: Data from the sources were reanalyzed in many cases in order to create comparable analysis across cases. Thus, the results reported in the base study will not necessarily mirror the results reported in this book. E = existing subsidy, S = simulation, * = analysis assumes all the eligible households are receiving the subsidy.

Type of subsidy: IBT = increasing block tariff; VDT = volume differentiated tariff; n.a. = not applicable.

Targeting method: Q = quantity, G = geography, M = means testing, O = other.

Quintiles: PCC = per capita consumption, HI = household income, PCE = per capita expenditure, HE = hh expenditure, PCI = per capita income.

Appendix A.3 Connection Subsidy Cases: Electricity and Water

Country, city	Types of subsidy and targeting methods studied	Year	Base study for subsidy analysis	Households assigned to quintiles by
Latin America				
Paraguay, Urban	Water: universal, geographic targeting, means testing	2001	Robles 2001	PCI
Argentina	Water and sewer: universal, means testing	2002	Foster 2004	HI
Argentina, Buenos Aires (E)	Water and sewer: universal	2002	Foster 2004	HI
South Asia				
Nepal, Kathmandu	Water: universal, geographic targeting, means testing	2001	Pattanayak and Yang 2002; Pattanayak and others 2001	HI
India, Bangalore	Water: universal, geographic targeting, means testing	2001	Prokopy 2002	HE
Sub-Saharan Africa				
Cape Verde	Water and electricity: universal, targeted to households that currently have access	2001–2	Angel-Urdinola and Wodon 2005a	PCE
Rwanda, Urban	Electricity: universal, targeted to to households that currently have access	2000–1	Angel-Urdinola and others 2005	PCE
Saõ Tomé and Principe	Electricity: universal, targeted to households that currently have access	2000–1	Angel-Urdinola and Wodon 2005b	PCE

Note: Data from the sources were reanalyzed in many cases in order to create comparable analysis across cases. Thus, the results reported in the base study will not necessarily mirror the results reported in this book.

In addition to these cases, simulations of connection subsidies for water, sewer, and electricity were done on all cases for which connection information by quintile was available (see appendixes B and C). The results of this analysis are presented in graphical form in chapter 7.

Unless identified with an E, these are all simulated subsidies.

Quintiles: HI = household income, HE = household expenditure, PCE = per capita expenditure, PCI = per capita income.

Appendix A.4 Consumption Subsidy Cases: Multisector Burden Limit

Country, city	Type of subsidy	Year	Base study for subsidy analysis	Households assigned to quintiles by
Latvia, Riga	Burden limit at 15%	1997	Shkaratan 2005	PCE
Latvia, Riga	Burden limit at 30%	1997	Shkaratan 2005	PCE
Latvia, Riga	Burden limit at 45%	1997	Shkaratan 2005	PCE
Ukraine, Odessa (E)	Burden limit	1998	Komives 1998	PCI

Note: Unless identified with an E, these are all simulated subsidies.

Quintiles: PCE = per capita expenditure, PCI = per capita income.

Appendix B: Electricity: Coverage, Expenditure, and Consumption

Appendix B.1 Electricity Coverage: Percentage of Households with Electricity or Nonzero Expenditure on Electricity

Country, city	Year	Total (%)	Poor (%)	Nonpoor (%)	Quintiles 1 (%)	2 (%)	3 (%)	4 (%)	5 (%)	Source
Latin America										
Argentina	2002	100.0	98.0	100.0	97.0	99.0	100.0	100.0	100.0	Foster 2004
Argentina, Greater Buenos Aires	2002	100.0	99.0	100.0	97.0	100.0	100.0	100.0	100.0	Foster 2004
Bolivia, Urban	1999	99.0	97.0	100.0	97.0	97.0	100.0	100.0	100.0	Barja, McKenzie, and Urquiola 2002
Brazil	2000	95.0	91.0	99.0	86.0	95.0	97.0	99.0	100.0	World Bank 2004a
Chile	2000	98.0	96.0	99.0	95.0	97.0	98.0	99.0	100.0	World Bank 2004a
Colombia, Bogota	2003	100.0	99.0	100.0	99.0	100.0	100.0	100.0	100.0	Melendez and others 2004; Melendez 2005
Colombia, Urban	2003	100.0	99.0	100.0	99.0	100.0	100.0	100.0	100.0	Melendez and others 2004; Melendez 2005
El Salvador	2000	84.0	73.0	92.0	68.0	77.0	87.0	92.0	98.0	World Bank 2004a
Guatemala	2000	73.0	52.0	87.0	40.0	64.0	77.0	89.0	95.0	Foster and Araujo 2004
Honduras	1999	69.0	45.0	85.0	30.0	59.0	76.0	86.0	93.0	Wodon Ajwad, and Siaens 2003
Mexico-ENIGH	2002	97.0	93.0	98.0	90.0	96.0	99.0	99.0	100.0	World Bank 2004b
Nicaragua	1998	65.0	35.0	85.0	20.0	49.0	75.0	90.0	89.0	Freije and Rivas 2002
Peru	2003	78.0	62.0	88.0	53.0	70.0	80.0	88.0	94.0	OSINERG 2005
Uruguay	2002–3	98.0	97.0	99.0	96.0	98.0	99.0	99.0	99.0	Ruggeri-Laderchi 2003
Venezuela, R. B. de	2000	98.0	98.0	99.0	97.0	98.0	99.0	99.0	99.0	World Bank 2004a

(Table continues on the following page.)

Appendix B.1 (continued)

Country, city	Year	Total (%)	Poor (%)	Nonpoor (%)	Quintiles 1 (%)	2 (%)	3 (%)	4 (%)	5 (%)	Source
South Asia										
India: State, Urban										
Kerala	2001–2	91.0	85.0	94.0	79.0	92.0	94.0	95.0	94.0	Santhakumar 2004a
Andhra Pradesh	2001–2	91.0	81.0	96.0	73.0	90.0	93.0	97.0	97.0	Santhakumar 2004a
Tamil Nadu	2001–2	92.0	84.0	96.0	78.0	90.0	95.0	96.0	98.0	Santhakumar 2004a
Karnataka	2001–2	91.0	80.0	96.0	75.0	93.0	95.0	97.0	97.0	Santhakumar 2004a
Maharashtra	2001–2	90.0	88.0	91.0	83.0	93.0	89.0	90.0	94.0	Santhakumar 2004a
Madhya Pradesh	2001–2	93.3	87.5	96.1	82.4	92.5	94.4	95.9	97.6	Santhakumar 2004a
Gujarat	2001–2	92.3	85.7	95.8	80.0	92.1	95.0	94.7	97.4	Santhakumar 2004a
Orissa	2001–2	81.6	65.4	90.8	47.5	75.5	86.4	92.3	92.2	Santhakumar 2004a
Punjab	2001–2	95.7	93.0	97.2	90.4	95.3	96.0	97.6	98.0	Santhakumar 2004a
Haryana	2001–2	92.7	87.4	96.2	83.3	91.8	95.3	83.3	91.8	Santhakumar 2004a
Rajasthan	2001–2	91.0	82.8	94.3	73.6	91.1	93.2	94.4	95.1	Santhakumar 2004a
Delhi	2001–2	92.0	90.3	92.7	86.6	93.9	92.3	91.6	94.3	Santhakumar 2004a
Uttar Pradesh	2001–2	84.2	72.9	89.5	66.9	77.6	84.4	89.7	92.3	Santhakumar 2004a
West Bengal	2001–2	84.4	71.3	92.2	59.5	81.7	87.2	90.4	96.7	Santhakumar 2004a
Bihar	2001–2	67.1	42.2	75.4	32.3	55.4	72.6	71.6	79.8	Santhakumar 2004a
Eastern and Central Europe										
Albania, Urban	2002	99.9	99.8	99.9	99.6	100.0	99.8	100.0	100.0	World Bank forthcoming b
Armenia, Urban	2002	99.2	98.9	99.4	98.3	99.5	99.8	99.3	99.1	World Bank forthcoming b
Azerbaijan, Urban	2002	99.8	99.9	99.8	99.9	99.9	99.9	99.7	99.8	World Bank forthcoming b
Belarus, Urban	2002	99.9	99.9	99.8	99.9	99.9	99.8	99.9	99.8	World Bank forthcoming b
Bulgaria, Urban	2003	99.9	99.5	100.0	99.0	100.0	100.0	100.0	100.0	World Bank forthcoming b
Croatia	1998	99.7	99.4	99.8	99.0	99.8	99.8	99.9	99.7	Shkaratan 2005

Country	Year									Source
Georgia, Urban	2002	100.0	100.0	100.0	100.0	100.0	100.0	100.0	100.0	World Bank forthcoming b
Hungary	1997	100.0	100.0	100.0	100.0	100.0	100.0	100.0	100.0	Shkaratan 2005
Hungary, Urban	2002	100.0	99.9	100.0	99.7	100.0	100.0	100.0	100.0	World Bank forthcoming b
Kazakhstan, Urban	2002	100.0	99.9	100.0	99.9	99.9	100.0	100.0	100.0	World Bank forthcoming b
Kyrgyz Republic, Urban	2002	98.2	97.4	98.2	97.6	97.1	97.7	97.6	99.2	World Bank forthcoming b
Latvia, Riga	1997	99.8	99.6	100.0	99.1	100.0	100.0	100.0	100.0	Shkaratan 2005
Moldova, Urban	2002	99.1	96.9	99.8	95.1	98.6	99.6	99.7	100.0	World Bank forthcoming b
Poland, Urban	2002	99.9	99.8	99.9	99.6	99.9	99.8	100.0	99.9	World Bank forthcoming b
Romania, Urban	2002	99.4	97.8	99.7	96.3	99.3	99.8	99.7	99.8	World Bank forthcoming b
Russian Federation, Urban	2002	100.0	100.0	100.0	100.0	100.0	100.0	100.0	100.0	World Bank forthcoming b
Serbia and Montenegro, Urban	2002	100.0	99.9	100.0	99.8	100.0	100.0	100.0	100.0	World Bank forthcoming b
Tajikistan, Urban	2003	99.9	99.8	99.9	100.0	99.6	100.0	100.0	99.8	World Bank forthcoming b
Turkey, Urban	2002	99.9	99.8	100.0	99.5	100.0	100.0	100.0	100.0	World Bank forthcoming b
Ukraine, Urban	2002	95.9	92.6	97.3	90.4	94.7	96.8	97.8	97.3	World Bank forthcoming b
Sub-Saharan Africa										
Rwanda, Urban	2000–1	32.0	12.8	45.0	4.0	21.7	28.6	45.3	60.8	Angel-Urdinola and others 2005
Cape Verde	2001–2	44.1	24.4	57.1	15.7	33.2	43.5	58.0	70.0	Angel-Urdinola and Wodon 2005a
Saõ Tomé and Principe	2000–1	42.3	23.2	55.0	14.1	32.4	43.3	56.1	65.7	Angel-Urdinola and Wodon 2005b
Middle East and North Africa										
Yemen, Urban	2003	90.1	86.1	92.8	80.0	92.1	89.5	93.7	95.2	ESMAP forthcoming
East Asia										
Philippines, Urban	1997	90.3	81.5	96.2	75.2	87.8	92.9	96.9	98.8	World Bank 2003
Philippines, Manila	1997	99.2	98.1	99.9	96.9	99.4	99.8	100.0	99.9	World Bank 2003
Vietnam, Urban	1998	98.4	96.5	99.7	94.9	98.1	99.4	99.8	100.0	World Bank 2003

Appendix B.2 Estimated Monthly Electricity Consumption in kWh

Country, City	Year	Total	Poor	Non-poor	Quintiles					Source
					1	2	3	4	5	
Latin America										
Colombia, Bogota	2003	146.7	101.1	177.0	94.4	107.9	130.9	163.0	237.0	Melendez and others 2004; Melendez 2005
Colombia, Urban	2003	145.0	100.5	174.7	99.0	102.0	126.0	163.0	235.0	Melendez and others 2004; Melendez 2005
Guatemala	2000	87.8	43.0	117.7	40.0	46.0	71.0	100.0	182.0	Foster and Araujo 2004
Mexico-CFE	2002	140.8	42.5	206.3	14.5	70.5	125.5	183.5	310.0	World Bank 2004b
Peru	2003	98.3	62.1	122.4	49.0	75.2	87.6	113.3	166.5	OSINERG 2005
Uruguay	2002–3	211.9	196.2	222.3	180.6	211.7	226.5	208.3	232.2	Ruggeri-Laderchi 2003
South Asia										
India: State, Urban										
Kerala	2001–2	107.0	68.1	126.7	59.4	78.0	80.1	116.1	154.0	Santhakumar 2004a
Andhra Pradesh	2001–2	85.7	55.5	97.0	48.4	61.4	70.7	94.5	123.0	Santhakumar 2004a
Tamil Nadu	2001–2	93.2	60.6	107.2	51.5	68.3	79.2	100.3	132.3	Santhakumar 2004a
Karnataka	2001–2	92.3	49.8	109.2	43.6	61.5	85.4	110.6	128.0	Santhakumar 2004a
Maharashtra	2001–2	124.3	74.0	161.2	59.1	88.0	99.1	121.2	253.1	Santhakumar 2004a
Madhya Pradesh	2001–2	99.4	66.6	113.7	55.1	76.8	89.5	109.0	137.5	Santhakumar 2004a
Gujarat	2001–2	86.6	58.0	99.8	45.1	70.5	76.1	93.6	122.6	Santhakumar 2004a
Orissa	2001–2	112.9	88.1	123.2	72.3	93.7	115.1	118.7	129.9	Santhakumar 2004a
Punjab	2001-2	122.6	93.7	138.9	80.4	104.7	109.4	129.9	n.a.	Santhakumar 2004a

	Year									Source
Haryana	2001–2	95.8	64.8	114.3	109.4	129.9	165.7	122.6	147.0	Santhakumar 2004a
Rajasthan	2001–2	86.1	62.4	94.3	53.7	68.8	79.3	96.0	104.2	Santhakumar 2004a
Delhi	2001–2	165.2	98.9	193.1	85.2	111.0	129.8	146.2	293.5	Santhakumar 2004a
Uttar Pradesh	2001–2	86.0	58.1	96.5	51.7	62.4	68.8	81.9	123.5	Santhakumar 2004a
West Bengal	2001–2	79.0	50.0	92.3	38.9	57.2	60.0	67.7	128.1	Santhakumar 2004a
Bihar	2001–2	69.1	51.7	72.4	44.5	57.4	60.5	69.0	80.6	Santhakumar 2004a
Eastern and Central Europe										
Croatia	1998	494.7	328.2	568.8	338.7	319.8	611.5	581.5	527.1	Shkaratan 2005
Sub-Saharan Africa										
Rwanda, Urban	2000–1	92.5	60.6	98.6	37.3	64.9	64.2	83.6	125.8	Angel-Urdinola and others 2005
Cape Verde	2001–2	111.7	56.8	127.4	41.0	64.3	95.0	115.0	157.7	Angel-Urdinola and Wodon 2005a
Saõ Tomé and Principe	2000–1	153.4	98.3	169.0	64.8	112.9	136.8	164.5	193.9	Angel-Urdinola and Wodon 2005b
Middle East and North Africa										
Yemen, Urban	2003	273.0	207.8	288.2	192.5	223.0	246.0	279.0	339.5	ESMAP forthcoming
Yemen	2003	183.0	143.3	186.7	134.0	152.5	162.5	181.0	216.5	ESMAP forthcoming

Note: n.a. = not applicable.

Appendix B.3 Monthly Expenditure per Household on Electricity in US$

Country, city	Year	Total	Poor	Nonpoor	Quintiles					Source
					1	2	3	4	5	
Latin America										
Colombia, Bogota	2003	11.32	5.57	12.88	5.25	5.70	7.33	9.71	16.70	Melendez and others 2004; Melendez 2005
Colombia, Urban	2003	11.12	8.29	13.01	8.28	8.30	9.87	11.60	17.55	Melendez and others 2004; Melendez 2005
Guatemala	2000	10.23	5.06	13.68	4.81	5.32	7.79	10.65	22.60	Foster and Araujo 2004
Peru	2003	9.51	4.49	12.86	3.04	5.94	8.96	11.70	17.94	OSINERG 2005
Uruguay	2002–3	22.17	21.85	22.39	21.67	22.03	23.16	21.14	22.86	Ruggeri-Laderchi 2003
Mexico-CFE	2002	9.54	2.09	14.50	1.59	2.59	4.63	9.00	29.87	World Bank 2004b
Argentina	2002	10.00	9.60	10.27	8.20	11.00	10.00	9.60	11.20	Foster 2004
South Asia										
India: State, Urban										
Kerala	2001–2	3.00	1.69	3.66	1.47	1.95	2.11	3.25	4.59	Santhakumar 2004a
Andhra Pradesh	2001–2	3.61	1.98	4.22	1.71	2.21	2.72	3.92	5.83	Santhakumar 2004a
Tamil Nadu	2001–2	2.21	1.22	2.63	0.99	1.42	1.69	2.34	3.50	Santhakumar 2004a
Karnataka	2001–2	4.11	1.89	4.98	1.63	2.39	3.49	4.83	6.41	Santhakumar 2004a
Maharashtra	2001–2	5.75	2.82	7.90	2.16	3.43	4.15	5.43	13.51	Santhakumar 2004a
Madhya Pradesh	2001–2	3.86	3.34	4.48	1.98	2.85	3.39	4.31	5.52	Santhakumar 2004a
Gujarat	2001–2	5.43	3.49	6.33	2.73	4.23	4.61	5.60	8.26	Santhakumar 2004a
Orissa	2001–2	3.34	2.58	2.58	2.09	2.75	3.27	3.47	3.95	Santhakumar 2004a
Punjab	2001–2	5.81	4.22	6.69	3.67	4.68	5.06	6.10	8.23	Santhakumar 2004a
Haryana	2001–2	6.79	4.22	6.69	3.67	5.48	5.76	6.66	10.58	Santhakumar 2004a
Rajasthan	2001–2	5.41	3.77	5.98	3.24	4.16	4.86	6.17	6.66	Santhakumar 2004a
Delhi	2001–2	5.27	3.18	6.15	2.66	3.65	4.03	4.80	9.28	Santhakumar 2004a
Uttar Pradesh	2001–2	3.63	2.38	4.10	2.12	2.55	2.89	3.47	5.27	Santhakumar 2004a
West Bengal	2001–2	3.61	2.04	4.33	1.55	2.36	2.61	3.00	6.25	Santhakumar 2004a
Bihar	2001–2	2.93	2.10	3.09	1.86	2.29	2.50	2.92	3.50	Santhakumar 2004a

Eastern Europe and Central Asia

Albania	2002	10.90	8.80	11.63	8.10	9.49	11.07	11.08	12.74	World Bank forthcoming b
Armenia	2002	5.62	4.64	5.97	4.45	4.84	5.21	5.53	7.16	World Bank forthcoming b
Azerbaijan	2002	2.19	2.22	2.17	2.26	2.18	2.18	2.14	2.20	World Bank forthcoming b
Belarus	2002	1.46	1.41	1.48	1.41	1.40	1.43	1.47	1.54	World Bank forthcoming b
Bulgaria	2003	17.87	14.03	19.42	11.91	16.16	17.47	18.23	22.55	World Bank forthcoming b
Croatia	1998	23.97	21.52	25.20	18.65	24.16	25.42	24.33	25.78	Shkaratan 2005
Georgia	2002	3.64	2.56	4.06	2.26	2.85	3.22	3.74	5.22	World Bank forthcoming b
Hungary	1997	12.86	11.88	13.50	11.15	12.62	13.19	12.95	14.37	Shkaratan 2005
Kazakhstan	2002	2.52	2.25	2.61	2.17	2.33	2.49	2.60	2.73	World Bank forthcoming b
Kyrgyz Republic	2002	1.24	0.93	1.35	0.86	1.00	1.26	1.33	1.46	World Bank forthcoming b
Latvia, Riga	1997	7.21	5.84	7.83	5.63	5.96	6.47	7.45	9.42	Shkaratan 2005
Moldova	2002	2.78	2.26	2.99	2.08	2.43	2.49	2.79	3.69	World Bank forthcoming b
Poland	2002	25.36	23.35	25.83	22.77	23.93	24.55	25.08	27.87	World Bank forthcoming b
Romania	2002	7.92	5.79	8.51	5.12	6.45	7.29	8.27	9.98	World Bank forthcoming b
Russian Federation	2002	2.13	1.79	2.27	1.70	1.89	2.01	2.23	2.57	World Bank forthcoming b
Serbia and Montenegro	2002	13.34	9.69	15.12	8.68	10.71	12.42	13.91	19.04	World Bank forthcoming b
Tajikistan	2003	1.40	1.24	1.47	1.14	1.34	1.31	1.41	1.68	World Bank forthcoming b
Turkey	2002	20.84	14.85	22.12	12.88	16.81	18.58	20.79	26.98	World Bank forthcoming b
Ukraine	2002	1.93	1.77	1.98	1.73	1.81	1.86	1.93	2.16	World Bank forthcoming b

Sub-Saharan Africa

Rwanda	2000–1	9.33	6.11	9.95	3.76	6.55	6.48	8.43	12.70	Angel-Urdinola and others 2005
Cape Verde	2001–2	19.71	9.56	22.60	6.73	10.90	16.57	20.27	28.29	Angel-Urdinola and Wodon 2005a
Saõ Tomé and Príncipe	2000–1	12.49	6.68	14.12	3.76	7.95	10.09	13.45	17.37	Angel-Urdinola and Wodon 2005b
Niger, Niamey	1998	19.49	n/r	n/r	n/r	n/r	n/r	n/r	n/r	Lauria and Kolb 1999

Middle East and North Africa

Yemen, Urban	2003	9.09	7.35	10.25	6.67	8.03	8.60	9.31	12.83	ESMAP forthcoming
Yemen	2003	7.32	6.00	8.21	5.39	6.61	6.60	7.62	10.41	ESMAP forthcoming

Appendix B.4 Monthly Expenditure on Electricity as a Percentage of Household Income

Country, city	Year	Total (%)	Poor (%)	Nonpoor (%)	Quintiles 1 (%)	2 (%)	3 (%)	4 (%)	5 (%)	Source
Latin Amercia										
Colombia, Bogota	2003	1.7	4.8	1.6	10.2	3.9	3.1	2.6	1.6	Melendez and others 2004; Melendez 2005
Colombia, Urban	2003	5.0	8.2	2.9	10.6	5.8	4.0	3.1	1.6	Melendez and others 2004; Melendez 2005
Guatemala	2000	3.0	3.0	3.0	3.0	3.0	3.0	3.0	3.0	Foster and Araujo 2004
Peru	2003	2.7	2.4	2.9	2.3	2.6	3.0	3.1	2.6	OSINERG 2005
Uruguay	2002–3	5.2	8.7	2.9	12.3	5.1	3.7	2.9	2.0	Ruggeri-Laderchi 2003
Mexico-ENIGH	2002	5.0	2.6	6.6	1.9	3.4	4.4	5.5	9.9	World Bank 2004b
Bolivia, Urban	1999	3.6	4.0	3.4	4.0	4.0	3.4	3.7	3.2	Barja, McKenzie, and Urquiola 2002
Nicaragua	1998	1.5	0.9	1.9	0.6	1.2	1.7	1.9	2.0	Freije and Rivas 2002
Argentina	2002	5.0	6.2	4.2	6.2	6.1	5.0	4.2	3.4	Foster 2004
South Asia										
India: State, Urban										
Kerala	2001–2	2.6	2.6	2.7	2.7	2.5	2.5	3.0	2.6	Santhakumar 2004a
Andhra Pradesh	2001–2	4.2	4.2	4.2	4.2	4.1	4.0	4.4	4.1	Santhakumar 2004a
Tamil Nadu	2001–2	2.7	2.8	2.6	2.9	2.6	2.6	2.8	2.6	Santhakumar 2004a
Karnataka	2001–2	3.9	3.5	4.0	3.6	3.5	3.9	4.0	4.1	Santhakumar 2004a
Maharashtra	2001–2	4.4	4.1	4.6	4.2	4.1	4.2	4.4	5.1	Santhakumar 2004a
Madhya Pradesh	2001–2	4.7	4.7	4.6	4.5	4.9	4.8	4.7	4.4	Santhakumar 2004a
Gujarat	2001–2	5.7	5.5	5.7	5.0	5.9	5.9	5.9	5.4	Santhakumar 2004a
Orissa	2001–2	4.3	5.2	4.0	5.3	5.1	4.8	4.3	3.4	Santhakumar 2004a
Punjab	2001–2	5.8	6.3	5.5	6.7	5.9	5.7	5.7	5.3	Santhakumar 2004a
Haryana	2001–2	6.6	6.7	6.5	6.6	6.9	6.5	6.6	6.4	Santhakumar 2004a
Rajasthan	2001–2	5.8	5.8	5.8	5.9	5.7	6.0	6.3	5.0	Santhakumar 2004a
Delhi	2001–2	4.6	4.7	4.5	4.6	4.8	4.7	4.3	4.5	Santhakumar 2004a
Uttar Pradesh	2001–2	4.1	4.2	4.1	4.2	4.2	4.1	4.0	4.0	Santhakumar 2004a
West Bengal	2001–2	4.0	4.0	4.0	4.2	3.9	4.0	3.9	4.2	Santhakumar 2004a
Bihar	2001–2	3.5	3.8	3.5	4.0	3.6	3.7	3.7	3.2	Santhakumar 2004a

Eastern Europe and Central Asia

	Year									Source
Albania, Urban	2002	6.7	9.0	6.4	9.8	8.1	7.7	6.6	5.0	World Bank forthcoming b
Armenia, Urban	2002	8.0	9.7	7.4	10.2	9.2	8.2	7.5	6.4	World Bank forthcoming b
Azerbaijan, Urban	2002	1.7	1.8	1.6	2.0	1.7	1.6	1.6	1.7	World Bank forthcoming b
Belarus, Urban	2002	1.2	1.6	1.0	1.9	1.3	1.1	1.0	0.8	World Bank forthcoming b
Bulgaria, Urban	2002	10.1	11.5	9.6	11.8	11.2	11.0	9.4	8.5	World Bank forthcoming b
Croatia	1998	3.1	3.7	2.7	4.0	3.5	3.1	2.8	2.4	Shkaratan 2005
Georgia, Urban	2002	5.2	7.1	4.7	8.2	6.1	5.3	4.7	4.0	World Bank forthcoming b
Hungary	1997	6.0	7.1	5.3	7.6	6.6	6.3	5.4	4.2	Shkaratan 2005
Hungary, Urban	2002	5.7	6.9	5.4	7.0	6.7	5.9	5.6	4.7	World Bank forthcoming b
Kazakhstan, Urban	2002	2.3	3.4	2.2	3.8	2.9	2.6	2.3	1.6	World Bank forthcoming b
Kyrgyz Republic, Urban	2002	2.3	2.9	2.2	3.2	2.7	2.5	2.4	1.8	World Bank forthcoming b
Latvia, Riga	1997	2.9	3.3	2.6	3.6	3.1	2.9	2.6	2.4	Shkaratan 2005
Moldova, Urban	2002	7.3	9.1	6.9	9.3	8.9	7.9	7.1	5.6	World Bank forthcoming b
Poland, Urban	2002	6.9	9.2	6.6	10.1	8.3	7.5	6.7	5.5	World Bank forthcoming b
Romania, Urban	2002	6.0	6.9	5.9	7.1	6.7	6.4	6.0	5.4	World Bank forthcoming b
Russian Federation, Urban	2002	1.4	2.0	1.2	2.2	1.7	1.4	1.2	0.9	World Bank forthcoming b
Serbia and Montenegro, Urban	2002	6.9	8.8	6.1	9.7	8.0	6.9	6.2	5.3	World Bank forthcoming b
Tajikistan, Urban	2002	2.3	3.1	2.1	3.4	2.8	2.3	2.1	1.9	World Bank forthcoming b
Turkey, Urban	2002	8.1	9.5	7.5	9.7	9.3	8.5	7.9	6.3	World Bank forthcoming b
Ukraine, Urban	2002	2.1	2.6	1.9	2.9	2.4	2.2	1.9	1.6	World Bank forthcoming b

(Table continues on the following page.)

193

Appendix B.4 *(continued)*

Country, city	Year	Total (%)	Poor (%)	Nonpoor (%)	1 (%)	2 (%)	3 (%)	4 (%)	5 (%)	Source
								Quintiles		
Sub-Saharan Africa										
Rwanda, Urban	2000–1	2.4	3.8	2.3	4.4	3.8	2.8	2.5	2.2	Angel-Urdinola and others 2005
Cape Verde	2001–2	3.7	4.6	3.6	4.2	4.7	5.1	4.6	2.9	Angel-Urdinola and Wodon 2005a
Saõ Tomé and Principe	2000–1	5.5	6.4	5.3	5.1	6.7	6.7	6.9	4.4	Angel-Urdinola and Wodon 2005b
Middle East and North Africa										
Yemen, Republic of	2003	1.7	1.4	1.8	1.3	1.6	1.8	2.0	1.8	ESMAP forthcoming
East Asia										
Philippines	2001	2.9	2.6	3.2	2.5	2.7	3.1	3.2	3.1	Chingcuanco 2001

Note: Poor = Poorest 40%; n/r = not reported.

Appendix C: Water: Coverage, Expenditure, and Consumption

Appendix C.1 Water Coverage: Percentage of Households with a Private Connection

Country, city	Year	Type of conn.	Total (%)	Poor (%)	Nonpoor (%)	Quintiles					Source
						1 (%)	2 (%)	3 (%)	4 (%)	5 (%)	
Latin America											
Argentina	2002	PWC	94.0	89.5	96.3	88.0	91.0	96.0	96.0	97.0	Foster 2004
Argentina, Buenos Aires	2002	PWC	85.0	76.0	90.3	73.0	79.0	89.0	89.0	93.0	Foster 2004
Bolivia, La Paz and El Alto	1999	PWC	94.4	91.1	100.0	88.8	93.3	95.6	100.0	100.0	Barja, McKenzie, and Urquiola 2002
Bolivia, Urban	1999	PWC	92.2	87.4	95.4	85.8	89.1	91.4	98.2	96.8	Barja, McKenzie, and Urquiola 2002
Chile	1998	PWC	89.1	81.5	93.8	78.0	86.0	90.5	94.0	97.0	Gomez-Lobo and Contreras 2000, 2003
Colombia	2000	PWC	84.8	75.0	91.3	70.0	80.0	86.0	92.0	96.0	World Bank 2004a
Colombia, Bogota	2003	PWC	99.4	98.5	99.7	97.6	99.1	99.7	99.6	99.7	Melendez and others 2004; Melendez 2005
Colombia, Urban	2003	PWC	98.2	97.8	98.4	97.5	98.1	98.2	98.8	98.3	Melendez and others 2004; Melendez 2005
El Salvador, San Miguel	1996	PWC	70.0	59.5	77.3	54.0	65.0	67.0	79.0	86.0	Walker and others 2000
El Salvador, Santa Ana	1996	PWC	95.0	88.0	99.0	84.0	92.0	98.0	99.0	100.0	Walker and others 2000

196

Country	Year										Source
El Salvador, Sonsonate	1996	PWC	84.0	75.5	90.3	71.0	80.0	84.0	93.0	94.0	Walker and others 2000
Guatemala	2000	PWC	70.4	58.5	78.3	57.0	60.0	68.0	75.0	92.0	World Bank 2004a
Mexico—ENIGH	2002	PWC	61.3	32.1	80.8	20.0	44.2	65.3	82.6	94.6	World Bank 2004b
Nicaragua, Managua	1995	PWC	97.0	95.0	97.7	93.0	97.0	98.0	97.0	98.0	Walker and others 2000
Panama, Panama City and Colon	1998	PWC	98.0	96.5	99.7	98.0	95.0	99.0	100.0	100.0	Walker and others 2000
Paraguay, Urban	2001	PWC	65.0	56.4	68.6	53.0	59.7	58.0	69.8	78.1	Robles 2001
Peru	2000	PWC	74.4	57.5	85.7	51.0	64.0	79.0	85.0	93.0	World Bank 2004a
Uruguay	2002–3	PWC	98.1	96.8	99.0	95.5	98.0	98.5	99.3	99.3	Ruggeri-Laderchi 2003
Venezuela, R. B. de, Merida	1996	PWC	100.0	100.0	100.0	100.0	100.0	100.0	100.0	100.0	Walker and others 2000
Venezuela, R. B. de	2000	PWC	92.8	89.0	95.3	87.0	91.0	93.0	96.0	97.0	World Bank 2004a
Eastern and Central Europe											
Albania	2002	PWC	91.7	82.6	94.5	80.2	85.0	93.2	94.8	95.4	World Bank forthcoming b
Armenia	2002	PWC	97.1	95.7	98.0	94.7	96.6	96.8	98.6	98.6	World Bank forthcoming b
Azerbaijan	2002	PWC	87.1	88.2	86.3	89.7	86.8	86.2	84.8	87.8	World Bank forthcoming b
Belarus	2002	PWC	89.6	87.7	90.5	85.9	89.5	89.3	90.6	91.7	World Bank forthcoming b
Bulgaria	2003	PWC	98.7	96.0	99.9	93.1	98.9	99.8	100.0	99.8	World Bank forthcoming b

(Table continues on the following page.)

Appendix C.1 (*continued*)

Country, city	Year	Type of conn.	Total (%)	Poor (%)	Nonpoor (%)	Quintiles					Source
						1 (%)	2 (%)	3 (%)	4 (%)	5 (%)	
Croatia	1998	PWC	92.4	83.7	97.0	76.5	90.5	95.5	96.7	98.5	Shkaratan 2005
Georgia	2002	PWC	94.4	92.0	95.2	90.4	93.5	92.8	95.6	97.2	World Bank forthcoming b
Hungary	2002	PWC	98.4	95.9	99.2	94.3	97.5	99.0	99.2	99.4	World Bank forthcoming b
Kazakhstan	2002	PWC	88.4	77.9	90.7	73.4	82.5	88.3	91.0	92.7	World Bank forthcoming b
Kyrgyz Republic	2002	PWC	81.5	61.9	85.2	64.5	59.4	78.9	86.8	89.9	World Bank forthcoming b
Latvia, Riga	1997	PWC	98.8	98.2	99.2	97.3	98.9	99.0	99.2	99.4	Shkaratan 2005
Moldova	2002	PWC	78.5	66.2	81.4	64.5	67.9	70.4	83.5	90.4	World Bank forthcoming b
Poland	2002	PWC	99.2	98.0	99.5	97.3	98.6	99.2	99.4	99.8	World Bank forthcoming b
Romania	2002	PWC	92.8	83.2	94.5	78.8	87.7	91.5	94.6	97.4	World Bank forthcoming b
Russian Federation	2002	PWC	96.4	94.4	97.1	93.8	95.0	95.9	97.3	98.0	World Bank forthcoming b
Serbia and Montenegro	2002	PWC	98.2	96.7	98.7	96.4	97.0	98.1	98.9	99.1	World Bank forthcoming b
Tajikistan	2003	PWC	83.5	80.3	83.8	81.0	79.5	78.6	85.5	87.3	World Bank forthcoming b

198

	Year	Method									Source
Turkey	2002	PWC	90.0	82.4	94.4	76.5	88.4	92.2	94.3	96.7	World Bank forthcoming b
Ukraine	2002	PWC	89.8	86.1	91.1	85.1	87.2	89.3	90.1	93.9	World Bank forthcoming b
Sub-Saharan Africa											
Cape Verde	2001–2	PWC	26.5	10.3	37.3	6.6	14.1	23.5	35.6	52.8	Angel-Urdinola and Wodon 2005a
Niger, Niamey	1998	PWC	44.0	15.0	55.3	n/r	n/r	n/r	n/r	n/r	Lauria and Kolb 1999
Niger, Niamey	1998	PT	15.0	32.0	9.0	n/r	n/r	n/r	n/r	n/r	Lauria and Kolb 1999
South Asia											
Nepal, Kathmandu	2001	PWC	65.5	48.3	77.1	42.7	56.6	71.5	77.0	83.3	Pattanayak and Yang 2002; Pattanayak and others 2001
Nepal, Kathmandu	2001	PT	34.5	51.7	22.9	57.3	43.4	28.5	23.0	16.7	Pattanayak and Yang 2002; Pattanayak and others 2001
India, Bangalore	2001	PWC	53.8	39.5	63.2	31.8	47.2	56.6	63.8	69.3	Prokopy 2002
India, Bangalore	2001	PT	24.0	44.0	10.0	57.0	31.0	18.5	9.0	3.5	Prokopy 2002
Sri Lanka	2003	PWC	37.4	31.2	41.6	27.7	34.6	42.4	39.7	42.5	Pattanayak and Yang 2005; Pattanayak and others 2004; Brocklehurst 2004
Sri Lanka	2003	PT	5.8	6.9	5.0	6.9	6.9	6.9	4.7	3.6	Pattanayak and Yang 2005; Pattanayak and others 2004; Brocklehurst 2004

Note: n/r = not reported.

199

Appendix C.2 Estimated Monthly Water Consumption per Household in m³

Country, City	Year	Sample	Total	Poor	Non-poor	Quintiles 1	2	3	4	5	Source
Latin America											
Colombia, Bogota	2003	AC	12.2	7.7	13.4	6.8	8.1	9.9	12.1	15.5	Melendez and others 2004; Melendez 2005
Colombia, Urban	2003	AC	8.0	4.5	10.3	4.0	5.0	7.0	10.0	14.0	Melendez and others 2004; Melendez 2005
El Salvador, San Miguel	1996	AC	29.0	30.5	28.0	30.0	31.0	27.0	30.0	27.0	Walker and others 2000
El Salvador, San Miguel	1996	AM	28.6	32.0	27.3	30.0	34.0	27.0	29.0	26.0	Walker and others 2000
El Salvador, Santa Ana	1996	AC	29.8	27.0	31.7	25.0	29.0	30.0	31.0	34.0	Walker and others 2000
El Salvador, Santa Ana	1996	AM	30.4	28.0	31.3	25.0	31.0	33.0	30.0	31.0	Walker and others 2000
El Salvador, Sonsonate	1996	AC	28.0	28.0	28.0	30.0	26.0	30.0	27.0	27.0	Walker and others 2000
El Salvador, Sonsonate	1996	AM	29.4	30.5	29.7	35.0	26.0	34.0	27.0	28.0	Walker and others 2000
Nicaragua, Managua	1995	AC	26.8	28.5	25.7	23.0	34.0	25.0	26.0	26.0	Walker and others 2000
Nicaragua, Managua	1995	AM	33.7	41.0	29.3	25.0	57.0	29.0	31.0	28.0	Walker and others 2000
Panama, Panama City and Colon	1998	AC	30.6	28.0	32.3	28.0	28.0	30.0	31.0	36.0	Walker and others 2000
Panama, Panama City and Colon	1998	AM	31.4	29.5	32.7	30.0	29.0	31.0	30.0	37.0	Walker and others 2000
Paraguay, Urban	2001	AC	27.0	21.4	30.8	18.7	24.1	26.7	28.7	37.1	Robles 2001

	Year									Source
Uruguay	2002–3	AC	11.5	11.4	11.7	11.8	10.9	11.6	10.6	12.8	Ruggeri-Laderchi 2003
Venezuela, R. B. de, Merida	1996	AC	39.6	40.5	39.0	43.0	38.0	38.0	40.0	39.0	Walker and others 2000
Venezuela, R. B. de, Merida	1996	AM	40.8	42.0	40.0	49.0	35.0	37.0	43.0	40.0	Walker and others 2000
Eastern and Central Europe											
Croatia	1998	AC	14.90	14.77	14.95	13.70	15.61	15.39	14.95	14.63	Shkaratan 2005
Sub-Saharan Africa											
Cape Verde	2001–2	AC	6.37	3.36	6.92	3.17	3.45	4.86	6.19	8.33	Angel-Urdinola and Wodon 2005a
South Asia											
Nepal, Kathmandu	2001	AC	22.1	16.9	24.3	15.0	19.0	19.1	21.7	31.9	Pattanayak and Yang 2002; Pattanayak and others 2001
Nepal, Kathmandu	2001	AM	25.9	23.1	26.9	18.1	30.2	22.7	23.4	33.1	Pattanayak and Yang 2002; Pattanayak and others 2001
Nepal, Kathmandu	2001	AUM	16.9	11.2	19.7	10.3	11.9	14.2	18.7	25.8	Pattanayak and Yang 2002; Pattanayak and others 2001
Nepal, Kathmandu	2001	PT	1.6	1.2	1.8	0.8	1.6	0.9	0.8	3.4	Pattanayak and Yang 2002; Pattanayak and others 2001
India, Bangalore	2001	AC	15.2	11.6	17.5	10.4	13.0	15.1	16.7	20.8	Prokopy 2002
India, Bangalore	2001	AM	20.3	17.9	21.3	n/r	n/r	n/r	n/r	n/r	Prokopy 2002
India, Bangalore	2001	PT	3.8	4.3	2.4	n/r	n/r	n/r	n/r	n/r	Prokopy 2002
Sri Lanka	2003	AC	28.8	22.6	33.0	20.9	24.3	29.5	32.8	36.7	Pattanayak and Yang 2005; Pattanayak and others 2004; Brocklehurst 2004
Sri Lanka	2003	AM	20.0	18.1	21.0	17.8	18.4	20.0	21.4	21.6	Pattanayak and Yang 2005; Pattanayak and others 2004; Brocklehurst 2004

Note: n/r = not reported.

Appendix C.3 Monthly Expenditure per Household on Water in US$

Country, City	Year	Sample	Total	Poor	Non-poor	Quintiles					Source
						1	2	3	4	5	
Latin America											
Nicaragua, Managua	1995	n/r	4.44	3.75	4.90	3.50	4.00	3.90	5.00	5.80	Walker and others 2000
Venezuela, R. B. de, Merida	1996	n/r	2.44	2.30	2.53	2.90	1.70	2.10	2.00	3.50	Walker and others 2000
El Salvador, Sonsonate	1996	n/r	5.84	5.15	6.30	5.60	4.70	7.40	5.30	6.20	Walker and others 2000
El Salvador, Santa Ana	1996	n/r	6.42	6.25	6.53	5.00	7.50	6.90	6.00	6.70	Walker and others 2000
El Salvador, San Miguel	1996	n/r	6.34	6.55	6.20	5.70	7.40	5.30	6.30	7.00	Walker and others 2000
Panama, Panama City and Colon	1998	n/r	10.72	9.55	11.50	8.40	10.70	11.20	10.70	12.60	Walker and others 2000
Colombia, Bogota	2003	n/r	7.59	3.98	8.55	3.74	4.10	5.22	6.70	10.79	Melendez and others 2004; Melendez 2005
Colombia, Urban	2003	n/r	5.50	3.92	6.55	3.84	4.00	4.80	5.78	9.07	Melendez and others 2004; Melendez 2005
Uruguay	2002–3	n/r	13.18	13.19	13.17	12.69	13.69	14.46	11.80	13.27	Ruggeri-Laderchi 2003
Paraguay, Urban	2001	n/r	5.38	2.50	7.31	2.58	2.42	5.34	5.65	10.93	Robles 2001
Mexico—ENIGH	2002	AC	9.97	5.64	12.85	4.76	6.52	9.77	11.29	17.50	World Bank 2004b
Guatemala	2000	AC	1.53	0.39	2.29	0.13	0.65	0.91	1.56	4.42	Foster and Araujo 2004
Bolivia, Urban	1994	AC	3.78	2.05	4.84	1.67	2.43	2.94	4.02	7.55	Israel 2002
Argentina	2002	AC	5.53	4.89	5.97	4.67	5.10	5.70	5.40	6.80	Foster 2004

Eastern and Central Europe

Albania	2002	AC	2.58	2.61	2.60	2.68	2.53	2.66	2.64	2.49	World Bank forthcoming b
Armenia	2002	AC	2.03	1.27	2.12	1.08	1.46	1.70	1.84	2.82	World Bank forthcoming b
Azerbaijan	2002	AC	1.42	1.49	1.41	1.50	1.49	1.45	1.47	1.29	World Bank forthcoming b
Bulgaria	2003	AC	6.56	5.92	6.80	5.67	6.17	6.29	6.84	7.27	World Bank forthcoming b
Croatia	1998	AC	10.83	10.72	10.87	9.94	11.34	11.20	10.87	10.64	Shkaratan 2005
Georgia	2002	AC	0.98	0.86	1.01	0.80	0.92	0.99	1.04	1.02	World Bank forthcoming b
Hungary	1997	AC	4.60	4.03	4.98	3.66	4.40	4.83	4.74	5.36	Shkaratan 2005
Kazakhstan	2002	AC	1.63	1.61	1.64	1.56	1.66	1.69	1.61	1.63	World Bank forthcoming b
Kyrgyz Republic	2002	AC	0.52	0.44	0.52	0.37	0.50	0.51	0.51	0.55	World Bank forthcoming b
Latvia, Riga	1997	AC	9.36	9.05	9.50	8.37	9.40	8.75	9.35	10.29	Shkaratan 2005
Moldova	2002	AC	1.65	1.27	1.63	1.29	1.25	1.22	1.61	2.05	World Bank forthcoming b
Poland	2002	AC	11.59	10.63	11.75	10.02	11.25	11.20	11.57	12.47	World Bank forthcoming b
Romania	2002	AC	7.24	5.71	7.34	4.97	6.45	6.73	7.39	7.89	World Bank forthcoming b
Russian Federation	2002	AC	2.48	2.25	2.56	2.15	2.35	2.51	2.49	2.69	World Bank forthcoming b
Tajikistan	2003	AC	1.32	0.95	1.43	0.86	1.04	1.32	1.39	1.58	World Bank forthcoming b
Turkey	2002	AC	10.34	7.66	10.95	6.97	8.35	9.45	11.22	12.16	World Bank forthcoming b
Ukraine	2002	AC	1.67	1.52	1.72	1.48	1.57	1.67	1.71	1.78	World Bank forthcoming b

(Table continues on the following page.)

Appendix C.3 (continued)

Country, City	Year	Sample	Total	Poor	Non-poor	Quintiles					Source
						1	2	3	4	5	
Sub-Saharan Africa											
Cape Verde	2001–2	AC	13.93	6.60	15.28	6.16	6.81	10.21	12.99	19.09	Angel-Urdinola and Wodon 2005a
Niamey, Niger	1998	AC	10.85	n/r	n/r	n/r	n/r	n/r	n/r	n/r	Lauria and Kolb 1999
Niamey, Niger	1998	AM	11.82	n/r	n/r	n/r	n/r	n/r	n/r	n/r	Lauria and Kolb 1999
South Asia											
Nepal, Kathmandu	2001	AM	2.59	2.23	2.72	1.58	3.14	2.18	2.27	3.52	Pattanayak and Yang 2002; Pattanayak and others 2001
Nepal, Kathmandu	2001	AUM	1.79	1.35	1.99	1.27	1.43	1.68	1.82	2.46	Pattanayak and Yang 2002; Pattanayak and others 2001
India, Bangalore	2001	AC	1.78	1.51	1.90	1.39	1.59	1.75	1.76	2.17	Prokopy 2002
India, Bangalore	2001	AM	1.89	1.65	2.01	n/r	n/r	n/r	n/r	n/r	Prokopy 2002
India, Bangalore	2001	OPC	1.48	1.28	1.59	n/r	n/r	n/r	n/r	n/r	Prokopy 2002
India, Bangalore	2001	PT	0.42	0.35	0.70	n/r	n/r	n/r	n/r	n/r	Prokopy 2002
Sri Lanka	2003	AM	2.26	1.64	2.58	1.55	1.71	2.16	2.75	2.83	Pattanayak and Yang 2005; Pattanayak and others 2004; Brocklehurst 2004

Note: n/r = not reported.

Appendix C.4 Monthly Expenditure on Water as a Percentage of Household Income (%)

Country, City	Year	Sample	Total	Poor	Non-poor	1	2	3	4	5	Source
Latin America											
Argentina	2002	AC	2.7	3.2	2.4	3.5	2.8	2.8	2.3	2.1	Foster 2004
Bolivia, Urban	1999	AH	1.8	1.8	1.9	1.8	1.9	2.0	1.9	1.7	Barja, McKenzie, and Urquiola 2002
Colombia, Bogota	2003	AC	1.2	3.4	1.1	7.1	2.8	2.2	1.8	1.0	Melendez and others 2004; Melendez 2005
Colombia, Urban	2003	AC	2.4	3.8	1.4	4.8	2.7	2.0	1.5	0.8	Melendez and others 2004; Melendez 2005
Guatemala	2000	AC	0.3	0.2	0.4	0.1	0.3	0.3	0.4	0.6	Foster and Araujo 2004
Mexico	1998	AH	1.1	1.2	0.9	1.1	1.3	1.2	1.1	0.8	López-Calva and Rosellón 2002
Paraguay, Urban	2001	AC	2.0	3.0	1.0	4.4	1.6	1.9	1.1	0.8	Robles 2001
Uruguay	2002–3	AC	4.3	7.3	2.3	10.4	4.1	3.2	2.2	1.5	Ruggeri-Laderchi 2003
Eastern and Central Europe											
Albania	2002	AC	1.2	1.8	1.1	2.1	1.6	1.4	1.2	0.8	World Bank forthcoming b
Armenia	2002	AC	2.3	2.5	2.3	2.4	2.5	2.7	2.1	2.1	World Bank forthcoming b
Azerbaijan	2002	AC	1.0	1.2	1.0	1.3	1.1	1.0	1.0	0.9	World Bank forthcoming b
Bulgaria	2003	AC	3.6	4.5	3.3	4.9	4.1	3.7	3.4	2.8	World Bank forthcoming b
Croatia	1998	AC	1.4	1.8	1.2	2.0	1.6	1.4	1.3	1.0	Shkaratan 2005

(Table continues on the following page.)

Appendix C.4: *(continued)*

Country, City	Year	Sample	Total	Poor	Non-poor	Quintiles (%)					Source
						1	2	3	4	5	
Georgia	2002	AC	1.1	1.9	0.9	2.5	1.4	1.3	1.0	0.6	World Bank forthcoming b
Hungary	1997	AC	2.1	2.3	1.9	2.4	2.2	2.3	1.9	1.5	Shkaratan 2005
Kazakhstan	2002	AC	1.3	1.9	1.2	2.1	1.7	1.5	1.2	0.9	World Bank forthcoming b
Kyrgyz Republic	2002	AC	0.9	1.1	1.0	1.1	1.0	1.1	1.0	0.8	World Bank forthcoming b
Latvia, Riga	1997	AC	3.5	4.6	3.0	5.1	4.4	3.5	3.1	2.4	Shkaratan 2005
Moldova	2002	AC	2.8	4.0	2.7	4.3	3.6	3.1	2.9	2.2	World Bank forthcoming b
Poland	2002	AC	3.2	4.1	3.0	4.4	3.8	3.5	3.2	2.5	World Bank forthcoming b
Romania	2002	AC	4.9	5.8	4.8	5.7	5.9	5.4	4.9	4.1	World Bank forthcoming b
Russian Federation	2002	AC	1.4	2.1	1.2	2.4	1.8	1.5	1.2	0.9	World Bank forthcoming b
Tajikistan	2003	AC	1.8	2.3	1.6	2.6	2.1	1.9	1.6	1.4	World Bank forthcoming b
Turkey	2002	AC	3.6	4.9	3.3	5.3	4.4	3.9	3.6	2.5	World Bank forthcoming b
Ukraine	2002	AC	1.6	2.1	1.5	2.3	1.9	1.8	1.5	1.2	World Bank forthcoming b
Sub-Saharan Africa											
Cape Verde	2001–2	AC	2.2	3.1	2.2	3.9	2.9	3.1	2.8	1.9	Angel-Urdinola and Wodon 2005a
Niamey, Niger	1998	AC	7.5	n/r	n/r	n/r	n/r	n/r	n/r	n/r	Lauria and Kolb 1999
Niamey, Niger	1998	AM	8.2	n/r	n/r	n/r	n/r	n/r	n/r	n/r	Lauria and Kolb 1999

South Asia

	Year	Sample									Source
India, Bangalore	2001	AC	0.8	1.1	0.7	1.2	1.0	0.8	0.7	0.6	Prokopy 2002
Nepal, Kathmandu	2001	AM	1.2	3.0	1.1	2.7	3.2	1.5	1.1	0.6	Pattanayak and Yang 2002; Pattanayak and others 2001
Nepal, Kathmandu	2001	AUM	0.8	1.8	0.8	2.2	1.4	1.2	0.9	0.4	Pattanayak and Yang 2002; Pattanayak and others 2001
Sri Lanka	2003	AM	0.9	1.0	0.9	1.2	0.9	0.9	1.0	0.8	Pattanayak and Yang 2005; Pattanayak and others 2004; Brocklehurst 2004

Note: Sample: AC = All connected; AM = All metered; AUM = All unmetered; AH = All households, including those without access.

Type of connection: PT = Public taps; PWC = Private water connection; OPC = Other private connection.

Poor = Poorest 40%.

Other: n/r = not reported.

Appendix D: Electricity: Consumption Subsidy Data

Appendix D.1 Percentage of Households Receiving Subsidy

Country, city	Type of subsidy	Total (%)	Poor (%)	Nonpoor (%)	Quintiles				
					1 (%)	2 (%)	3 (%)	4 (%)	5 (%)
Latin America									
Colombia									
Colombia, Bogota (E)	Geographically defined tariffs with IBTs	83.0	96.3	74.1	96.7	95.8	92.9	82.3	47.0
Colombia, Bogota (S)	Geographically defined tariffs with IBTs and limited use of means testing	57.3	83.8	39.7	87.8	79.7	65.6	41.8	11.6
Colombia, Urban (E)	Geographically defined tariffs with IBTs	88.4	98.0	82.1	97.9	98.1	95.8	90.1	60.3
Guatemala									
Guatemala (E)	VDT with 300 kWh threshold	62.9	44.6	75.1	33.5	56.3	69.9	80.5	73.9
Guatemala (S)	VDT with 100 kWh threshold	47.6	41.5	48.2	31.9	51.2	58.1	51.1	31.5
Honduras (E)	VDT with 300 kWh threshold	57.4	41.5	51.1	n/r	n/r	n/r	n/r	n/r
Peru (E)	IBT	41.0	40.1	41.5	35.9	44.2	44.3	44.4	36.8
Argentina									
Argentina (E*)	Average of provincial means-tested subsidy	n/r	6.0	n/r	n/r	n/r	n/r	n/r	n/r
Argentina (S)	Discount for means-tested households	n/r	64.0	n/r	n/r	n/r	n/r	n/r	n/r

(Table continues on the following page.)

Appendix D.1 (continued)

Country, city	Type of subsidy	Total (%)	Poor (%)	Nonpoor (%)	Quintiles				
					1 (%)	2 (%)	3 (%)	4 (%)	5 (%)
South Asia									
India: State, Urban (E)									
Kerala	State IBTs	90.2	84.3	93.5	78.8	91.6	93.6	93.8	92.9
Andhra Pradesh	State IBTs	90.2	80.9	94.3	72.5	89.1	91.6	96.0	95.1
Tamil Nadu	State IBTs	90.2	82.8	93.9	77.0	88.7	93.6	93.2	93.6
Karnataka	State IBTs	88.4	78.9	92.9	73.2	92.0	94.0	92.6	90.5
Maharashtra	State IBTs	87.6	86.7	88.2	82.3	91.6	87.0	88.1	89.3
Madhya Pradesh	State IBTs	92.0	86.6	94.6	81.7	91.3	93.3	94.1	96.0
Gujarat	State IBTs	76.4	76.3	76.4	74.1	81.4	79.0	76.7	66.6
Orissa	State IBTs	72.6	58.7	80.5	42.7	67.9	79.5	79.9	79.8
Punjab	State IBTs	83.5	86.8	81.5	84.3	87.9	84.8	83.0	75.7
Haryana	State IBTs	88.2	84.5	90.7	79.9	88.7	94.0	77.6	84.2
Rajasthan	State IBTs	84.3	78.3	86.6	71.0	81.0	86.8	87.2	87.5
Delhi	State IBTs	91.3	90.3	91.7	86.6	93.4	91.2	91.1	92.7
Uttar Pradesh	State IBTs	83.9	72.6	89.1	66.4	77.6	84.1	89.3	91.8
West Bengal	State IBTs	80.6	68.5	87.8	57.5	78.0	84.3	86.6	90.0
Bihar	State IBTs	66.1	41.4	74.4	31.7	55.2	70.9	71.0	78.0

Eastern and Central Europe

Croatia (E)	Uniform volumetric tariff	99.7	99.7	99.8	99.0	99.8	99.8	99.9	99.7
Hungary (S)	IBT	98.7	98.3	99.0	97.7	98.9	99.2	99.1	98.7
Georgia									
Georgia, Tbilisi (E)	Winter heating allowance	20.8	25.0	18.0	27.0	23.0	21.0	19.0	14.0
Georgia, Tbilisi (E)	Discount on bill for targeted households	13.0	13.0	13.0	10.0	16.0	18.0	11.0	10.0

Sub-Saharan Africa

Rwanda

Rwanda, Urban (E)	Uniform volumetric tariff	32.0	12.8	45.0	4.0	21.7	28.6	45.3	60.8
Rwanda, Urban (S)	IBT with 40 kWh first block	32.0	12.8	n/r	n/r	n/r	n/r	n/r	n/r
Rwanda, Urban (S)	VDT with 40 kWh threshold	8.8	5.7	n/r	n/r	n/r	n/r	n/r	n/r

Cape Verde

Cape Verde (E)	IBT with 40 kWh first block	44.1	24.4	57.1	15.7	33.2	43.5	58.0	70.0
Cape Verde (S)	VDT with 40 kWh first block	10.4	11.4	n/r	n/r	n/r	n/r	n/r	n/r
Cape Verde (S)	Means-tested discount: housing and region	3.4	6.7	n/r	n/r	n/r	n/r	n/r	n/r

Saõ Tomé and Principe

Saõ Tomé and Principe (E)	IBT with 300 kWh first block	42.3	23.2	55.0	14.1	32.4	43.3	56.1	65.7
Saõ Tomé and Principe (S)	VDT with 300 kWh threshold	30.4	20.8	n/r	n/r	n/r	n/r	n/r	n/r
Saõ Tomé and Principe (S)	IBT with 200 kWh first block	37.2	22.5	n/r	n/r	n/r	n/r	n/r	n/r

Source: Authors' elaboration based on data from sources cited in appendix A.

Note: E = existing subsidy; S = simulation; poor = poorest 40%; IBT = increasing block tariff; VDT = volume differentiated tariff; n/r = not reported; kWh = electricity consumption.

*Assumes all eligible households are receiving the subsidy.

Appendix D.2. Percentage of Connected Households Receiving Subsidy

Country, city	Type of subsidy	Total (%)	Poor (%)	Nonpoor (%)	Quintiles				
					1 (%)	2 (%)	3 (%)	4 (%)	5 (%)
Colombia									
Colombia, Bogota (E)	Geographically defined tariffs with IBTs	83.1	96.8	74.1	97.8	96.0	93.2	82.4	47.0
Colombia, Bogota (S)	Geographically defined tariffs with IBTs and limited use of means testing	57.4	84.3	39.7	88.8	79.9	65.7	41.9	11.6
Colombia, Urban (E)	Geographically defined tariffs with IBTs	88.7	98.8	82.1	99.3	98.3	95.8	90.1	60.4
Guatemala									
Guatemala (E)	VDT with 300 kWh threshold	86.1	85.8	86.3	83.7	88.0	90.7	90.4	77.8
Guatemala (S)	VDT with 100 kWh threshold	65.2	79.9	55.4	79.8	79.9	75.5	57.4	33.2
Honduras (E)	VDT with 300 kWh threshold	83.5	93.3	60.2	n/r	n/r	n/r	n/r	n/r
Peru (E)	IBT	52.4	64.9	47.3	67.8	62.8	55.2	50.4	39.0
Mexico (E)	Geographically defined tariffs with IBTs	90.4	83.3	95.2	71.4	95.2	95.2	95.2	95.2
Argentina									
Argentina (E*)	Average of provincial means-tested subsidy	n/r	7.0	n/r	n/r	n/r	n/r	n/r	n/r
Argentina (S)	Discount for means-tested households	n/r	69.0	n/r	n/r	n/r	n/r	n/r	n/r

South Asia

India: State, Urban (E)

Kerala	State IBTs	99.3	99.6	99.1	99.4	100.0	100.0	98.2	98.8
Andhra Pradesh	State IBTs	98.8	99.8	98.4	99.8	99.3	98.7	98.7	97.6
Tamil Nadu	State IBTs	97.7	98.5	97.3	98.8	98.6	98.4	96.8	95.8
Karnataka	State IBTs	96.9	98.3	96.4	97.5	99.3	98.9	95.8	93.0
Maharashtra	State IBTs	97.6	99.0	96.5	99.4	98.9	97.5	97.3	94.7
Madhya Pradesh	State IBTs	98.6	98.9	98.5	99.1	98.6	98.8	98.2	98.4
Gujarat	State IBTs	82.7	89.1	79.8	92.6	88.4	83.2	81.0	68.4
Orissa	State IBTs	89.0	89.9	88.6	89.9	89.9	91.9	86.6	86.5
Punjab	State IBTs	87.2	93.3	83.9	93.2	92.3	88.4	85.0	77.3
Haryana	State IBTs	95.2	96.7	94.3	95.8	96.6	98.6	93.1	91.7
Rajasthan	State IBTs	92.6	94.6	91.9	96.6	88.9	93.1	92.4	92.0
Delhi	State IBTs	99.2	100.0	98.9	100.0	99.4	98.9	99.4	98.3
Uttar Pradesh	State IBTs	99.6	99.5	99.6	99.4	100.0	99.6	99.5	99.5
West Bengal	State IBTs	95.5	96.1	95.3	96.6	95.4	96.6	95.8	93.1
Bihar	State IBTs	98.5	98.1	98.6	98.1	99.6	97.8	99.3	97.8

Eastern Europe and Central Asia

Croatia (E)	Uniform volumetric tariff	100.0	100.0	100.0	100.0	100.0	100.0	100.0	100.0

(Table continues on the following page.)

Appendix D.2 (continued)

Country, city	Type of subsidy	Total (%)	Poor (%)	Nonpoor (%)	Quintiles				
					1 (%)	2 (%)	3 (%)	4 (%)	5 (%)
Sub-Saharan Africa									
Rwanda									
Rwanda, Urban (E)	Uniform volumetric tariff	100.0	100.0	100.0	100.0	100.0	100.0	100.0	100.0
Rwanda, Urban (S)	IBT with 40 kWh first block	100.0	100.0	n/r	n/r	n/r	n/r	n/r	n/r
Rwanda, Urban (S)	VDT with 40 kWh threshold	27.6	44.6	n/r	n/r	n/r	n/r	n/r	n/r
Cape Verde									
Cape Verde (E)	IBT with 40 kWh first block	100.0	100.0	100.0	100.0	100.0	100.0	100.0	100.0
Cape Verde (S)	VDT with 40 kWh first block	23.5	46.9	n/r	n/r	n/r	n/r	n/r	n/r
Cape Verde (S)	Means-tested discount: housing and region	7.7	27.4	n/r	n/r	n/r	n/r	n/r	n/r
Saõ Tomé and Principe									
Saõ Tomé and Principe (E)	IBT with 300 kWh first block	100.0	100.0	100.0	100.0	100.0	100.0	100.0	100.0
Saõ Tomé and Principe (S)	VDT with 300 kWh threshold	72.0	89.6	n/r	n/r	n/r	n/r	n/r	n/r
Saõ Tomé and Principe (S)	IBT with 200 kWh first block	88.0	97.0	n/r	n/r	n/r	n/r	n/r	n/r

Source: Authors' elaboration based on data from sources cited in appendix A.

Note: E = existing subsidy; S = simulation; poor = poorest 40%; IBT = increasing block tariff; VDT = volume differentiated tariff; n/r = not reported; kWh = electricity consumption.

*Assumes all eligible households are receiving the subsidy.

Appendix D.3 Average Value of Subsidy per Household, as Average Percentage of Household Income

Country, city	Type of subsidy	Total (%)	Poor (%)	Nonpoor (%)	Quintiles				
					1 (%)	2 (%)	3 (%)	4 (%)	5 (%)
Latin America									
Colombia									
Colombia, Bogota (E)	Geographically defined tariffs with IBTs	1.3	2.5	0.5	3.8	1.2	0.8	0.4	0.2
Colombia, Bogota (S)	Geographically defined tariffs with IBTs and limited use of means testing	1.3	2.5	0.5	3.8	1.2	0.8	0.4	0.2
Colombia, Urban (E)	Geographically defined tariffs with IBTs	1.9	3.7	0.8	5.4	1.9	1.3	0.8	0.3
Guatemala									
Guatemala (E)	VDT with 300 kWh threshold	4.4	4.0	4.7	4.0	4.0	4.5	5.9	3.7
Guatemala (S)	VDT with 100 kWh threshold	2.6	3.0	2.3	3.4	2.7	3.0	2.5	1.3
Peru (E)	IBT	1.4	2.2	0.8	2.7	1.7	1.2	0.8	0.4
South Asia									
India: State, Urban (E)									
Kerala	State IBTs	4.1	4.3	4.0	4.3	4.2	4.0	4.5	3.6
Andhra Pradesh	State IBTs	3.6	4.0	3.4	3.7	4.2	3.8	3.8	2.7
Tamil Nadu	State IBTs	5.0	5.4	4.7	5.7	5.2	5.2	5.0	4.1
Karnataka	State IBTs	3.0	3.0	3.1	2.9	3.3	3.6	3.2	2.5

(Table continues on the following page.)

Appendix D.3 (continued)

Country, city	Type of subsidy	Total (%)	Poor (%)	Nonpoor (%)	Quintiles				
					1 (%)	2 (%)	3 (%)	4 (%)	5 (%)
Maharashtra	State IBTs	3.5	3.9	3.2	4.0	3.9	3.5	3.3	2.7
Madhya Pradesh	State IBTs	3.4	3.6	3.3	3.3	3.8	3.6	3.3	3.1
Gujarat	State IBTs	1.3	1.3	1.3	1.1	1.5	1.5	1.6	0.9
Orissa	State IBTs	1.1	1.0	1.1	0.8	1.2	1.4	1.4	0.9
Punjab	State IBTs	1.6	1.9	1.4	1.8	2.0	1.6	1.5	1.1
Haryana	State IBTs	1.5	1.4	1.5	1.3	1.4	2.0	1.7	1.2
Rajasthan	State IBTs	1.2	1.2	1.2	1.1	1.3	1.5	1.2	1.0
Delhi	State IBTs	9.0	8.9	9.0	8.7	9.1	9.5	8.5	9.3
Uttar Pradesh	State IBTs	3.1	2.9	3.2	2.7	3.1	3.1	3.2	3.3
West Bengal	State IBTs	2.7	2.7	2.7	2.4	2.9	2.8	2.7	2.7
Bihar	State IBTs	2.1	1.5	2.3	1.2	1.9	2.5	2.2	2.2
Eastern Europe and Central Asia									
Croatia (E)	Uniform volumetric tariff	0.9	0.8	1.0	0.9	0.7	1.1	1.2	0.7
Hungary (S)	IBT	0.1	0.0	0.1	0.0	0.0	0.0	0.1	0.1
AFR									
Rwanda, Urban (E)	Uniform volumetric tariff	2.3	3.5	2.2	4.1	3.5	2.6	2.4	2.0
Cape Verde (E)	IBT with 40 kWh first block	0.2	0.5	0.2	0.6	0.5	0.4	0.3	0.1
Saõ Tomé and Principe (E)	IBT with 300 kWh first block	5.6	9.2	5.2	9.5	9.1	8.4	7.0	3.7

Source: Authors' elaboration based on data from sources cited in appendix A.

Note: E = existing subsidy; S = simulation; poor = poorest 40%; IBT = increasing block tariff; VDT = volume differentiated tariff; n/r = not reported; kWh = electricity consumption.

*Assumes all eligible households are receiving the subsidy.

Appendix D.4 Average Value of Subsidy per Household in US$

Country, city	Type of subsidy	Total	Poor	Nonpoor	Quintiles				
					1	2	3	4	5
Latin America									
Colombia									
Colombia, Bogota (E)	Geographically defined tariffs with IBTs	2.69	2.75	2.64	2.66	2.85	2.83	2.66	2.44
Colombia, Bogota (S)	Geographically defined tariffs with IBTs and limited use of means testing	2.50	2.38	2.57	2.30	2.46	2.53	2.50	2.68
Colombia, Urban (E)	Geographically defined tariffs with IBTs	3.28	3.30	3.27	3.18	3.42	3.43	3.33	3.06
Guatemala									
Guatemala (E)	VDT with 300 kWh threshold	2.94	0.67	4.29	0.70	1.14	1.89	3.90	7.09
Guatemala (S)	VDT with 100 kWh threshold	1.36	0.47	1.83	0.58	0.76	1.26	1.68	2.54
Peru (E)	IBT	0.42	0.47	0.38	0.45	0.48	0.44	0.40	0.30
Mexico (E)	Geographically defined tariffs with IBTs	9.61	5.75	12.18	3.03	8.46	12.76	15.03	8.74

(Table continues on the following page.)

Appendix D.4 (*continued*)

Country, city	Type of subsidy	Total	Poor	Nonpoor	Quintiles				
					1	2	3	4	5
South Asia									
India: State, Urban (E)									
Kerala	State IBTs	4.33	2.74	5.22	2.25	3.40	3.46	4.93	6.18
Andhra Pradesh	State IBTs	2.60	1.78	2.96	1.40	2.17	2.42	3.11	3.35
Tamil Nadu	State IBTs	3.53	2.26	4.15	1.82	2.70	3.27	4.00	4.94
Karnataka	State IBTs	2.84	1.61	3.42	1.34	2.24	3.03	3.70	3.50
Maharashtra	State IBTs	3.59	2.61	4.33	2.04	3.21	3.23	3.69	5.97
Madhya Pradesh	State IBTs	2.68	1.82	3.10	1.45	2.19	2.53	2.96	3.71
Gujarat	State IBTs	1.08	0.80	1.23	0.57	1.06	1.14	1.46	1.07
Orissa	State IBTs	0.83	0.54	1.00	0.33	0.65	1.02	1.03	0.98
Punjab	State IBTs	1.43	1.26	1.53	1.01	1.48	1.39	1.60	1.60
Haryana	State IBTs	1.35	0.88	1.66	0.66	1.11	1.61	1.22	2.00
Rajasthan	State IBTs	1.10	0.85	1.20	0.65	1.03	1.15	1.15	1.28
Delhi	State IBTs	10.05	5.88	11.85	4.93	6.80	8.02	8.74	18.39
Uttar Pradesh	State IBTs	2.74	1.66	3.25	1.35	1.90	2.21	2.77	4.27
West Bengal	State IBTs	2.20	1.35	2.71	0.90	1.75	1.84	2.10	3.70
Bihar	State IBTs	1.68	0.83	1.97	0.53	1.24	1.64	1.80	2.27
Eastern and Central Europe									
Croatia (E)	Uniform volumetric tariff	7.78	5.16	8.94	5.32	5.03	9.61	9.14	8.28
Hungary (S)	IBT	1.15	1.13	1.16	1.11	1.16	1.15	1.16	1.17

Sub-Saharan Africa

Rwanda

Rwanda, Urban (E)	Uniform volumetric tariff	8.67	5.67	9.24	3.49	6.08	6.02	7.83	11.79
Rwanda, Urban (S)	IBT with 40 kWh first block	3.36	2.93	3.65	n/r	n/r	n/r	n/r	n/r
Rwanda, Urban (S)	VDT with 40 kWh threshold	2.36	1.92	2.64	n/r	n/r	n/r	n/r	n/r

Cape Verde

Cape Verde (E)	IBT with 40 kWh first block	1.31	1.13	1.36	0.99	1.20	1.30	1.36	1.39
Cape Verde (S)	VDT with 40 kWh first block	0.78	0.75	0.79	n/r	n/r	n/r	n/r	n/r
Cape Verde (S)	Means-tested discount: housing and region	2.08	1.54	2.44	n/r	n/r	n/r	n/r	n/r

Saõ Tomé and Principe

Saõ Tomé and Principe (E)	IBT with 300 kWh first block	12.93	9.61	13.87	6.98	10.76	12.58	13.81	14.76
Saõ Tomé and Principe (S)	VDT with 300 kWh threshold	7.72	6.63	8.44	n/r	n/r	n/r	n/r	n/r
Saõ Tomé and Principe (S)	IBT with 200 kWh first block	8.58	7.08	9.57	n/r	n/r	n/r	n/r	n/r

Source: Authors' elaboration based on data from sources cited in appendix A.

Note: E = existing subsidy; S = simulation; poor = poorest 40%; IBT = increasing block tariff; VDT = volume differentiated tariff; n/r = not reported; kWh = electricity consumption.

*Assumes all eligible households are receiving the subsidy.

Appendix D.5 Percentage of Subsidy Pool Going to Each Quintile

Country, city	Type of subsidy	Total value of the subsidy (US$)	Poor (%)	Nonpoor (%)	Quintiles 1 (%)	2 (%)	3 (%)	4 (%)	5 (%)
Latin America									
Colombia									
Colombia, Bogota (E)	Geographically defined tariffs with IBTs	3,934,265	43.9	56.1	20.1	23.8	24.1	20.9	11.2
Colombia, Bogota (S)	Geographically defined tariffs with IBTs and limited use of means testing	2,401,971	53.8	46.2	25.8	28.0	24.9	16.4	4.9
Colombia, Urban (E)	Geographically defined tariffs with IBTs	20,780,802	42.8	57.2	19.2	23.6	25.0	23.6	8.6
Guatemala									
Guatemala (E)	VDT with 300 kWh threshold	4,005,010	8.0	92.0	2.2	5.8	11.4	28.1	52.4
Guatemala (S)	VDT with 100 kWh threshold	1,094,591	19.4	80.6	6.5	12.9	23.2	28.1	29.3
Peru (E)	IBT	1,488,635	32.8	67.2	13.2	19.6	21.2	24.8	21.2
Mexico (E)	Geographically defined tariffs with IBTs	2,748,771,930	23.9	76.1	6.3	17.6	26.6	31.3	18.2
Argentina									
Argentina (E*)	Average of provincial means-tested subsidy	18,376,338	60.0	40.0	28.0	32.0	20.0	12.0	8.0
Argentina (S)	Discount for means-tested households	98,000,000	55.0	45.0	29.0	26.0	20.0	15.0	10.0

South Asia

India: State, Urban (E)

Kerala	State IBTs	1,501,796	22.9	77.1	10.7	12.3	10.9	22.0	44.2
Andhra Pradesh	State IBTs	7,306,841	21.0	79.0	8.4	12.6	22.5	24.3	32.3
Tamil Nadu	State IBTs	11,746,016	21.1	78.9	8.4	12.6	20.8	18.0	40.1
Karnataka	State IBTs	5,939,065	18.2	81.8	10.7	7.6	22.1	30.4	29.3
Maharashtra	State IBTs	16,936,660	31.6	68.4	12.6	19.0	14.4	22.1	31.9
Madhya Pradesh	State IBTs	4,632,461	21.9	78.1	8.7	13.2	17.4	28.8	31.9
Gujarat	State IBTs	1,808,834	25.2	74.8	9.5	15.8	18.5	32.4	23.9
Orissa	State IBTs	668,664	23.5	76.5	5.2	18.3	18.8	22.9	34.9
Punjab	State IBTs	900,203	32.5	67.5	12.2	20.3	20.1	16.9	30.5
Haryana	State IBTs	660,422	25.8	74.2	10.2	15.5	19.4	16.7	38.1
Rajasthan	State IBTs	1,090,904	21.8	78.2	8.0	13.9	21.2	27.0	30.0
Delhi	State IBTs	12,595,868	17.6	82.4	7.2	10.4	15.0	23.6	43.8
Uttar Pradesh	State IBTs	9,377,700	19.1	80.9	6.8	12.3	13.7	23.3	43.9
West Bengal	State IBTs	6,866,694	22.8	77.2	7.1	15.7	13.2	19.9	44.1
Bihar	State IBTs	1,029,616	12.3	87.7	4.5	7.8	18.5	24.4	44.7

Eastern Europe and Central Asia

Croatia (E)	Uniform volumetric tariff	13,281	20.4	79.6	9.4	11.1	25.0	25.5	29.1
Hungary (S)	IBT	8,691	39.4	60.6	19.3	20.1	20.0	20.2	20.4
Georgia									
Georgia, Tbilisi (E)	Winter heating allowance	n/r	48.1	51.9	26.0	22.1	20.2	18.3	13.5
Georgia, Tbilisi (E)	Discount on bill for targeted households	n/r	40.0	60.0	15.4	24.6	27.7	16.9	15.4

(Table continues on the following page.)

Appendix D.5 (continued)

Country, city	Type of subsidy	Total value of the subsidy (US$)	Poor (%)	Nonpoor (%)	1 (%)	2 (%)	3 (%)	4 (%)	5 (%)
							Quintiles		
Sub-Saharan Africa									
Rwanda									
Rwanda, Urban (E)	Uniform volumetric tariff	442,202	10.5	89.7	1.0	9.5	12.4	25.6	51.7
Rwanda, Urban (S)	IBT with 40 kWh first block	171,292	14.0	86.0	n/r	n/r	n/r	n/r	n/r
Rwanda, Urban (S)	VDT with 40 kWh threshold	33,153	21.2	78.8	n/r	n/r	n/r	n/r	n/r
Cape Verde									
Cape Verde (E)	IBT with 40 kWh first block	54,827	19.2	80.9	5.4	13.8	19.7	27.4	33.8
Cape Verde (S)	VDT with 40 kWh first block	7,655	42.5	57.5	n/r	n/r	n/r	n/r	n/r
Cape Verde (S)	Means-tested discount: housing and region	6,739	58.4	41.6	n/r	n/r	n/r	n/r	n/r
Saõ Tomé and Principe									
Saõ Tomé and Principe (E)	IBT with 300 kWh first block	148,832	16.2	83.8	3.6	12.6	20.1	28.4	35.3
Saõ Tomé and Principe (S)	VDT with 300 kWh threshold	63,901	23.5	76.5	n/r	n/r	n/r	n/r	n/r
Saõ Tomé and Principe (S)	IBT with 200 kWh first block	86,795	20.0	80.0	n/r	n/r	n/r	n/r	n/r

Source: Authors' elaboration based on data from sources cited in appendix A.

Note: E = existing subsidy; S = simulation; poor = poorest 40%; IBT = increasing block tariff; VDT = volume differentiated tariff; n/r = not reported; kWh = electricity consumption.

*Assumes all eligible households are receiving the subsidy.

Appendix D.6 Targeting Indicators: Electricity Subsidies

Country, city	Type of subsidy	Benefit targeting performance indicator (Ω)	Error of inclusion (%)	Error of exclusion (%)	Income Gini	Subsidy Quasi-Gini
Latin America						
Colombia						
Colombia, Bogota (E)	Geographically defined tariffs with IBTs	1.10	48.1	3.7	n/r	(0.04)
Colombia, Bogota (S)	Geographically defined tariffs with IBTs and limited use of means testing	1.35	26.1	16.8	n/r	(0.17)
Colombia, Urban (E)	Geographically defined tariffs with IBTs	1.01	51.2	2.0	n/r	0.02
Guatemala						
Guatemala (E)	VDT with 300 kWh threshold	0.20	71.4	55.4	n/r	n/r
Guatemala (S)	VDT with 100 kWh threshold	0.48	62.5	58.7	n/r	n/r
Peru (E)	IBT	0.82	64.3	59.9	n/r	0.08
Mexico (E)	Geographically defined tariffs with IBTs	0.60	n/r	n/r	0.50	n/r
Argentina						
Argentina (E*)	Average of provincial means-tested subsidy	1.50	39.0	94.0	0.44	(0.37)
Argentina (S)	Discount for means-tested households	1.38	41.0	36.0	0.44	(0.24)

(Table continues on the following page.)

Appendix D.6 (*continued*)

Country, city	Type of subsidy	Benefit targeting performance indicator (Ω)	Error of inclusion (%)	Error of exclusion (%)	Income Gini	Subsidy Quasi-Gini
South Asia						
India: State, Urban (E)						
Kerala	State IBTs	0.65	62.1	14.5	0.47	0.31
Andhra Pradesh	State IBTs	0.78	62.9	16.4	0.43	0.24
Tamil Nadu	State IBTs	0.53	62.5	15.3	0.42	0.27
Karnataka	State IBTs	0.74	63.2	18.6	0.41	0.24
Maharashtra	State IBTs	0.66	60.6	13.8	0.35	0.17
Madhya Pradesh	State IBTs	0.70	61.9	12.4	0.39	0.25
Gujarat	State IBTs	1.00	59.0	21.6	0.39	0.18
Orissa	State IBTs	0.71	67.0	40.1	0.44	0.26
Punjab	State IBTs	0.91	58.5	13.4	0.37	0.13
Haryana	State IBTs	0.66	61.6	15.4	0.35	0.23
Rajasthan	State IBTs	0.84	62.4	20.7	0.41	0.23
Delhi	State IBTs	0.57	60.1	9.1	0.42	0.34
Uttar Pradesh	State IBTs	0.66	64.6	25.8	0.45	0.34
West Bengal	State IBTs	0.62	65.6	30.5	0.40	0.31
Bihar	State IBTs	0.43	68.4	47.7	0.50	0.39

Eastern Europe and Central Asia

Croatia (E)	Uniform volumetric tariff	0.51	65.7	0.6	0.25	0.22
Hungary (S)	IBT	0.98	59.4	1.7	0.04	0.01
Georgia						
Georgia, Tbilisi (E)	Winter heating allowance	1.20	n/r	75.0	n/r	n/r
Georgia, Tbilisi (E)	Discount on bill for targeted households	1.00	n/r	87.0	n/r	n/r

Sub-Saharan Africa

Rwanda						
Rwanda, Urban (E)	Uniform volumetric tariff	0.26	45.0	87.2	n/r	n/r
Rwanda, Urban (S)	IBT with 40 kWh first block	0.35	n/r	87.2	n/r	n/r
Rwanda, Urban (S)	VDT with 40 kWh threshold	0.53	n/r	94.3	n/r	n/r
Cape Verde						
Cape Verde (E)	IBT with 40 kWh first block	0.48	57.1	75.6	n/r	n/r
Cape Verde (S)	VDT with 40 kWh first block	1.06	n/r	88.6	n/r	n/r
Cape Verde (S)	Means-tested discount: housing and region	1.46	n/r	93.3	n/r	n/r
Saõ Tomé and Principe						
Saõ Tomé and Principe (E)	IBT with 300 kWh first block	0.41	55.0	76.8	n/r	n/r
Saõ Tomé and Principe (S)	VDT with 300 kWh threshold	0.59	n/r	79.2	n/r	n/r
Saõ Tomé and Principe (S)	IBT with 200 kWh first block	0.51	n/r	77.5	n/r	n/r

Source: Authors' elaboration based on data from sources cited in appendix A.

Note: E = existing subsidy; S = simulation; poor = poorest 40%; IBT = Increasing block tariff; VDT = Volume differentiated tariff; n/a = not applicable; n/r = not reported.

*Assumes all eligible households are receiving the subsidy.

Appendix E: Water: Consumption Subsidy Data

Appendix E.1 Percentage of Households Receiving Subsidy

Country, city	Type of subsidy	Total (%)	Poor (%)	Nonpoor (%)	Quintiles				
					1 (%)	2 (%)	3 (%)	4 (%)	5 (%)
Latin America									
Nicaragua, Managua (E)	IBT with slum discount	97.0	95.0	97.7	93.0	97.0	98.0	97.0	98.0
Venezuela, R. B. de, Merida (E)	IBT with slum discount	100.0	100.0	100.0	100.0	100.0	100.0	100.0	100.0
Panama, Panama City and Colon (E)	IBT with slum and pensioner discount	98.0	96.5	99.7	98.0	95.0	99.0	100.0	100.0
Colombia									
Colombia, Bogota (E)	Geographically defined tariffs with IBTs	92.0	98.1	88.0	98.1	98.1	97.5	94.3	72.2
Colombia, Bogota (S)	Geographically defined tariffs with IBTs and limited use of means testing	55.9	81.8	38.7	86.2	77.4	64.4	40.5	11.2
Colombia, Urban (E)	Geographically defined tariffs with IBTs	94.6	99.0	91.6	98.9	99.1	98.3	96.0	80.6
Chile (E)	Discounts of 40–70% on lifeline block for means-tested recipients	11.9	18.9	7.2	20.3	17.5	13.3	6.6	1.5
Paraguay									
Paraguay, Urban (E)	Discount for means-tested households (housing characteristics)	4.1	7.3	1.9	10.1	4.6	4.0	0.8	0.8
Paraguay, Urban (S)	IBT with 15 m³ first block	1.7	2.0	1.6	2.0	1.9	1.4	1.8	1.4
Paraguay, Urban (S)	IBT with 5 m³ first block	1.9	3.4	0.9	4.6	2.3	0.6	1.4	0.6
Paraguay, Urban (S)	Discount for households in targeted areas	0.8	1.2	0.5	1.4	1.0	0.4	0.7	0.3

(Table continues on the following page.)

Appendix E.1 (*continued*)

Country, city	Type of subsidy	Total (%)	Poor (%)	Nonpoor (%)	Quintiles				
					1 (%)	2 (%)	3 (%)	4 (%)	5 (%)
Paraguay, Urban (S)	Discount for means-tested households (housing + household characteristics)	1.8	4.1	0.4	3.8	4.4	1.1	0.0	0.0
Argentina									
Argentina (E*)	Average of provincial means-tested subsidy	n/r	24.0	n/r	n/r	n/r	n/r	n/r	n/r
Argentina, Buenos Aires (E*)	Average of provincial means-tested subsidy	n/r	24.3	n/r	n/r	n/r	n/r	n/r	n/r
Argentina (S)	Discount for means-tested households	n/r	44.0	n/r	n/r	n/r	n/r	n/r	n/r
Eastern Europe and Central Asia									
Croatia (E)	Uniform volumetric tariff	92.4	83.7	97.0	76.5	90.5	95.5	96.7	98.5
Sub-Saharan Africa									
Cape Verde									
Cape Verde (E)	IBT with 7 m³ first block	26.5	10.3	37.3	6.6	14.1	23.5	35.6	52.8
Cape Verde (S)	VDT with 7 m³ threshold	21.4	9.8	n/r	n/r	n/r	n/r	n/r	n/r
Cape Verde (S)	Means-tested discount on 10 m³	1.1	2.0	n/r	n/r	n/r	n/r	n/r	n/r
South Asia									
Nepal									
Kathmandu (E)	IBT with 10 m³ first block	64.3	47.2	75.8	41.6	54.5	70.9	75.7	82.6

228

Kathmandu (E)	Subsidy on public taps	18.3	28.5	11.6	31.7	23.1	17.5	10.5	6.4
Kathmandu (S)	Uniform volumetric tariff	64.3	47.2	75.8	41.6	54.5	70.9	75.7	82.6
Kathmandu (S)	IBT with 7 m³ first block	64.3	47.2	75.8	41.6	54.5	70.9	75.7	82.6
Kathmandu (S)	Discount for slums (revenue neutral)	64.3	47.2	75.8	41.6	54.5	70.9	75.7	82.6
Kathmandu (S)	Discount for means-tested households	64.9	47.9	76.4	42.4	56.2	71.2	76.0	82.6
Kathmandu (S)	Discount for slums (all others pay cost recovery price)	37.1	23.5	46.4	21.5	26.4	38.2	43.1	58.9
Kathmandu (S)	Discount for means-tested households (all others pay cost recovery)	34.3	26.9	39.2	24.5	30.6	37.9	38.5	41.5

India

Bangalore (E)	IBT with 25 m³ first block	53.8	39.5	63.2	31.8	47.2	56.6	63.8	69.3
Bangalore (E)	Subsidy on public taps	20.5	39.1	8.0	50.5	27.1	14.8	6.9	2.4
Bangalore (S)	Uniform volumetric tariff	54.3	40.0	63.8	31.8	48.1	56.9	64.5	69.9
Bangalore (S)	IBT with 18 m³ first block	54.3	40.0	63.8	31.8	48.1	56.9	64.5	69.9
Bangalore (S)	Discounts for households in poor areas	54.3	40.0	63.8	31.8	48.1	56.9	64.5	69.9
Bangalore (S)	Discount for means-tested households	54.3	40.0	63.8	31.8	48.1	56.9	64.5	69.9
Bangalore (S)	IBT with 6 m³ first block	54.3	40.0	63.8	31.8	48.1	56.9	64.5	69.9
Sri Lanka (E)	IBT	36.4	30.5	40.4	27.2	33.8	41.3	37.8	42.0

Source: Authors' elaboration based on data from sources cited in appendix A.

Note: E = existing subsidy; S = simulation; poor = poorest 40%; IBT = increasing block tariff; VDT = volume differentiated tariff; m = meter.

*Assumes all eligible households are receiving the subsidy.

Appendix E.2 Percentage of Connected Households Receiving Subsidy

Country, city	Type of subsidy	Total (%)	Poor (%)	Nonpoor (%)	1 (%)	2 (%)	3 (%)	4 (%)	5 (%)
						Quintiles			
Latin America									
Nicaragua, Managua (E)	IBT with slum discount	100.0	100.0	100.0	100.0	100.0	100.0	100.0	100.0
Venezuela, R. B. de, Merida (E)	IBT with slum discount	100.0	100.0	100.0	100.0	100.0	100.0	100.0	100.0
Panama, Panama City and Colon (E)	IBT with slum and pensioner discount	100.0	100.0	100.0	100.0	100.0	100.0	100.0	100.0
Colombia									
Colombia, Bogota (E)	Geographically defined tariffs with IBTs	92.5	99.5	88.2	100.5	99.0	97.7	94.6	72.4
Colombia, Bogota (S)	Geographically defined tariffs with IBTs and limited use of means testing	56.2	83.0	38.8	88.2	78.1	64.6	40.7	11.2
Colombia, Urban (E)	Geographically defined tariffs with IBTs	96.3	101.2	93.1	101.4	101.0	100.1	97.2	82.0
Chile (E)	Discounts of 40–70% on lifeline block for means-tested recipients	13.3	23.2	7.6	26.0	20.4	14.7	7.1	1.6
Paraguay									
Paraguay, Urban (E)	Discount for means-tested households (housing characteristics)	7.3	13.8	3.0	19.1	8.6	6.8	1.2	1.0
Paraguay, Urban (S)	IBT with 15 m^3 first block	2.8	3.5	2.3	3.8	3.2	2.5	2.6	1.9
Paraguay, Urban (S)	IBT with 5 m^3 first block	3.3	6.3	1.2	9.1	3.6	1.0	2.0	0.7

		Col1	Col2	Col3	Col4	Col5	Col6	Col7	Col8
Paraguay, Urban (S)	Discount for households in targeted areas	1.3	2.3	0.7	2.8	1.8	0.7	1.0	0.4
Paraguay, Urban (S)	Discount for means-tested households (housing + household characteristics)	3.5	7.7	0.6	7.2	8.3	1.9	0.0	0.0
Argentina									
Argentina (E*)	Average of provincial means-tested subsidy	n/r	27.0	n/r	n/r	n/r	n/r	n/r	n/r
Argentina, Buenos Aires (E*)	Average of provincial means-tested subsidy	n/r	32.0	n/r	n/r	n/r	n/r	n/r	n/r
Argentina (S)	Discount for means-tested households	n/r	62.0	n/r	n/r	n/r	n/r	n/r	n/r
Eastern Europe and Central Asia									
Croatia (E)	Uniform volumetric tariff	100.0	100.0	100.0	100.0	100.0	100.0	100.0	100.0
Sub-Saharan Africa									
Cape Verde									
Cape Verde (E)	IBT with 7 m³ first block	100.0	100.0	100.0	100.0	100.0	100.0	100.0	100.0
Cape Verde (S)	VDT with 7 m³ threshold	80.6	94.9	n/r	n/r	n/r	n/r	n/r	n/r
Cape Verde (S)	Means-tested discount on 10 m³	4.2	19.7	n/r	n/r	n/r	n/r	n/r	n/r
South Asia									
Nepal									
Nepal, Kathmandu (E)	IBT with 10 m³ first block	98.3	96.9	98.8	97.4	96.4	99.1	98.3	99.1
Nepal, Kathmandu (E)	Subsidy on public taps	18.3	28.5	11.6	31.7	23.1	17.5	10.5	6.4

(Table continues on the following page.)

Appendix E.2 (*continued*)

Country, city	Type of subsidy	Total (%)	Poor (%)	Nonpoor (%)	Quintiles				
					1 (%)	2 (%)	3 (%)	4 (%)	5 (%)
Nepal, Kathmandu (S)	Uniform volumetric tariff	98.3	96.9	98.8	97.4	96.4	99.1	98.3	99.1
Nepal, Kathmandu (S)	IBT with 7 m³ first block	98.3	96.9	98.8	97.4	96.4	99.1	98.3	99.1
Nepal, Kathmandu (S)	Discount for slums (revenue neutral)	98.3	96.9	98.8	97.4	96.4	99.1	98.3	99.1
Nepal, Kathmandu (S)	Discount for means-tested households	99.2	99.3	99.1	99.4	99.3	99.5	98.7	99.1
Nepal, Kathmandu (S)	Discount for slums (all others pay cost recovery price)	56.7	48.6	60.1	50.3	46.7	53.4	56.0	70.6
Nepal, Kathmandu (S)	Discount for means-tested households (all others pay cost recovery)	52.3	55.8	50.9	57.4	54.0	52.9	50.0	49.8
India									
India, Bangalore (E)	IBT with 25 m³ first block	100.0	100.0	100.0	100.0	100.0	100.0	100.0	100.0
India, Bangalore (E)	Subsidy on public taps	20.5	39.1	8.0	50.5	27.1	14.8	6.9	2.4
India, Bangalore (S)	Uniform volumetric tariff	100.0	100.0	100.0	100.0	100.0	100.0	100.0	100.0
India, Bangalore (S)	IBT with 18 m³ first block	100.0	100.0	100.0	100.0	100.0	100.0	100.0	100.0
India, Bangalore (S)	Discounts for households in poor areas	100.0	100.0	100.0	100.0	100.0	100.0	100.0	100.0
India, Bangalore (S)	Discount for means-tested households	100.0	100.0	100.0	100.0	100.0	100.0	100.0	100.0
India, Bangalore (S)	IBT with 6 m³ first block	100.0	100.0	100.0	100.0	100.0	100.0	100.0	100.0
Sri Lanka (E)	IBT	97.4	97.8	97.1	98.0	97.6	97.4	95.2	98.7

Source: Authors' elaboration based on data from sources cited in appendix A.

Note: E = existing subsidy; S = simulation; poor = poorest 40%; IBT = increasing block tariff; VDT = volume differentiated tariff; m = meter.

*Assumes all eligible households are receiving the subsidy.

Appendix E.3 Average Value of Subsidy per Household, as Average Percentage of Household Income

Country, city	Type of subsidy	Total (%)	Poor (%)	Nonpoor (%)	Quintiles				
					1 (%)	2 (%)	3 (%)	4 (%)	5 (%)
Latin America									
Colombia									
Colombia, Bogota (E)	Geographically defined tariffs with IBTs	1.8	3.7	0.6	5.6	1.8	1.0	0.5	0.2
Colombia, Bogota (S)	Geographically defined tariffs with IBTs and limited use of means testing	1.8	3.7	0.6	5.6	1.8	1.0	0.5	0.2
Colombia, Urban (E)	Geographically defined tariffs with IBTs	1.9	3.9	0.6	6.0	1.8	1.1	0.6	0.2
Chile (E)	Discounts of 40–70% on lifeline block for means-tested recipients	1.5	3.5	0.6	5.0	2.0	0.9	1.0	0.0
Eastern Europe and Central Asia									
Croatia (E)	Uniform volumetric tariff	0.9	1.2	0.8	1.4	1.1	1.0	0.9	0.7
Sub-Saharan Africa									
Cape Verde (E)	IBT with 7 m³ first block	1.0	2.0	1.0	2.5	1.8	1.7	1.5	0.7
South Asia									
Nepal									
Nepal, Kathmandu (E)	IBT with 10 m³ first block	2.6	4.2	2.3	4.1	4.3	3.8	3.2	1.7
Nepal, Kathmandu (E)	Subsidy on public taps	0.1	0.3	0.0	0.4	0.2	0.1	0.0	0.0

(Table continues on the following page.)

Appendix E.3 *(continued)*

Country, city	Type of subsidy	Total (%)	Poor (%)	Nonpoor (%)	Quintiles				
					1 (%)	2 (%)	3 (%)	4 (%)	5 (%)
Nepal, Kathmandu (S)	Uniform volumetric tariff	2.6	4.1	2.4	3.9	4.4	3.7	3.1	1.7
Nepal, Kathmandu (S)	IBT with 7 m³ first block	2.6	4.2	2.3	4.1	4.3	3.8	3.2	1.7
Nepal, Kathmandu (S)	Discount for slums (revenue neutral)	2.6	4.5	2.3	4.7	4.4	3.9	3.1	1.6
Nepal, Kathmandu (S)	Discount for means-tested households	2.6	4.9	2.2	5.3	4.6	4.0	3.1	1.5
Nepal, Kathmandu (S)	Discount for slums (all others pay cost recovery price)	0.8	1.7	0.7	2.1	1.3	1.1	0.8	0.5
Nepal, Kathmandu (S)	Discount for means-tested households (all others pay cost recovery)	1.1	3.0	0.8	3.6	2.4	1.9	1.1	0.5
India									
India, Bangalore (E)	IBT with 25 m³ first block	4.8	4.9	4.7	4.5	5.3	5.1	4.9	4.1
India, Bangalore (E)	Subsidy on public taps	0.6	1.3	0.1	2.0	0.6	0.2	0.1	0.0
India, Bangalore (S)	Uniform volumetric tariff	4.7	4.7	4.7	4.3	5.0	5.0	4.8	4.3
India, Bangalore (S)	IBT with 18 m³ first block	4.7	4.9	4.6	4.5	5.2	5.0	4.8	4.0
India, Bangalore (S)	Discounts for households in poor areas	4.8	5.0	4.7	4.7	5.3	5.1	4.9	4.1
India, Bangalore (S)	Discount for means-tested households	4.7	4.9	4.7	4.5	5.2	5.1	4.9	4.1
India, Bangalore (S)	IBT with 6 m³ first block	0.7	0.8	0.6	0.9	0.8	0.7	0.7	0.5
Sri Lanka (E)	IBT	2.2	3.4	1.8	4.0	2.9	2.3	2.0	1.4

Source: Authors' elaboration based on data from sources cited in appendix A.

Note: E = existing subsidy; S = simulation; poor = poorest 40%; IBT = increasing block tariff; VDT = volume differentiated tariff; m = meter.

*Assumes all eligible households are receiving the subsidy.

Appendix E.4 Average Value of Subsidy per Household in US$

Country, city	Type of subsidy	Total	Poor	Nonpoor	Quintiles				
					1	2	3	4	5
Latin America									
Nicaragua, Managua (E)	IBT with slum discount	8.08	9.66	7.03	7.28	12.04	7.75	7.20	6.14
Venezuela, R. B. de, Merida (E)	IBT with slum discount	2.72	2.97	2.56	2.72	3.21	2.85	3.19	1.64
Panama, Panama City and Colon (E)	IBT with slum and pensioner discount	10.88	10.19	11.34	11.13	9.25	10.24	11.03	12.75
Colombia									
Colombia, Bogota (E)	Geographically defined tariffs with IBTs	3.48	4.19	3.00	4.23	4.16	3.71	3.09	2.20
Colombia, Bogota (S)	Geographically defined tariffs with IBTs and limited use of means testing	3.13	3.12	3.13	3.08	3.17	3.07	3.04	3.28
Colombia, Urban (E)	Geographically defined tariffs with IBTs	2.72	3.03	2.52	2.99	3.07	2.94	2.53	2.09
Chile (E)	Discounts of 40–70% on lifeline block for means-tested recipients	7.10	6.36	7.59	6.30	6.43	7.16	8.61	6.98
Paraguay									
Paraguay, Urban (E)	Discount for means-tested households (housing characteristics)	3.04	3.37	2.81	3.04	3.70	3.79	1.59	3.07
Paraguay, Urban (S)	IBT with 15 m³ first block	7.07	7.04	7.09	6.36	7.73	7.92	6.95	6.41
Paraguay, Urban (S)	IBT with 5 m³ first block	2.30	2.29	2.31	2.07	2.51	2.57	2.26	2.08
Paraguay, Urban (S)	Discount for households in targeted areas	4.41	4.39	4.42	3.97	4.82	4.94	4.33	4.00
Paraguay, Urban (S)	Discount for means-tested households (housing + household characteristics)	1.14	2.19	0.44	1.98	2.40	1.33	0.00	0.00

(Table continues on the following page.)

Appendix E.4 (*continued*)

Country, city	Type of subsidy	Total	Poor	Nonpoor	Quintiles				
					1	2	3	4	5
Eastern Europe and Central Asia									
Croatia (E)	Uniform volumetric tariff	7.45	7.38	7.47	6.85	7.80	7.69	7.47	7.31
Sub-Saharan Africa									
Cape Verde									
Cape Verde (E)	IBT with 7 m³ first block	6.52	4.18	6.95	4.01	4.26	5.42	6.89	7.67
Cape Verde (S)	VDT with 7 m³ threshold	4.69	3.66	5.38	n/r	n/r	n/r	n/r	n/r
Cape Verde (S)	Means-tested discount on 10 m³	2.58	1.97	2.98	n/r	n/r	n/r	n/r	n/r
South Asia									
Nepal									
Nepal, Kathmandu (E)	IBT with 10 m³ first block	8.88	6.75	9.76	5.81	7.70	7.46	9.00	12.66
Nepal, Kathmandu (E)	Subsidy on public taps	0.71	0.69	0.72	0.67	0.77	0.70	0.47	1.09
Nepal, Kathmandu (S)	Uniform volumetric tariff	8.88	6.63	9.81	5.45	7.84	7.32	8.88	13.05
Nepal, Kathmandu (S)	IBT with 7 m³ first block	8.88	6.75	9.76	5.81	7.70	7.46	9.00	12.66
Nepal, Kathmandu (S)	Discount for slums (revenue neutral)	8.88	7.24	9.56	6.58	7.88	7.59	8.80	12.16

Nepal, Kathmandu (S)	Discount for means-tested households	8.79	7.71	9.24	7.28	8.09	7.77	8.62	11.22
Nepal, Kathmandu (S)	Discount for slums (all others pay cost recovery price)	4.71	5.44	4.45	5.61	4.95	4.09	3.92	5.10
Nepal, Kathmandu (S)	Discount for means-tested households (all others pay cost recovery)	7.31	8.32	6.84	8.62	7.88	6.76	6.03	7.41
India									
India, Bangalore (E)	IBT with 25 m³ first block	15.74	14.22	16.38	14.07	14.38	15.08	15.51	18.16
India, Bangalore (E)	Subsidy on public taps	3.74	4.19	2.30	4.62	3.36	2.31	2.30	1.59
India, Bangalore (S)	Uniform volumetric tariff	15.56	13.42	16.44	13.28	13.54	14.82	15.07	18.94
India, Bangalore (S)	IBT with 18 m³ first block	15.46	14.02	16.05	14.06	14.03	14.88	15.21	17.74
India, Bangalore (S)	Discounts for households in poor areas	15.68	14.37	16.22	14.72	14.21	15.12	15.39	17.84
India, Bangalore (S)	Discount for means-tested households	15.50	13.90	16.15	14.02	13.88	14.93	15.35	17.83
India, Bangalore (S)	IBT with 6 m³ first block	2.18	2.38	2.07	2.81	2.17	2.14	2.08	2.04
Sri Lanka (E)	IBT	5.42	5.39	5.43	5.35	5.42	5.50	5.46	5.33

Source: Authors' elaboration based on data from sources cited in appendix A.

Note: E = existing subsidy; S = simulation; poor = poorest 40%; IBT = increasing block tariff; VDT = volume differentiated tariff; m = meter.

*Assumes all eligible households are receiving the subsidy.

Appendix E.5 Percentage of Subsidy Pool Going to Each Quintile

		Total value of the subsidy (US$)	Poor (%)	Nonpoor (%)	Quintiles				
Country, city	Type of subsidy				1 (%)	2 (%)	3 (%)	4 (%)	5 (%)
Latin America									
Nicaragua, Managua (E)	IBT with slum discount	1,334,525	47.2	52.8	17.3	29.9	19.5	17.9	15.4
Venezuela, R. B. de, Merida (E)	IBT with slum discount	94,304	43.6	56.4	20.0	23.6	20.9	23.5	12.0
Panama, Panama City and Colon (E)	IBT with slum and pensioner discount	2,422,508	36.7	63.3	20.4	16.3	18.9	20.6	23.8
Colombia									
Colombia, Bogota (E)	Geographically defined tariffs with IBTs	4,734,116	43.6	56.4	19.7	23.9	23.6	20.9	11.8
Colombia, Bogota (S)	Geographically defined tariffs with IBTs and limited use of means testing	2,434,489	52.4	47.6	24.5	27.9	25.1	17.3	5.1
Colombia, Urban (E)	Geographically defined tariffs with IBTs	7,693,262	40.3	59.7	15.7	24.6	27.7	26.3	5.7
Chile (E)	Discounts of 40–70% on lifeline block for means-tested recipients	9,255	65.0	35.0	36.0	29.0	22.0	11.0	2.0
Paraguay									
Paraguay, Urban (E)	Discount for means-tested households (housing characteristics)	83,249	65.5	34.4	42.8	22.7	24.2	4.8	5.4
Paraguay, Urban (S)	IBT with 15 m³ first block	83,335	38.5	61.5	18.1	20.4	17.9	23.7	19.9
Paraguay, Urban (S)	IBT with 5 m³ first block	27,080	66.8	33.1	40.9	25.9	7.3	17.9	7.9

Paraguay, Urban (S)	Discount for households in targeted areas	21,867	56.6	43.4	30.4	26.2	12.6	20.9	9.9
Paraguay, Urban (S)	Discount for means-tested households (housing + household characteristics)	23,872	85.4	14.6	36.6	48.8	14.6	0.0	0.0
Argentina									
Argentina (E*)	Average of provincial means-tested subsidy	46,884,000	49.0	51.0	37.0	12.0	14.0	16.0	21.0
Argentina, Buenos Aires (E*)	Average of provincial means-tested subsidy	11,239,721	43.0	57.0	34.0	9.0	14.0	17.0	26.0
Argentina (S)	Discount for means-tested households	21,300,000	52.0	48.0	27.0	25.0	19.0	17.0	12.0
Eastern Europe and Central Asia									
Croatia (E)	Uniform volumetric tariff	17,062	28.2	71.8	11.5	16.7	20.9	23.2	27.7
Sub-Saharan Africa									
Cape Verde									
Cape Verde (E)	IBT with 7 m³ first block	164,607	10.7	89.3	3.4	7.2	15.3	28.6	45.5
Cape Verde (S)	VDT with 7 m³ threshold	95,448	14.3	85.7	n/r	n/r	n/r	n/r	n/r
Cape Verde (S)	Means-tested discount on 10 m³	2,736	55.7	44.3	n/r	n/r	n/r	n/r	n/r
South Asia									
Nepal									
Nepal, Kathmandu (E)	IBT with 10 m³ first block	8,570	22.3	77.7	10.4	11.9	19.2	24.1	34.4
Nepal, Kathmandu (E)	Subsidy on public taps	194	61.5	38.6	39.8	21.7	19.5	7.7	11.4

(Table continues on the following page.)

Appendix E.5 (*continued*)

Country, city	Type of subsidy	Total value of the subsidy (US$)	Poor (%)	Nonpoor (%)	Quintiles				
					1 (%)	2 (%)	3 (%)	4 (%)	5 (%)
Nepal, Kathmandu (S)	Uniform volumetric tariff	8,559	21.8	78.1	9.7	12.1	18.8	23.8	35.5
Nepal, Kathmandu (S)	IBT with 7 m³ first block	8,569	22.3	77.7	10.4	11.9	19.2	24.1	34.4
Nepal, Kathmandu (S)	Discount for slums (revenue neutral)	8,568	23.9	76.1	11.8	12.1	19.4	23.6	33.0
Nepal, Kathmandu (S)	Discount for means-tested households	8,559	26.1	73.9	13.3	12.9	20.2	23.3	30.5
Nepal, Kathmandu (S)	Discount for slums (all others pay cost recovery price)	2,624	29.5	70.5	17.3	12.2	18.2	19.7	32.7
Nepal, Kathmandu (S)	Discount for means-tested households (all others pay cost recovery)	3,758	36.1	63.9	20.6	15.5	21.4	18.8	23.7
India									
India, Bangalore (E)	IBT with 25 m³ first block	24,591	26.5	73.5	10.5	16.0	20.1	23.3	30.0
India, Bangalore (E)	Subsidy on public taps	1,786	85.6	14.4	62.0	23.5	9.0	4.4	1.0
India, Bangalore (S)	Uniform volumetric tariff	24,504	25.4	74.6	10.0	15.4	20.0	23.0	31.6
India, Bangalore (S)	IBT with 18 m³ first block	24,358	26.7	73.3	10.6	16.1	20.2	23.4	29.8
India, Bangalore (S)	Discounts for households in poor areas	24,709	27.0	73.0	11.0	16.0	20.2	23.3	29.5
India, Bangalore (S)	Discount for means-tested households	24,411	26.4	73.6	10.6	15.8	20.2	23.5	29.9
India, Bangalore (S)	IBT with 6 m³ first block	3,421	32.4	67.6	14.8	17.6	20.6	22.7	24.3
Sri Lanka (E)	IBT	3,585	33.4	66.6	14.8	18.6	23.0	21.0	22.6

Source: Authors' elaboration based on data from sources cited in appendix A.

Note: E = existing subsidy; S = simulation; poor = poorest 40%; IBT = increasing block tariff; VDT = volume differentiated tariff; m = meter.

Appendix E.6 Targeting Indicators: Water Consumption Subsidies

Country, city	Type of subsidy	Benefit targeting performance indicator (Ω)	Error of inclusion (%)	Error of exclusion (%)	Income Gini	Subsidy Quasi-Gini
Latin America						
Nicaragua, Managua (E)	IBT with slum discount	1.18	52.8	5.0	0.45	n/r
Venezuela, R. B. de, Merida (E)	IBT with slum discount	1.09	56.4	0.0	0.45	0.24
Panama, Panama City and Colon (E)	IBT with slum and pensioner discount	0.92	63.3	3.5	n/r	n/r
Colombia						
Colombia, Bogota (E)	Geographically defined tariffs with IBTs	1.09	49.2	1.9	n/r	(0.04)
Colombia, Bogota (S)	Geographically defined tariffs with IBTs and limited use of means testing	1.31	22.6	19.0	n/r	(0.16)
Colombia, Urban (E)	Geographically defined tariffs with IBTs	0.95	51.1	1.0	n/r	0.11
Chile (E)	Discounts of 40–70% on lifeline block for means-tested recipients	1.50	32.0	78.0	n/r	n/r
Paraguay						
Paraguay, Urban (E)	Discount for means-tested households (housing characteristics)	1.64	34.4	93.1	n/r	n/r
Paraguay, Urban (S)	IBT with 15 m³ first block	0.96	8.0	98.1	n/r	n/r
Paraguay, Urban (S)	IBT with 5 m³ first block	1.67	33.1	96.6	n/r	n/r
Paraguay, Urban (S)	Discount for households in targeted areas	1.42	43.4	98.8	n/r	n/r
Paraguay, Urban (S)	Discount for means-tested households (housing + household characteristics)	2.14	14.6	96.0	n/r	n/r

(Table continues on the following page.)

241

Appendix E.6 (continued)

Country, city	Type of subsidy	Benefit targeting performance indicator (Ω)	Error of inclusion (%)	Error of exclusion (%)	Income Gini	Subsidy Quasi-Gini
Argentina						
Argentina (E*)	Average of provincial means-tested subsidy	1.23	44.0	76.0	0.44	(0.15)
Argentina, Buenos Aires (E*)	Average of provincial means-tested subsidy	1.08	10.0	n/r	n/r	(0.63)
Argentina (S)	Discount for means-tested households	1.30	43.0	56.0	0.44	(0.15)
Eastern Europe and Central Asia						
Croatia (E)	Uniform volumetric tariff	0.71	68.7	16.3	0.25	0.16
Sub-Saharan Africa						
Cape Verde						
Cape Verde (E)	IBT with 7 m³ first block	0.24	37.3	89.7	n/r	n/r
Cape Verde (S)	VDT with 7 m³ threshold	0.36	n/r	90.2	n/r	n/r
Cape Verde (S)	Means-tested discount on 10 m³	1.39	n/r	98.0	n/r	n/r
South Asia						
Nepal						
Nepal, Kathmandu (E)	IBT with 10 m³ first block	0.56	71.0	53.0	0.45	0.24
Nepal, Kathmandu (E)	Subsidy on public taps	1.54	38.0	72.0	0.45	(0.30)
Nepal, Kathmandu (S)	Uniform volumetric tariff	0.55	71.0	53.0	0.45	0.25
Nepal, Kathmandu (S)	IBT with 7 m³ first block	0.56	71.0	53.0	0.45	0.24

Nepal, Kathmandu (S)	Discount for slums (revenue neutral)	0.60	71.0	53.0	0.45	0.22
Nepal, Kathmandu (S)	Discount for means-tested households	0.65	70.2	52.1	0.45	0.18
Nepal, Kathmandu (S)	Discount for slums (all others pay cost recovery price)	0.74	74.5	76.5	0.45	0.17
Nepal, Kathmandu (S)	Discount for means-tested households (all others pay cost recovery)	0.90	68.3	73.1	0.45	0.04
India						
India, Bangalore (E)	IBT with 25 m^3 first block	0.66	71.0	60.5	0.32	n/r
India, Bangalore (E)	Subsidy on public taps	2.14	23.0	61.0	0.32	(0.30)
India, Bangalore (S)	Uniform volumetric tariff	0.64	70.6	60.0	0.32	0.16
India, Bangalore (S)	IBT with 18 m^3 first block	0.67	70.6	60.0	0.32	0.14
India, Bangalore (S)	Discounts for households in poor areas	0.67	70.6	60.0	0.32	0.14
India, Bangalore (S)	Discount for means-tested households	0.66	70.6	60.0	0.32	0.14
India, Bangalore (S)	IBT with 6 m^3 first block	0.81	70.6	60.0	0.32	(0.13)
Sri Lanka (E)	IBT	0.83	66.5	69.5	0.19	0.07

Source: Authors' elaboration based on data from sources cited in appendix A.

Note: E = existing subsidy; S = simulation; poor = poorest 40%; IBT = increasing block tariff; VDT = volume differentiated tariff; n/a = not applicable; n/r = not reported; HH = household; PT = public taps.

*Assumes all eligible households are receiving the subsidy.

Appendix F: Water: Connection Subsidy Data

Appendix F.1 Percentage of Households Receiving Subsidy

Country, city	Type of subsidy	Total (%)	Poor (%)	Nonpoor (%)	Quintiles				
					1 (%)	2 (%)	3 (%)	4 (%)	5 (%)
Latin America									
Paraguay, Urban	Geographic targeting	25.5	25.1	25.7	26.0	24.3	29.6	26.4	21.2
Paraguay, Urban	Means tested	27.3	34.8	22.3	39.7	29.9	36.1	20.6	10.3
Argentina	Water: means tested	n/r	10.0	n/r	n/r	n/r	n/r	n/r	n/r
Argentina	Sewer: means tested	n/r	40.0	n/r	n/r	n/r	n/r	n/r	n/r
South Asia									
Nepal, Kathmandu	Geographic targeting	34.5	51.7	22.9	57.3	43.4	28.5	23.0	16.7
Nepal, Kathmandu	Means tested	24.8	51.7	6.6	57.3	43.4	8.4	6.6	4.6
India, Bangalore	Geographic targeting	26.0	40.7	16.1	50.6	30.9	23.4	15.5	9.4
India, Bangalore	Means tested	24.1	46.7	9.0	58.9	34.5	17.4	7.1	9.4

Source: Authors' elaboration based on data from sources cited in appendix A.

Note: n/r = not reported.

Appendix F.2 Percentage of Unconnected Households Receiving Subsidy

Country, city	Type of subsidy	Total (%)	Poor (%)	Nonpoor (%)	Quintiles				
					1 (%)	2 (%)	3 (%)	4 (%)	5 (%)
Latin America									
Paraguay, Urban	Geographic targeting	76.0	58.0	87.0	55.0	62.0	72.0	87.0	103.0
Paraguay, Urban	Means tested	72.0	80.0	68.0	84.0	75.0	87.0	68.0	47.0
Argentina	Water: means tested	n/r	100.0	n/r	n/r	n/r	n/r	n/r	n/r
Argentina	Sewer: means tested	n/r	100.0	n/r	n/r	n/r	n/r	n/r	n/r
South Asia									
Nepal, Kathmandu	Geographic targeting	100.0	100.0	100.0	100.0	100.0	100.0	100.0	100.0
Nepal, Kathmandu	Means tested	71.8	100.0	28.8	100.0	100.0	29.5	28.6	27.7
India, Bangalore	Geographic targeting	56.1	67.4	43.8	74.2	58.5	54.0	42.9	30.7
India, Bangalore	Means tested	52.0	77.2	24.5	86.4	65.4	40.1	19.5	30.7

Source: Authors' elaboration based on data from sources cited in appendix A.
Note: n/r = not reported.

Appendix F.3 Average Value of Subsidy per Household, as Average Percentage of Household Income

Country, city	Type of subsidy	Total (%)	Poor (%)	Nonpoor (%)	Quintiles				
					1 (%)	2 (%)	3 (%)	4 (%)	5 (%)
South Asia									
Nepal, Kathmandu	Geographic targeting	0.8	3.7	0.4	5.2	2.4	1.1	0.6	0.1
Nepal, Kathmandu	Means tested	0.8	5.2	0.2	7.2	3.3	0.5	0.2	0.1
India, Bangalore	Geographic targeting	1.3	2.4	0.5	3.3	1.5	0.9	0.5	0.2
India, Bangalore	Means tested	1.3	2.8	0.3	3.8	1.7	0.6	0.2	0.1

Source: Authors' elaboration based on data from sources cited in appendix A.

Appendix F.4 Average Value of Subsidy per Household in US$

| Country, city | Type of subsidy | Total | Poor | Nonpoor | Quintiles | | | | |
					1	2	3	4	5
Latin America									
Paraguay, Urban	Geographic targeting	84.00	84.00	84.00	84.00	84.00	84.00	84.00	84.00
Paraguay, Urban	Means tested	84.00	84.00	84.00	84.00	84.00	84.00	84.00	84.00
Argentina	Water: means tested	135.50	135.50	135.50	135.50	135.50	135.50	135.50	135.50
Argentina	Sewer: means tested	203.30	203.30	203.30	203.30	203.30	203.30	203.30	203.30
South Asia									
Nepal, Kathmandu	Geographic targeting	5.36	5.36	5.36	5.36	5.36	5.36	5.36	5.36
Nepal, Kathmandu	Means tested	7.51	7.51	7.51	7.51	7.51	7.51	7.51	7.51
India, Bangalore	Geographic targeting	6.26	6.26	6.26	6.26	6.26	6.26	6.26	6.26
India, Bangalore	Means tested	6.26	6.26	6.26	6.26	6.26	6.26	6.26	6.26

Source: Authors' elaboration based on data from sources cited in appendix A.

Appendix F.5 Percentage of Subsidy Pool Going to Each Quintile

| | | Total value of the | Poor | Nonpoor | | | Quintiles | | |
Country, city	Type of subsidy	subsidy (US$)	(%)	(%)	1 (%)	2 (%)	3 (%)	4 (%)	5 (%)
Latin America									
Paraguay, Urban	Geographic targeting	10,081,092	32.9	67.1	15.3	17.6	25.0	22.7	19.4
Paraguay, Urban	Means tested	10,036,152	43.9	56.1	22.8	21.1	29.7	17.3	9.1
Argentina	Water: means tested	21,300,000	74.0	26.0	49.0	25.0	14.0	9.0	3.0
Argentina	Sewer: Means Tested	21,300,000	62.0	38.0	37.0	25.0	22.0	11.0	5.0
South Asia									
Nepal, Kathmandu	Geographic targeting	2,775	60.4	39.6	40.2	20.3	17.0	13.5	9.1
Nepal, Kathmandu	Means tested	2,790	84.1	15.9	55.9	28.2	7.0	5.4	3.5
India, Bangalore	Geographic targeting	4,713	62.7	37.3	39.0	23.7	18.0	11.9	7.3
India, Bangalore	Means tested	4,369	77.5	22.5	48.9	28.6	14.4	5.9	2.1

Source: Authors' elaboration based on data from sources cited in appendix A.

Appendix F.6 Targeting Indicators: Connection Subsidies

Country, city	Type of subsidy	Benefit targeting performance indicator (Ω)	Error of inclusion (%)	Error of exclusion (%)	Income Gini	Subsidy Quasi-Gini
Latin America						
Paraguay, Urban	Geographic targeting	0.82	67.1	75.1	n/r	n/r
Paraguay, Urban	Means tested	1.10	56.1	65.9	n/r	n/r
Argentina	Water: means tested	1.85	28.0	90.0	0.44	(0.28)
Argentina	Sewer: means tested	1.55	42.0	60.0	0.44	(0.16)
South Asia						
Nepal, Kathmandu	Geographic targeting	1.51	39.6	48.3	0.45	(0.28)
Nepal, Kathmandu	Means tested	2.10	15.9	48.3	0.45	(0.51)
India, Bangalore	Geographic targeting	1.57	37.3	59.3	0.32	(0.32)
India, Bangalore	Means tested	1.94	22.5	53.3	0.32	(0.48)

Source: Authors' elaboration based on data from sources cited in appendix A.

Note: Poor = Poorest 40%. *Other:* n/a = not applicable; n/r = not reported.

Appendix G: Burden Limit: Consumption Subsidy Data

Appendix G.1 Percentage of Households Receiving Subsidy

Country, city	Type of subsidy	Total (%)	Poor (%)	Nonpoor (%)	Quintiles				
					1 (%)	2 (%)	3 (%)	4 (%)	5 (%)
Latvia, Riga (S)	Income support—burden limit at 15%	90.8	91.0	90.6	88.4	93.4	93.1	93.3	85.8
Latvia, Riga (S)	Income support—burden limit at 30%	59.9	62.2	58.5	61.1	63.3	63.0	61.3	51.6
Latvia, Riga (S)	Income support—burden limit at 45%	34.1	32.4	35.1	30.9	33.9	34.3	39.9	31.3

Source: Authors' elaboration based on data from sources cited in appendix A.

Appendix G.2 Percentage of Connected Households Receiving Subsidy

Country, city	Type of subsidy	Total (%)	Poor (%)	Nonpoor (%)	Quintiles				
					1 (%)	2 (%)	3 (%)	4 (%)	5 (%)
Latvia, Riga (S)	Income support—burden limit at 15%	91.9	92.7	91.4	90.9	94.4	94.1	94.0	86.3
Latvia, Riga (S)	Income support—burden limit at 30%	60.6	63.4	59.0	62.8	64.0	63.7	61.8	51.9
Latvia, Riga (S)	Income support—burden limit at 45%	34.5	33.0	35.4	31.7	34.3	34.7	40.2	31.5

Source: Authors' elaboration based on data from sources cited in appendix A.

Appendix G.3 Average Value of Subsidy per Household, as Average Percentage of Household Income

Country, city	Type of subsidy	Total (%)	Poor (%)	Nonpoor (%)	Quintiles				
					1 (%)	2 (%)	3 (%)	4 (%)	5 (%)
Latvia, Riga (S)	Income support—burden limit at 15%	36.0	34.5	37.0	37.4	31.9	39.0	33.7	38.2
Latvia, Riga (S)	Income support—burden limit at 30%	35.9	32.2	38.3	36.4	28.3	38.8	32.3	44.4
Latvia, Riga (S)	Income support—burden limit at 45%	43.6	46.7	55.2	54.3	39.4	61.3	40.9	65.4

Source: Authors' elaboration based on data from sources cited in appendix A.

Appendix G.4 Average Value of Subsidy per Household in US$

Country, city	Type of subsidy	Total	Poor	Nonpoor	Quintiles				
					1	2	3	4	5
Latvia, Riga (S)	Income support—burden limit at 15%	51.85	44.78	56.65	40.70	48.70	47.48	53.40	70.22
Latvia, Riga (S)	Income support—burden limit at 30%	38.43	31.11	43.98	28.71	33.52	32.74	38.30	64.06
Latvia, Riga (S)	Income support—burden limit at 45%	35.38	28.58	39.97	28.25	28.90	27.70	28.96	65.91

Source: Authors' elaboration based on data from sources cited in appendix A.

Appendix G.5 Targeting Indicators: Burden Limit

Country, city	Type of subsidy	Benefit targeting performance indicator (Ω)	Error of inclusion (%)	Error of exclusion (%)	Income Gini	Subsidy Quasi-Gini
Latvia, Riga (S)	Income support—burden limit at 15%	0.81	54.0	9.0	0.24	n/r
Latvia, Riga (S)	Income support—burden limit at 30%	0.78	33.9	37.8	0.24	n/r
Latvia, Riga (S)	Income support—burden limit at 45%	0.71	20.1	67.6	0.24	n/r

Source: Authors' elaboration based on data from sources cited in appendix A.
Note: Poor = poorest 40%. *Other:* n/a = not applicable; n/r = not reported.

Appendix H: Increasing Block Tariff Structures

Appendix H.1 Electricity

Utility	Country	Geographic area	Type	Fixed charge (US$)	Min. con. (kWh)	Capacity charge	Peak tariff	No. of blocks	Threshold for first block	Threshold for last block	Price for first block (US$)	Price for last block (US$)
LATIN AMERICA												
EDELAP	Argentina	La Plata	<300 kWh	0.75	0	No	No	1	—	—	0.03	0.03
EDELAP	Argentina	La Plata	>300 kWh	2.73	0	No	No	1	—	—	0.01	0.01
EDEMSA	Argentina	Mendoza	<600 kWh	0.52	0	No	No	1	—	—	0.03	0.03
EDEMSA	Argentina	Mendoza	>600 kWh	4.01	0	No	No	1	—	—	0.02	0.02
EDENOR	Argentina	Buenos Aires	<150 kWh	0.76	0	No	No	1	—	—	0.03	0.03
EDENOR	Argentina	Buenos Aires	>150 kWh	2.78	0	No	No	1	—	—	0.01	0.01
EDESUR	Argentina	Buenos Aires	<150 kWh	0.75	0	No	No	1	—	—	0.03	0.03
EDESUR	Argentina	Buenos Aires	>150 kWh	2.74	0	No	No	1	—	—	0.01	0.01
EDET	Argentina	Tucuman	—	0.63	0	No	No	2	300	300	0.03	0.04
EPESF	Argentina	Santa Fe	<120 kWh	1.56	0	No	No	2	60	60	0.02	0.03
EPESF	Argentina	Santa Fe	>120 kWh	2.03	0	No	No	3	60	120	0.02	0.07
EPESF	Argentina	Santa Fe	Social	1.00	0	No	No	2	60	60	0.01	0.02
Bandeirante	Brazil	Saõ Paulo	Normal	—	0	No	No	1	—	—	0.08	0.08
Bandeirante	Brazil	Saõ Paulo	Social	—	0	No	No	3	30	200	0.03	0.08
CELESC	Brazil	Santa Catarina	Normal	—	0	No	No	1	—	—	0.08	0.08
CELESC	Brazil	Santa Catarina	Social	—	0	No	No	3	30	100	0.03	0.07
CEMIG	Brazil	Minas Gerais	Normal	—	0	No	No	1	—	—	0.07	0.07
CEMIG	Brazil	Minas Gerais	Social	—	0	No	No	3	30	100	0.02	0.06
COELCE	Brazil	Ceara	Normal	—	0	No	No	2	50	50	0.06	0.09
COELCE	Brazil	Ceara	Social	—	0	No	No	4	30	140	0.02	0.09

COPEL	Brazil	Parana	Normal	—	0	No	No	1	—	—	0.09	0.09
COPEL	Brazil	Parana	Social	—	0	No	No	3	30	100	0.03	0.08
COSERN	Brazil	Rio Grande do Norte	Normal	—	0	No	No	1	—	—	0.06	0.06
COSERN	Brazil	Rio Grande do Norte	Social	—	0	No	No	3	30	100	0.02	0.05
CPFL	Brazil	Saõ Paulo	Normal	—	0	No	No	1	—	—	0.07	0.07
CPFL	Brazil	Saõ Paulo	Social	—	0	No	No	4	30	200	0.03	0.07
CGE	Chile	Concepcion	Type 1	1.13	0	No	Yes	2	—	Seasonal	0.08	0.14
CGE	Chile	Concepcion	Type 2	1.13	0	Yes	Yes	1	—	—	0.03	0.03
Chilectra	Chile	Santiago	<10 kW	0.69	0	No	Yes	2	—	Seasonal	0.08	0.14
Chilectra	Chile	Santiago	Load specific	0.69	0	Yes	Yes	1	—	—	0.03	0.03
CONAFE	Chile	Vina del Mar	Single phase	0.99	0	No	Yes	2	—	Seasonal	0.07	0.12
CONAFE	Chile	Vina del Mar	Three phase	0.99	0	Yes	Yes	1	—	—	0.03	0.03
EMEC	Chile	Valparaiso	Single phase	1.43	0	No	Yes	2	—	Seasonal	0.07	0.14
EMEC	Chile	Valparaiso	Three phase	1.43	0	Yes	Yes	1	—	—	0.03	0.03
Emelectric	Chile	Santiago	<10 kW	0.81	0	No	Yes	2	—	Seasonal	0.09	0.16
Emelectric	Chile	Santiago	Load specific	0.81	0	Yes	Yes	1	—	—	0.03	0.03
CODENSA	Colombia	Bogota	Stratum 1	—	0	No	No	2	200	200	0.03	0.07
CODENSA	Colombia	Bogota	Stratum 2	—	0	No	No	2	200	200	0.04	0.07
CODENSA	Colombia	Bogota	Stratum 3	—	0	No	No	2	200	200	0.06	0.07
CODENSA	Colombia	Bogota	Stratum 4	—	0	No	No	1	—	—	0.07	0.07
CODENSA	Colombia	Bogota	Stratum 5	—	0	No	No	1	—	—	0.08	0.08
CODENSA	Colombia	Bogota	Stratum 6	—	0	No	No	1	—	—	0.08	0.08
EPM	Colombia	Medellin	Stratum 1	—	0	No	No	2	200	200	0.03	0.06
EPM	Colombia	Medellin	Stratum 2	—	0	No	No	2	200	200	0.04	0.06

(Table continues on the following page.)

Appendix H.1 (continued)

Utility	Country	Geographic area	Type	Fixed charge (US$)	Min. con. (kWh)	Capacity charge	Peak tariff	No. of blocks	Threshold for first block	Threshold for last block	Price for first block (US$)	Price for last block (US$)
EPM	Colombia	Medellin	Stratum 3	—	0	No	No	2	200	200	0.05	0.06
EPM	Colombia	Medellin	Stratum 4	—	0	No	No	1	—	—	0.06	0.06
EPM	Colombia	Medellin	Stratum 5	—	0	No	No	1	—	—	0.08	0.08
EPM	Colombia	Medellin	Stratum 6	—	0	No	No	1	—	—	0.08	0.08
ESSA	Colombia	Santander	Stratum 1	—	0	No	No	2	200	200	0.04	0.08
ESSA	Colombia	Santander	Stratum 2	—	0	No	No	2	200	200	0.05	0.08
ESSA	Colombia	Santander	Stratum 3	—	0	No	No	2	200	200	0.07	0.08
ESSA	Colombia	Santander	Stratum 4	—	0	No	No	1	—	—	0.08	0.08
ESSA	Colombia	Santander	Stratum 5	—	0	No	No	1	—	—	0.09	0.09
ESSA	Colombia	Santander	Stratum 6	—	0	No	No	1	—	—	0.09	0.09
Centrosur	Ecuador	Centro sur	—	2.73	20	No	No	6	50	300	0.07	0.12
EEASA	Ecuador	Centro norte	—	1.29	0	No	No	6	50	300	0.08	0.13
EEQSA	Ecuador	Quito	—	1.29	0	No	No	7	50	300	0.06	0.09
EERSA	Ecuador	Sur	—	1.26	0	No	No	7	50	300	0.08	0.12
EMELGUR	Ecuador	Duran	—	1.29	0	No	No	5	50	250	0.08	0.10
CAESS	El Salvador	San Salvador	<200 kWh	2.32	0	No	No	1	—	—	0.11	0.11
CAESS	El Salvador	San Salvador	>200 kWh	2.60	0	No	No	1	—	—	0.11	0.11
ENEE (2)	Honduras	National	<500 kWh	1.00	1	No	No	3	100	300	0.05	0.08
ENEE (2)	Honduras	National	>500 kWh	1.00	1	No	No	4	100	500	0.05	0.10
EEGSA (3)	Guatemala	Metro area	Normal	1.00	0	No	No	1	—	—	0.18	0.18
EEGSA (3)	Guatemala	Metro area	Social	1.00	0	No	No	1	—	—	0.09	0.09

DEOCSA (3)	Guatemala	Western region	Normal	1.00	0	No	No	1	—	—	0.15	0.15
DEOCSA (3)	Guatemala	Western region	Social	1.00	0	No	No	1	—	—	0.09	0.09
DEORSA (3)	Guatemala	Eastern region	Normal	1.00	0	No	No	1	—	—	0.15	0.15
DEORSA (3)	Guatemala	Eastern region	Social	1.00	0	No	No	1	—	—	0.09	0.09
LFC (4)	Mexico	Federal District	—	1.00	0	No	No	3	50	100	0.11	0.15
CFE (4)	Mexico	Rest of Country	—	—	0	No	Yes	3	75	125	0.05	0.17
INE (5)	Nicaragua	National	—	—	0	No	No	6	25	1,000	0.04	0.26
ANDE (6)	Paraguay	National	Normal	—	0	No	No	3	50	150	0.05	0.06
ANDE (6)	Paraguay	National	Social	—	0	No	No	2	20	50	0.02	0.03
Electrosureste	Peru	Cusco	—	0.52	0	No	No	3	30	100	0.07	0.10
Electrosurmedio	Peru	—	—	0.52	0	No	No	3	30	100	0.07	0.10
Electronoroeste	Peru	Piura	—	0.52	0	No	No	3	30	100	0.08	0.11
Hidrandina	Peru	Cajamarca	—	0.52	0	No	No	3	30	100	0.08	0.10
Luz del Sur	Peru	Lima	—	0.54	0	No	No	3	30	100	0.07	0.09
UTE	Uruguay	National	Normal	1.82	0	Yes	No	3	100	600	0.04	0.07
UTE	Uruguay	National	Time of day	3.55	0	Yes	Yes	1	—	—	0.03	0.08
CADAFE	Venezuela, R. B. de	National	<200 kWh	1.26	200	No	No	0	—	—	0.00	0.00
CADAFE	Venezuela, R. B. de	National	Normal	1.87	100	No	No	3	300	500	0.06	0.07
CADAFE	Venezuela, R. B. de	National	>500 kWh	29.40	500	No	No	1	—	—	0.08	0.08
ELEVAL	Venezuela, R. B. de	Valencia	<200 kWh	1.79	0	No	No	1	—	—	0.07	0.07
ELEVAL	Venezuela, R. B. de	Valencia	Normal	8.89	200	No	No	2	600	600	0.05	0.09

(Table continues on the following page.)

Appendix H.1 (continued)

Utility	Country	Geographic area	Type	Fixed charge (US$)	Min. con. (kWh)	Capacity charge	Peak tariff	No. of blocks	Threshold for first block	Threshold for last block	Price for first block (US$)	Price for last block (US$)
ELEVAL	Venezuela, R. B. de	Valencia	>600 kWh	10.59	600	No	No	2	—	—	0.06	0.09
ENELVEN	Venezuela, R. B. de	Costa	<300 kWh	1.78	100	No	No	2	300	300	0.03	0.04
ENELVEN	Venezuela, R. B. de	Costa	>300 kWh	3.57	100	No	No	2	600	600	0.04	0.04
S. ASIA/MIDDLE EAST AND N. AFRICA												
CEB	Sri Lanka	—	Domestic	—	—	No	No	5	30	180	0.03	0.16
	Egypt, Arab Rep. of	—	Residential	—	—	No	—	6	100	1,000	0.86	4.29
EAST ASIA AND PACIFIC												
	Brunei Darussalam	National	—	2.00	0	No	No	4	10	170	0.25	0.05
	Cambodia	Phnom Penh	—	—	0	No	No	3	60	101	0.09	0.17
	Cambodia	Siem Reap	—	—	0	No	No	3	20	110	0.22	0.16
	Indonesia	—	450 VA	—	—	Yes	No	3	30	60	0.02	0.04
	Indonesia	—	900 VA	—	—	Yes	No	3	20	60	0.02	0.04
	Indonesia	—	1.300 VA	—	—	Yes	No	3	20	60	0.03	0.04
	Indonesia	—	2.200 VA	—	—	Yes	No	3	20	60	0.04	0.04
	Indonesia	—	2.0–6.6 VA	—	—	Yes	No	1	—	—	0.06	0.06
	Lao PDR	—	—	—	—	No	No	3	50	151	0.02	0.11

Tenaga Nas Berhad	Malaysia		—	—	—	No	No	3	200	1,000	0.06	0.07
SESB	Malaysia		—	—	—	No	No	3	40	200	0.06	0.07
SESCO	Malaysia		—	—	—	No	No	3	100	400	0.09	0.09
	Myanmar			2.00	—	Yes	No	3	50	200	0.40	4.00
	Philippines		Manila	—	10	No	No	3	10	300	0.07	0.13
	Singapore		Low tension	—	—	Yes	Yes	0	—	—	0.16	—
	Thailand		<150 kWh	—	—	Yes	Yes	8	6	400	0.00	0.07
	Thailand		>150 kWh	—	—	Yes	Yes	3	150	400	0.04	0.07
	Vietnam		Residential	—	—	No	Yes	5	100	310	0.04	0.10
AFRICA												
UEDCL	Uganda	National	Domestic	—	0	No	No	2	30	30	0.03	0.10
KPLC	Kenya	National	Domestic	—	0	No	No	4	50	7,000	0.02	0.19
ZESA	Zimbabwe	Harare	Domestic	—	0	No	No	4	50	1,000	0.02	0.05
ZESCO	Zambia	National	Domestic	—	0	No	No	3	300	700	0.01	0.03
ELÉCTRA	Cape Verde	National	Domestic	—	—	No	No	2	40	40	0.15	0.19
Empresa de Agua e Electricidade	Saõ Tomé and Principe	National	Domestic	—	—	No	No	3	100	300	0.07	0.17

Sources: CIER 2003; Empresa Nacional de Energía Eléctrica 2005; Empresa Eléctrica de Guatemala 2005; CFE 2005; Luz y Fuerza del Centro 2005; INE 2005; CAESS 2005; Ceylon Electricity Board 2005; Egyptian Electric Utility and Consumer Protection Regulatory Agency 2005; ACE 2005; Kyokutamba 2004; Kenya Power and Light Company 2005; "ZESA Bills Shock Residents" 2004; ZESCO Ltd. 2005; and Angel-Urdinola and Wodon 2005a, 2005b.

Note: kW: kilowatt; kWh: kilowatt-hour; VA: volt-ampere; — = not available or not applicable.

Appendix H.2 Water

Utility	Country	Geographic area	Type	Fixed charge (US$)	Min. con. (m³)	Peak tariff	No. of blocks	Threshold for first block	Threshold for last block	Price for first block (US$)	Price for last block (US$)
LATIN AMERICA (1)											
SEMAPA	Bolivia	Cochabamba	Social	5.91	12	No	6	25	400	0.23	0.33
SEMAPA	Bolivia	Cochabamba	Residential 1	1.08	12	No	6	25	150	0.07	0.22
SEMAPA	Bolivia	Cochabamba	Residential 2	2.15	12	No	6	25	150	0.12	0.31
SEMAPA	Bolivia	Cochabamba	Residential 3	4.03	12	No	6	25	150	0.14	0.36
SEMAPA	Bolivia	Cochabamba	Residential 4	6.71	12	No	6	25	150	0.17	0.40
Aguas del Illimani	Bolivia	La Paz	—	—	0	No	4	30	300	0.22	1.19
SAGUAPAC	Bolivia	Santa Cruz	—	4.35	0	No	10	15	135	0.29	0.73
COMPESA	Brazil	Pernambuco	Normal	2.57	10	No	5	20	90	0.54	2.00
COMPESA	Brazil	Pernambuco	Social	1.94	10	No	5	20	90	0.54	2.00
SABESP	Brazil	Saõ Paulo	Social	1.10	10	No	4	20	50	0.19	1.06
SABESP	Brazil	Saõ Paulo	Shanty	0.84	10	No	4	20	50	0.09	1.06
SABESP	Brazil	Saõ Paulo	Normal	3.24	10	No	3	20	50	0.51	1.39
ESSCO	Chile	Concepcion	—	1.04	0	Yes	2	40	40	0.39	0.80
Aguas Andinas	Chile	Santiago	—	0.77	0	Yes	2	40	40	0.35	0.87
ESVAL	Chile	Valparaiso	—	1.07	0	Yes	2	40	40	0.74	1.39
EAAB	Colombia	Bogota	Stratum 1	2.61	0	No	3	20	40	0.17	0.69
EAAB	Colombia	Bogota	Stratum 2	3.48	0	No	3	20	40	0.28	0.69
EAAB	Colombia	Bogota	Stratum 3	5.79	0	No	3	20	40	0.48	0.69
EAAB	Colombia	Bogota	Stratum 4	7.21	0	No	3	20	40	0.53	0.69
EAAB	Colombia	Bogota	Stratum 5	17.84	0	No	3	20	40	0.64	0.82
EAAB	Colombia	Bogota	Stratum 6	25.43	0	No	3	20	40	0.74	0.82
EPM	Colombia	Medellin	Stratum 1	1.12	0	No	2	20	20	0.13	0.35
EPM	Colombia	Medellin	Stratum 2	1.41	0	No	2	20	20	0.17	0.35

EPM	Colombia	Medellin	Stratum 3	2.46	0	No	1	—	—	0.35	0.35
EPM	Colombia	Medellin	Stratum 4	2.49	0	No	1	—	—	0.35	0.35
EPM	Colombia	Medellin	Stratum 5	5.92	0	No	1	—	—	0.44	0.44
EPM	Colombia	Medellin	Stratum 6	10.71	0	No	1	—	—	0.44	0.44
EMCALI	Colombia	Cali	Stratum 1	0.95	0	No	2	20	20	0.11	0.27
EMCALI	Colombia	Cali	Stratum 2	2.21	0	No	2	20	20	0.20	0.27
EMCALI	Colombia	Cali	Stratum 3	2.49	0	No	2	20	20	0.22	0.27
EMCALI	Colombia	Cali	Stratum 4	2.69	0	No	1	—	—	0.27	0.27
EMCALI	Colombia	Cali	Stratum 5	4.48	0	No	2	20	20	0.38	0.42
EMCALI	Colombia	Cali	Stratum 6	5.64	0	No	2	40	40	0.41	0.42
ICAA	Costa Rica	National	—	10.74	15	No	4	25	60	0.31	0.70
ENACAL	Nicaragua	Metropolitan	Subsidized	0.07	0	No	2	20	20	0.13	0.16
ENACAL	Nicaragua	Metropolitan	Domestic	0.27	0	No	3	20	50	0.23	0.67
ENACAL	Nicaragua	Metropolitan	Residential	0.55	0	No	2	50	50	0.38	0.85
ENACAL	Nicaragua	Interior	Subsidized	0.07	0	No	2	20	20	0.14	0.18
ENACAL	Nicaragua	Interior	Domestic	0.27	0	No	3	20	50	0.31	0.84
IDAAN	Panama	National	—	6.40	38	No	4	57	115	0.36	0.44
SEDAPAR	Peru	Arequipa	—	0.84	6	No	4	15	60	0.14	0.51
SEDAPAL	Peru	Lima	Normal	1.19	0	No	5	20	80	0.26	0.98
SEDAPAL	Peru	Lima	Social	1.19	0	No	1	—	—	0.26	0.26
SEDALIB	Peru	Trujillo	Normal	1.89	7	No	3	20	100	0.27	0.69
SEDALIB	Peru	Trujillo	Social	0.40	5	No	1	—	—	0.08	0.08
SOUTH ASIA (2)											
Hyderabad	India	Andhra Pradesh	—	1.31	15	No	3	25	500	0.09	0.33
Jaipur	India	Jaipur	—	—	0	No	3	15	40	0.04	0.09
Delhi	India	Delhi	—	0.47	20	No	2	30	30	0.03	0.07

(Table continues on the following page.)

Appendix H.2 (continued)

Utility	Country	Geographic area	Type	Fixed charge (US$)	Min. con. (m³)	Peak tariff	No. of blocks	Threshold for first block	Threshold for last block	Price for first block (US$)	Price for last block (US$)
Vadorara	India	Gujarat	—	—	0	No	1	—	—	0.03	0.03
Surat	India	Gujarat	—	0	0	No	—	—	—	0.05	0.05
Vishakapatnam	India	Vishakapatnam	—	0	0	No	—	—	—	0.12	0.12
Indore	India	Madhya Pradesh	—	0	0	No	—	—	—	0.05	0.05
Mumbai	India	Maharashtra	—	0	0	No	—	—	—	0.06	0.06
Pune	India	Maharashtra	—	0	0	No	—	—	—	0.06	0.06
Nagpur	India	Maharashtra	—	0	0	No	10	40	—	0.02	0.03
Chennai	India	Tamil Nadu	—	0	0	No	10	25	—	0.06	0.58
Madurai	India	Tamil Nadu	—	0	0	No	—	—	—	0.12	0.12
Coimbatore	India	Tamil Nadu	—	0	0	No	3	200	—	—	0.09
Bangalore	India	Karnataka	—	1.51	18	No	5	25	100	0.08	0.77
Kanpur	India	Uttar Pradesh	—	0	0	No	—	—	—	0.05	0.05
Lucknow	India	Uttar Pradesh	—	0	0	No	—	—	—	0.05	0.05
Varanasi	India	Uttar Pradesh	—	0	0	No	—	—	—	0.05	0.05
Ahmedabad	India	Gujarat	—	0	0	No	—	—	—	0.07	0.07
NWSDB	Sri Lanka	Colombo	—	0	0	No	10	25	—	0.01	0.48
DWSSA	Bangladesh	Dhaka	—	0	0	No	—	—	—	0.08	0.08
NWSC	Nepal	Kathmandu	By diameter	0.65	10	No	1	—	—	0.16	0.16
EAST ASIA (3)											
CMWSGC	China	Chengdu	—	0	0	No	—	—	—	0.13	0.13
HCMWSC	Vietnam	Ho Chi Minh City	—	0	0	No	20	50	—	0.11	0.27
Water Supplies Dept.	Hong Kong, China	China	—	0	0	No	12	62	—	—	1.16

Pam Jaya	Indonesia	Jakarta	Public taps	—	0	No	3	10	20	0.04	0.04
Pam Jaya	Indonesia	Jakarta	Very modest	—	0	No	3	10	20	0.04	0.08
Pam Jaya	Indonesia	Jakarta	Modest	—	0	No	3	10	20	0.10	0.15
Pam Jaya	Indonesia	Jakarta	Moderate	—	0	No	3	10	20	0.13	0.20
Pam Jaya	Indonesia	Jakarta	Luxurious	—	0	No	3	10	20	0.24	0.34
Selangor	Malaysia	Kuala Lumpur	Houses	1.32	0	No	3	20	35	0.15	0.45
Selangor	Malaysia	Kuala Lumpur	Apartments	7.89	0	No	1	—	—	0.18	0.18
Selangor	Malaysia	Kuala Lumpur	Condominiums	39.47	0	No	1	—	—	0.32	0.32
MWSS	Philippines	Manila	—	0.29	10	No	8	20	200	0.04	0.12
PPWSA	Cambodia	Phnom Penh	—	—	0	No	4	7	50	0.14	0.33
SMG	Korea, Rep. of	Seoul	By diameter	0.82	0	No	4	30	100	0.24	0.60
SWB	China	Shanghai	—	—	0	No	1	—	—	0.12	0.12
UCWSSSC	Mongolia	Ulaanbataar	Houses	—	0	No	1	—	—	0.12	0.12
UCWSSSC	Mongolia	Ulaanbataar	Apartments	—	0	No	1	—	—	0.10	0.10
AFRICA (4,5)											
Venda De Água	Niger	Niamey	Social/Normale	—	—	No	4	15	75	0.22	0.70
	Cape Verde	—	Domestic	—	—	—	3	6	10	1.84	3.21

Note: — = not available or not applicable.

(1) ADERASA 2004.

(2) Ragupathi and Foster 2002.

(3) Asian Development Bank 2004.

(4) Bardasi and Wodon forthcoming.

(5) Angel-Urdinola and Wodon 2005a.

Bibliography

ACE (ASEAN Center for Energy). 2005. Electricity Tariff Database. ASEAN, Jakarta, Indonesia. Available at http://www.aseanenergy.org/publications_statistics/electricity_database/ (accessed January 2005).

ADB (Asian Development Bank). 2004. *Water in Asian Cities: Utilities Performance and Civil Society Views.* Water for All Series, no. 10. Manila, Philippines: Asian Development Bank.

ADERASA (Association of Water and Sanitary Regulatory Entities of the Americas). 2005. "Situación Actual de la Regulación de las Tarifas de los Servicios de Agua, Alcantarrillado y Tratamiento de Aguas Residuales en Latinoamérica." Grupo de Tarifas y Subsidios, Consultant's draft report, World Bank, Washington, DC.

Ajwad, M. I., and Q. Wodon. 2001. "Marginal Benefit Incidence Analysis Using a Single Cross-Section of Data." Background paper for Regional Report on Infrastructure Reform and the Poor, World Bank, Washington, DC.

———. 2002a. "Do Local Governments Maximize Access Rates to Public Services across Areas? A Test Based on Marginal Benefit Incidence Analysis." Background paper for the Bolivian Poverty Assessment, World Bank, Washington, DC.

———. 2002b. "Who Benefits from Increased Access to Public Services at the Local Level? A Marginal Benefit Analysis for Education and Basic Infrastructure." *World Bank Economists Forum 2:* 155–75.

Ajwad, M. I., and Q. Wodon. 2003. "Infrastructure Services and the Poor: Providing Connection or Consumption Subsidies?" Mimeo, Africa Region, World Bank, Washington, DC.

Andres, L., V. Foster, and J. L. Guasch. Forthcoming. "The Impact of Privatization on Performance of Firms in the Infrastructure Sector in Latin America." Finance, Private Sector, and Infrastructure Department, Latin America and Caribbean Region, World Bank, Washington, DC.

Angel-Urdinola, D., and Q. Wodon. 2005a. "Do Utility Subsidies Reach the Poor? Framework and Evidence for Cape Verde." Paper prepared by the Poverty Reduction and Economic Management Department, Africa Region, World Bank, Washington, DC.

———. 2005b. "The Targeting Performance of Utility Subsidies in Africa: A Cross-Country Study." Paper prepared by the Poverty Reduction and Economic Management Department, Africa Region, World Bank, Washington, DC.

Angel-Urdinola, D., M. Cosgrove-Davies, and Q. Wodon. 2005. "Electricity Tariffs and Poverty in Rwanda." Paper prepared by the Poverty Reduction and Economic Management Department, Africa Region, World Bank, Washington, DC.

Auriol, E., and M. Warlters. 2005. "Taxation Base in Developing Countries." *Journal of Public Economics* 89 (4): 567–727.

Ballard, C. L., J. B. Shoven, and J. Whalley. 1985. "General Equilibrium Computations of the Marginal Welfare Costs of Taxes in the United States." *American Economic Review* 75 (1): 128–38.

Bardasi, Elena, and Q. Wodon. Forthcoming. "Comparing Subsidies for Access or Consumption in Basic Infrastructure: A Simple Approach." Poverty Reduction and Economic Management Department, Africa Region, World Bank, Washington, DC.

Barja, G., D. McKenzie, and M. Urquiola. 2002. "Capitalization and Privatization in Bolivia." Unpublished paper. Cornell University, Ithaca, NY.

Barnes, D. F. 1988. *Electric Power for Rural Growth: How Electricity Affects Rural Life in Developing Countries.* Boulder, CO: Westview Press.

Barnes, D. F., K. B. Fitzgerald, and H. M. Peskin. 2002. "The Benefits of Rural Electrification in India: Implications for Education, Household Lighting, and Irrigation" Mimeo, South Asia Energy and Infrastructure Unit (SASEI), World Bank, Washington, DC.

Barnes, D. F., K. Krutilla, and W. F. Hyde. 2005. *The Urban Household Energy Transition: Social and Environmental Impacts in the Developing World.* Washington, DC: Resources for the Future.

Boiteux, M. 1971. "On the Management of Public Monopolies Subject to Budget Constraints." *Journal of Economic Theory* 3 (3): 219–40.

Boland, J., and D. Whittington. 2000. "The Political Economy of Water Tariff Design in Developing Countries: Increasing Block Tariff versus Uniform Price with Rebate." In *The Political Economy of Water Pricing Reform*, ed. A. Dinar, 215–35. New York: Oxford University Press.

Black, R. E., S. S. Morris, and J. Bryce. 2003. "Where and Why Are 10 Million Dying Every Year?" Child Survival I. *Lancet* 361: 2226–34.

Brocklehurst, C. 2001. "Durban Metro Water: Private Sector Partnerships to Serve the Poor." Nairobi, Kenya: Water and Sanitation Program.

———. 2004. "Addressing the Needs of the Poor in the Context of Water Sector Reform in Greater Negombo and the Kalutara to Galle Coastal Strip, Sri Lanka." Mimeo, Energy and Water Department, Infrastructure Vice Presidency, World Bank, Washington, DC.

Brodman, J. 1982. "Rural Electrification and the Commercial Sector in Indonesia." Discussion Paper D-73L, Resources for the Future, Washington, DC.

CAESS (Compania de Alumbrado Electrico de San Salvador). 2005. "Electricity Tariff Structure." CAESS, San Salvador, El Salvador. http://www.caess.com.sv (accessed January 2005).

Cairncross, S., D. O'Neill, A. McCoy, and D. Sethi. 2003. *Health Environment and the Burden of Disease: A Guidance Note.* London: Department for International Development.

Calderon, C., and L. Serven. 2004. "The Effects of Infrastructure Development on Growth and Income Distribution." Policy Research Working Paper 3400, World Bank, Washington, DC.

Ceylon Electricity Board. 2005. "Electricity Tariff Structure." Ceylon Electricity Board, Colombo, Sri Lanka. http://www.ceb.lk/Tariff/Tariffpage1.htm (accessed January 2005).

CFE (Comisión Federal de Electricidad). 2005. "Electricity Tariff Structure." Comisión Federal de Electricidad, Mexico City, Mexico. http://www.cfe.gob.mx (accessed January 2005).

Charles River Associates. 2004. "Primer on Demand Side Management." Energy and Water Department, Infrastructure Vice Presidency, World Bank, Washington, DC.

Chingcuanco, D. B. 2001. "A Technical Paper on Lifeline Rates." Consultant's Report for the Energy Regulatory Commission, Manila, Philippines.

Choe, K., R. C. G. Varley, and H. U. Biljlani. 1996. "Coping with Intermittent Water Supply: Problems and Prospects." Activity Report 26, Environmental Health Project, U.S. Agency for International Development, Washington, DC.

CIER (Comisión de Integración Energética Regional), 2003, Tarifas Eléctricas en los Países de la CIER 2003. Montevideo, Uruguay: CIER.

Clert, C., and Q. Wodon. 2001. The Targeting of Government Programs in Chile: A Quantitative and Qualitative Assessment. Washington, DC: World Bank.

Coady, D., M. Grosh, and J. Hoddinott. 2003. "The Targeting of Transfers in Developing Countries: Review of Experience and Lessons." Social Protection Discussion Paper, World Bank, Washington, DC.

Coase, R. H. 1946. "The Marginal Cost Controversy." Economica 13: 169–89.

DEFRA (Department for Environment, Food, and Rural Affairs). 2004. United Kingdom Cross-Government Review of Water Affordability Report. London: DEFRA.

de la Fuente, A. 2004. "Infrastructure Productivity and Growth." Unpublished paper, World Bank Institute Governance, Regulation, and Finance Division, World Bank, Washington, DC.

DTI (Department of Trade and Industry). 2001. United Kingdom Fuel Poverty Strategy. London: DTI.

Ebinger, J. 2005. Data Collected for the Infrastructure and Energy Department, Europe and Central Asia Region. Washington, DC: World Bank.

Egyptian Electric Utility and Consumer Protection Regulatory Agency. 2005. "Electricity Tariff Structure." Egyptian Electric Utility and Consumer Protection Regulatory Agency, the Arab Republic of Egypt. http://www.egyptera.com/en/Bill_Tariffs.htm (accessed January 2005).

Empresa Eléctrica de Guatemala. 2005. "Electricity Tariff Structure." Empresa Eléctrica de Guatemala, S.A. (EEGSA). http://www.cnee.gob.gt (accessed January 2005).

Empresa Nacional de Energía Eléctrica. 2005. "Electricity Tariff Structure." Empresa Nacional de Energía Eléctrica, Honduras, CA. http://www.enee.hn (accessed January 2005).

ERM (Environmental Resources Management). 2002. "Emerging Lessons in Private Infrastructure Provision in Rural Areas: Water and Electricity Services in Gabon." Consultants' report, World Bank and Public Private Infrastructure Advisory Facility, Washington, DC.

ERRA (Energy Regulators Regional Association). 2004. "Database of Electricity and Natural Gas Prices in Central/Eastern Europe and the Newly Independent States." Energy Regulators Regional Association, Budapest, Hungary. http://www.erranet.org.

ESMAP (Energy Sector Management Assistance Programme). 2002. *Rural Electrification and Development in the Philippines: Measuring the Social and Economic Benefits.* Washington, DC: Energy Sector Management Assistance Programme. World Bank.

————. 2004. *Sustainable Energy.* Energy Sector Management Assistance Programme. Washington, DC: World Bank.

————. Forthcoming. "Energy Access for Poverty Reduction in Yemen." Draft final report, ESMAP Publication, World Bank. Washington, DC.

Esrey, S. A., J. B. Potash, L. Roberts, and C. Schiff. 1991. "Effects of Improved Water Supply and Sanitation on Ascariasis, Diarrhoea, Dracunculiasis, Hookworm Infection, Schistosomiasis, and Trachoma." *Bulletin of the World Health Organization* 69 (5): 609–21.

Estache, A. 2002. "Argentina's 1990s Privatization: A Cure or a Disease?" Unpublished paper, Infrastructure Vice Presidency, World Bank, Washington, DC.

Estache, A., V. Foster, and Q. Wodon. 2002. *Accounting for Poverty in Infrastructure Reform: Learning from Latin America's Experience.* World Bank Institute Development Studies. Washington, DC: World Bank.

Estache, A., and K. Gassner. 2004. "The Electricity Sector of Sub-Saharan Africa: Basic Facts and Emerging Issues." Unpublished paper, Infrastructure Vice Presidency, World Bank, Washington, DC.

Estache, A., and E. Kouassi. 2002. "Sector Organization, Governance, and the Efficiency of African Water Utilities." Policy Research Working Paper 2890, World Bank, Washington, DC.

Estache, A., M. A. Rossi, and C. A. Ruzzier. 2004. "The Case for International Coordination of Electricity Regulation: Evidence from the Measurement of Efficiency in South America." *Journal of Regulatory Economics* 25 (3): 271–95.

Faulhaber, G. R., and S. B. Levinson. 1981. "Subsidy-Free Prices and Anonymous Equity." *American Economic Review* 71 (5): 1083–91.

Fewtrell, L., and J. Colford. 2004. *Water Sanitation and Hygiene: Interventions and Diarrhea—A Review and Meta-Analysis.* Washington, DC: World Bank.

Foley, Gerald. 1990. *Electricity for Rural People.* London: Panos Institute.

Foster, V. 2002. "Condominial Water and Sewer Systems: Costs of Implementation of the Model." Economic and Financial Evaluation of the El Alto Pilot Project, Water and Sanitation Program, Lima, Peru.

————. 2003a. "Hacia una Política Social para los Sectores de Infraestructura en Argentina: Evaluando el Pasado y Explorando el Futuro." Working Paper

10/03, World Bank Office for Argentina, Chile, Paraguay, and Uruguay, Buenos Aires, Argentina.

———. 2003b. "Impacto Social de la Crisis Argentina en los Sectores de Infraestructura." Working Paper 5/03, World Bank Office for Argentina, Chile, Paraguay, and Uruguay, Buenos Aires, Argentina.

———. 2004. "Toward a Social Policy for Argentina's Infrastructure Sectors. Evaluating the Past, Exploring the Future." Policy Research Working Paper 3422, World Bank, Washington, DC.

Foster, V., and M. C. Araujo. 2004. "Does Infrastructure Reform Work for the Poor? A Case Study from Guatemala." Policy Research Working Paper 3185, World Bank, Washington, DC.

Foster, V., A. Gomez-Lobo, and J. Halpern. 2000. "Designing Direct Subsidies for Water and Sanitation: Panama: A Case Study." Policy Research Working Paper 2344, World Bank, Washington, DC.

Foster, V., and K. Homman. 2001. "The Design of Pro-Poor Subsidies for Water and Sanitation Services in India: Maximizing the Social Dividends of Reform." Unpublished paper, Energy and Infrastructure Department, South Asia Region, South Asia Energy and Infrastructure Department, World Bank, Washington, DC.

Foster, V., S. Pattanayak, and L. S. Prokopy. 2003. "Water Tariffs and Subsidies in South Asia: Do Current Water Subsidies Reach the Poor?" Water and Sanitation Program, New Delhi, India.

Foster, V., and T. Yepes. 2005. "Is Cost Recovery a Feasible Objective for Water and Electricity?" Finance, Private Sector, and Infrastructure Department, Latin America and the Caribbean Region, World Bank, Washington, DC.

Freeman, A. M. III. 1994. *The Measurement of Environmental and Resource Values: Theory and Methods.* Washington, DC: Resources for the Future.

Freije, S., and L. Rivas. 2002. "Privatization, Inequality, and Welfare: Evidence from Nicaragua." Unpublished paper, IESA (Institute for Advanced Studies in Administration), Caracas, República Bolivariana de Venezuela.

Galiani, S., P. J. Gertler, and E. Schargrodsky. 2005. "Water for Life: The Impact of the Privatization of Water Services on Child Mortality," *Journal of Political Economy* 113:83–120.

Gomez-Lobo, A. 2001. "Incentive-Based Subsidies: Designing Output-Based Subsidies for Water Consumption." *Public Policy for the Private Sector.* Note no. 232, June 2001. World Bank, Washington, DC.

Gomez-Lobo, A., and D. Contreras. 2000. "Subsidy Policies for the Utility Industries: A Comparison of the Chilean and Colombian Water Subsidy Schemes." Draft, Department of Economics, University of Chile, Santiago, Chile.

———. 2003. "Water Subsidy Policies: A Comparison of the Chilean and Colombian Schemes." *World Bank Economic Review* 17 (3): 391–407.

Gomez-Lobo, A., V. Foster, and J. Halpern. 2000. "Information and Modeling Issues in Designing Water and Sanitation Subsidy Schemes." Policy Research Working Paper 2345, World Bank, Washington, DC.

GWI (Global Water Intelligence). 2004. *Tariffs: Half Way There.* Oxford, U.K.: GWI.

Howard, G., and J. Bartram. 2003. *Domestic Water Quantity, Service Level, and Health.* Geneva: World Health Organization.

Huttley, S. R. A. 1994. "Water, Sanitation, and Health in Developing Countries." In *Water and Public Health,* ed. A. M. B. Golding, N. Noah, and R. Stanwell-Smith, 251–58. London: Smith-Gordon and Co.

IEA (International Energy Association). 1999. "World Energy Outlook—Looking at Subsidies: Getting the Prices Right." IEA, Paris, France.

———. 2002. *World Energy Outlook.* Paris: Organisation for Economic Co-operation and Development/International Energy Agency.

Ijjaz, E. 2003. "Rapid Assessment of Energy Efficiency in Urban Water Utilities of Bakhara and Samarkand, Uzbekistan." Unpublished paper, Europe and Central Asia Region, World Bank, Washington, DC.

INE (Instituto Nicaragüense de Energía). 2005. "Electricity Tariff Structure." INE, Managua, Nicaragua. http://www.ine.gob.ni (accessed January 2005).

IRC (International Resource Center). 2004. "Results from School Sanitation Programmes in Kenya." Delft: IRC. http://www.irc.nl/page/9963.

Israel, D. K. 2002. "The Distributional Impact of Price Ceilings on Water in Developing Countries: An Analysis of Household Water Expenditures in Urban Bolivia." Draft paper, Indiana State University, Terre Haute, IN.

James, K., C. E. Godlove, and S. L. Campbell. 2003. *Watergy: Taking Advantage of Untapped Energy and Water Efficiency Opportunities in Municipal Water Utilities.* Washington, DC: Alliance to Save Energy.

Kariuki, M., and G. Acolor. 2000. "Delivery of Water Supply to Low-Income Urban Communities through the Teshie Tankers Owners Association: A Case Study of Public–Private Initiatives in Ghana." Paper for conference on Infrastructure for Development: Private Solutions and the Poor, Public Private Infrastructure Advisory Facility, London, May 2000.

Kariuki, M., and J. Schwartz. 2005. "Small-Scale Private Service Providers of Water Supply and Electricity: A Review of Incidence, Structure, Pricing, and Operating Characteristics." Energy and Water Department, World Bank, Washington, DC.

Keener, S. C., and S. G. Banerjee. Forthcoming. "Measuring Consumer Benefits from Utility Reform: An Exploration of Consumer Assessment Methodology in Sub-Saharan Africa." World Bank, Washington, DC.

Kelley, P., S. Hicks, J. Oloya, and L. Sikakwa. 2003. "*Escherichia coli* Enterovirulent Phenotypes in Zambians with AIDS-Related Diarrhea." *Transcripts of the Royal Society for Tropical Medicine and Hygiene* 97 (5): 573–76.

Kenya Power and Light Company. 2005. "Schedule of Tariffs and Rates for Supply of Electricity by the Kenya Power and Lighting Company Limited." The Kenya Power & Lighting Co. Ltd., Nairobi, Kenya. http://www.kplc.co.ke/corporate/tarrifsintro.htm (accessed January 2005).

Komives, K. 1998. "Serving the Poor in Transition Economies: An Evaluation of Targeted Municipal Service Subsidy Programs." Master's thesis, Department of City and Regional Planning, University of North Carolina, Chapel Hill, NC.

————. 1999. "Designing Pro-Poor Water and Sewer Concessions: Early Lessons from Bolivia." *Water Policy* 3: 61–79.

Komives, K., L. Prokopy, and D. Lauria. 2004. "Pricing Water to Subsidize the Poor: Testing the Potential of Increasing Block Tariffs." Unpublished paper, Institute of Social Studies (ISS), The Hague, Netherlands.

Komives, K., D. Whittington, and X. Wu. 2001. "Infrastructure Coverage and the Poor: A Global Perspective." Policy Research Working Paper 2551, World Bank, Washington, DC.

Kosek, M., C. Bern, and R. L. Guerrant. 2003. "The Global Burden of Diarrhoeal Disease, as Estimated from Studies Published between 1992 and 2000." *Bulletin of the World Health Organization* 81: 197–204.

Kulkarni, V., and D. F. Barnes. 2004. "The Impact of Electricity on School Participation in Rural Nicaragua." Working paper, University of Maryland, College Park, MD.

Kyokutamba, J. 2004. "Uganda Country Study." In *Energy Services for the Urban Poor in Africa: Issues and Policy Implications*, ed. Bereket Kebede and Ikhupuleng Dube. London: ZED Books Ltd.

Lampietti, J., ed. 2004. "Power's Promise: Electricity Reforms in Eastern Europe and Central Asia." Working Paper 40, World Bank, Washington, DC.

Lampietti, J. A., H. Gonzalez, E. Hamilton, and M. Wilson. 2003. "Revisiting Reform in the Energy Sector, Lessons from Georgia." Working Paper 21, World Bank, Washington, DC.

Lampietti, J. A., A. Kolb, S. Gulyani, and V. Avenesyan. 2001. "Utility Pricing and the Poor: Lessons from Armenia." Technical Paper 497, World Bank, Washington, DC.

Lauria, D., and O. Hopkins. 2004. "Pro-Poor Subsidies for Water Connections: Cases from West Africa." Consultant's Report, University of North Carolina, Chapel Hill, NC.

Lauria, D., and A. Kolb. 1999. "Willingness to Pay for Improved Water Supply in Niger." Executive Summary and Final Report, World Bank, Washington, DC.

Levin, J. 2003. "ASTAE/ESMAP Cross-Sector Initiative Energy Efficiency at Water Supply/Wastewater Utilities in China." Energy Sector Management Advisory Program, World Bank, Washington, DC.

Listorti, J. A. 1996. "Bridging Environmental Health Gaps." AFTES Working Papers 20–22, Urban Environmental Management, Africa Technical Department, World Bank, Washington, DC.

López-Calva, L. F., and J. Rosellón. 2002. "Privatization and Inequality: The Mexican Case." Unpublished paper, Universidad de las Américas, Puebla, Mexico.

Lovei, L., E. Gurenko, M. Haney, P. O'Keefe, and M. Shkaratan. 2000. *Maintaining Utility Services for the Poor: Policies and Practices in Central and Eastern Europe and the Former Soviet Union*. Washington, DC: World Bank.

Low, J. W., J. L. Garrett, and V. Ginja. 1999. "Can Cash Transfer Programs Work in Resource Poor Countries? The Experience of Mozambique." FCND Discussion

Paper 74, Food Consumption and Nutrition Division, International Food Policy Research Institute, Washington, DC.

Luz y Fuerza del Centro. 2005. "Electricity Tariff Structure." Luz y Fuerza del Centro, Mexico. http://www.lfc.gob.mx (accessed January 2005).

Makdissi, P., and Q. Wodon. 2000. "Consumption Dominance Curves: Testing for the Impact of Indirect Tax Reform on Poverty." *Economics Letters* 75: 227–35

McIntosh, Arthur. 2003. *Asian Water Supplies: Reaching the Urban Poor*. London: Asian Development Bank and IWA Publishing. http://www.adb.org/Documents/Books/Asian_Water_Supplies/default.asp.

McIntosh, A. C., and C. E. Yñiquez. 1997. *Second Water Utilities Date Book: Asian and Pacific Region*. Manila: Asian Development Bank.

Melendez, M. 2005. "Distributional Incidence of Water and Electricity Tariffs in Colombia: Subsidy Data Template." World Bank, Washington, DC.

Melendez, M., C. Casas, and P. Medina. 2004. "Subsidios al Consumo de los Servicios Públicos en Colombia: Hacia donde Movernos?" Final report of Finance, Private Sector, and Infrastructure Unit, Latin America and the Caribbean Region, World Bank, Washington, DC.

Murray, C. J. L., and A. D. Lopez. 1996. *Global Health Statistics: Global Burden of Disease and Injury Series*. Vol. 2. Cambridge, MA: Harvard University Press.

Musgrave, R. 1959. *The Theory of Public Finance*. New York: McGraw-Hill.

NIUA (National Institute of Urban Affairs). 1999. *Status of Water Supply, Sanitation and Solid Waste Management in Urban India*. New Delhi: NIUA.

Noll, R. G., M. M. Shirley, and S. Cowan. 2000. "Reforming Urban Water Systems in Developing Countries." In *Economic Policy Reform: The Second Stage*, ed. A. O. Krueger, 243–91. Chicago: University of Chicago Press.

Noth, R. Forthcoming. "Plan Estratégico de Ampliación de Cobertura en los Asentamientos Humanos de Lima." Consultant's report to Lima Water Utility (SEDAPAL), Lima, Peru.

OECD (Organisation for Economic Co-operation and Development). 1999. *The Price of Water: Trends in OECD Countries*. Paris: OECD.

———. 2004. "Electricity Tariffs Database." OECD, Paris, France. http://www.oecd.org/statsportal.

OLADE (Organización Latinoamericano de Energia). 2004. "Regional Database of Electricity Tariffs." OLADE, Quito, Ecuador. http://www.olade.org (accessed January 200).

OSINERG (Organismo Supervisor de la Inversión en Energía). 2005. "Evaluación del Impacto del FOSE." Unpublished paper, OSINERG, Lima, Peru.

Palmer Development Group. 2001. "Free Basic Water: Implementation Strategy Document, Version 1." South Africa Department of Water Affairs and Forestry, Pretoria, South Africa. http://www.dwaf.gov.za/FreeBasicWater/docs/Implementation%20Strategy%20version%208.3.pdf.

Pattanayak, S., and J.-C. Yang. 2002. "Distributional Incidence of Water Tariffs and Subsidies in Kathmandu, Nepal." RTI International, Durham, NC.

————. 2005. "Distributional Incidence of Water Subsidies in Sri Lanka: Subsidy Data Template." World Bank, Washington, DC.

Pattanayak, S. K., J.-C. Yang, C. Agarwal, H. M. Gunatilake, H. Bandara, and T. Ranasinghe. 2004. "Water, Sanitation, and Poverty in Southwest Sri Lanka." Revised Final Report, submitted to the Energy and Water Department, Infrastructure Vice Presidency, and funded by Bank Netherlands Water Partnership, World Bank, Washington, DC.

Pattanayak, S. K., J.-C. Yang, D. Whittington, B. Kumar K. C., G. Subedi, Y. B. Gurung, K. P. Adhikari, D. V. Shakya, L. S. Kunwar, and B. K. Mabuhang. 2001. "Willingness to Pay for Improved Water Supply in Kathmandu Valley, Nepal." Final Report. RTI International, Durham, NC.

PPIAF (Public–Private Infrastructure Advisory Facility). 2001. "The Design of Pro-Poor Subsidies in Urban Water and Sanitation Services in India: Maximizing the Social Dividends of Reform." Unpublished paper, Energy and Infrastructure Department, South Asia Region, World Bank, Washington, DC.

Prokopy, L. 2002. "Distributional Incidence of Current and Potential Water Tariffs and Subsidies in Bangalore, India." Unpublished paper, Energy and Infrastructure Department, South Asia Region, World Bank, Washington, DC.

Ragupathi, U. P., and V. Foster. 2002. "Water Tariffs and Subsidies in South Asia— A Scorecard for India." Water and Sanitation Program, New Delhi, India.

Ramsey, F. P. 1927. "A Contribution to the Theory of Taxation." *Economic Journal* 37: 66–83.

Reiche, K., E. Martinot, and A. Covarrubias. 2000. *Expanding Access to Remote Areas: Off-Grid Rural Electrification in Developing Countries.* WorldPower 2000. London: Isherwood.

Robles, M. 2001. "Simulation of Strategies for Targeting Water and Sewerage Subsidies by CORPOSANA Paraguay." Consultant's report, World Bank, Washington, DC.

Ruggeri-Laderchi, C. 2003. "Public Utilities and the Poor: Evidence from Uruguay." Background Paper 6 for the Uruguay Poverty Update 2003, World Bank, Washington, DC.

SAD-ELEC. Ltd. 2003. "Electricity Prices in Southern and Eastern Africa." South Africa: SAD-ELEC. http://www.sad-elec.com/Publications.htm (accessed January 2005).

Santhakumar, V. 2004a. "Distributional Incidence of Electricity Subsidies in India: Subsidy Data Template." World Bank: Washington, DC.

————. 2004b. "Electricity Subsidies in India." Presentation for India Development Foundation, Gurgaon, India.

————. 2005. "Impact of the Distribution of Cost of Reforms on the Pace of Institutional Reforms: A Study of Power Sector Reforms in Indian States." CDS (Centre for Development Studies), Kerala, India.

Sen, A. 1995. "The Political Economy of Targeting." In *Public Spending and the Poor: Theory and Evidence,* ed. D. van de Walle and K. Nead, 11–24. Baltimore, MD, and London: Johns Hopkins University Press for the World Bank.

Shkaratan, M. 2005. "Distributional Incidence of Utility Subsidies in Croatia, Hungary, and Latvia: Subsidy Data Template." World Bank, Washington, DC.

Singh, N., and R. Thomas. 2000. "Welfare Policy: Cash versus Kind, Self-Selection, and Notches." *Southern Economic Journal* 66 (4): 976–90.

Smith, N. 1999. "Low-Cost Electrification: Affordable Electricity Installation for Low-Income Households in Developing Countries." ITDG (Intermediate Technology Development Group) Working Papers, Intermediate Technology Development Group Publishing, Warwickshire, UK.

Solo, T. 1999. "Small-Scale Entrepreneurs in the Urban Water and Sanitation Market." *Environment and Urbanization* 11 (1): 117–31.

Strand, J., and I. Walker. 2005. "Water Markets and Demand in Central American Cities." *Environment and Development Economics* 10: 313–35.

Subbarao, K., A. Bonnerjee, K. Ezemerari, J. Braithwaite, C. Graham, S. Carvalho, and A. Thompson. 1997. *Safety Net Programs and Poverty Reduction: Lessons from Cross-Country Experience.* Directions in Development. Washington, DC: World Bank.

Thorne, S. 1995. "Electricity Dispensers and Affordable Electricity Services." *Energy for Sustainable Development* 1 (6): 30–32.

Thurow, L. C. 1974. "Cash versus In-Kind Transfers." *American Economic Review* 64 (2): 190–95.

Tremolet, S. 2002. "Multi-Utilities and Access: Can Private Multi-Utilities Help to Expand Access to Rural Areas?" Note 248, Public Policy for the Private Sector, World Bank, Washington, DC.

Ugaz, C., and C. Waddams Price. 2002. *Utility Privatization and Regulation: A Fair Deal for Customers?* Cheltenham, UK: Edward Elgar.

UN (United Nations) Millennium Project. 2005. *Investing in Development: A Practical Plan to Achieve the Millennium Development Goals.* London: EarthScan. Available at http://www.unmillenniumproject.org/documents/MainReportComplete-lowres.pdf.

UN-ESCAP (United Nations Economic and Social Commission for Asia and the Pacific). 2004. Electricity Tariffs Database. UN-ESCAP, Bangkok, Thailand. Available at http://www.unescap.org.

Van Humbeeck, P. 2000. "The Distributive Effects of Water Price Reform on Households in the Flanders Region of Belgium." In *The Political Economy of Water Pricing Reform,* ed. A. Dinar, 279–95. New York: Oxford University Press.

Venkataraman, K. 1990. "Rural Electrification in the Asian and Pacific Region." In *Power Systems in Asia and the Pacific, with Emphasis on Rural Electrification,* ed. Economic and Social Commission for Asia and the Pacific, 310–32. New York: United Nations.

Warlters, M., and E. Auriol. 2005. "The Marginal Cost of Public Funds in Africa." Policy Research Working Group Paper No. WPS 3679, World Bank, Washington, DC.

Walker, I., F. Ordonez, P. Serrano, and J. Halpern. 2000. "Potable Water Pricing and the Poor: Evidence from Central America on the Distribution of Subsidies and the Demand for Improved Services." Policy Working Paper 2468, World Bank, Washington, DC.

Water Aid. 2001. *Land Tenure*. London: Water Aid.

Whittington, D. 1992. "Possible Adverse Effects of Increasing Block Water Tariffs in Developing Countries." *Economic Development and Cultural Change* 41 (1): 75–87.

Whittington, D., J. Boland, and V. Foster. 2002. "Understanding the Basics: Water Tariffs and Subsidies in South Asia." Water and Sanitation Program, World Bank, Washington, DC.

Wodon, Q., M. I. Ajwad, and C. Siaens. 2003. "Lifeline or Means Testing? Electric Utility Subsidies in Honduras." In *Infrastructure for the Poor People: Public Policy for Private Provision*, ed. P. Brook and T. Irwin, 227–96. Washington, DC: World Bank and Public–Private Infrastructure Advisory Facility.

World Bank. 2003. "Urban Poverty in East Asia: A Review of Indonesia, the Philippines, and Vietnam." East Asia Urban Working Paper 11, Urban Sector Development Unit, East Asia Infrastructure Department, World Bank, Washington, DC.

———. 2004a. *Colombia: Recent Economic Developments in Infrastructure.* Washington, DC: Finance, Private Sector, and Infrastructure Unit, World Bank.

———. 2004b. *Mexico Public Expenditure Review (PER)*. Vol. 1 and 2. Colombia and Mexico Country Management Team, Poverty Reduction and Economic Management Unit, Latin America and the Caribbean Region, World Bank, Washington, DC.

———. Forthcoming a. "Implementation Completion Report: Lima Water Rehabilitation and Management Project." Finance, Private Sector, and Infrastructure Unit, Latin America and Caribbean Region, World Bank, Washington, DC.

———. Forthcoming b. "Infrastructure in Europe and Central Asia: Sustainable Reforms and Financing. Europe and Central Asia." Unpublished paper, Infrastructure and Energy Department, Europe and Central Asia Region, World Bank, Washington, DC.

WEC (World Energy Council). 2001. *Pricing Energy in Developing Countries.* London: WEC. http://www.worldenergy.org/wec-geis/global/downloads/pedc/PEDC.pdf.

WHO/UNICEF (World Health Organization and United Nations Children's Fund). 2004. *Meeting the MDG Drinking Water and Sanitation Target: A Mid-Term Assessment of Progress.* Joint Monitoring Programme for Water Supply and Sanitation. Geneva, Switzerland: WHO/UNICEF. http://www.who.int/ water_sanitation_health/monitoring/jmp04.pdf.

"ZESA Bills Shock Residents." 2004. Kubatana, Harare, Zimbabwe. http://www.kubatana.net (accessed January 2005 and excerpted from *The Resident*, issue 33).

ZESCO Ltd. 2005. "Electricity Tariff Structure." ZESCO Ltd., Zambia. http://www.zesco.co.zm/tariffs.html (accessed January 2005).

Index